Change the world!

FURY'S HOUR

a (sort-of) punk manifesto

 random house canada

wArren kinsellA

All rights reserved under International and Pan-American Copyright Conventions. No
part of this book may be reproduced in any form or by any electronic or mechanical
means, including information storage and retrieval systems, without permission
in writing from the publisher, except by a reviewer, who may quote brief passages
in a review. Published in 2005 by Random House Canada, a division of
Random House of Canada Limited. Distributed in Canada by
Random House of Canada Limited.

Random House Canada and colophon are trademarks.

www.randomhouse.ca

LIBRARY AND ARCHIVES CANADA CATALOGUING IN PUBLICATION

Kinsella, Warren, 1960–
Fury's hour : a (sort-of) punk manifesto / Warren Kinsella.

ISBN 0-679-31325-7

1. Punk rock music—History and criticism. I. Title.

ML3534.K565 2005   781.66   C2005-903482-3

Cover and text design: Valerie Applebee

Printed and bound in Canada

10 9 8 7 6 5 4 3 2 1

My Dad, T. Douglas Kinsella,
died while I was writing this book.
I dedicate it to him. We all love him,
and we all miss him a lot.

*(He always tolerated the racket coming up
the basement stairs, and he always pushed us
to try and change the world.*

We didn't, but he did.)

Hey everyone would you look at me
At least what I'm supposed to be
Anything this, is it anything new?
Frustrated, confused, and acne, too
What do I think, I think someone said
Give me your hand, and touch my head
I think, I do not think, I do not care
I think what everyone put there

"I Am a Confused Teenager,"
the Hot Nasties

I AM A CONFUSED TEENAGER
(or, the punk's secret of immortality)

"NO, NO, NO, NO, NO! YOU PUNK!"

Now, *this* was going to be interesting.

"Listen, you little punk, you're going to get arrested for inciting a goddamned riot, *do you understand me?* Get these people off this stage *now,* punk!"

I have to admit, the police officer's bellowed threat sounded a lot more like an offer. To a rabble-rousing teenage punk like me—and to the anti-social bunch of punks that made up our band, the Hot Nasties—getting arrested for inciting a riot was *pretty fucking cool.* I kept playing, and kept hollering into the microphone, and kept looking at the cop, who in turn was glowering at me. He had his hand on his constable's utility belt, which suggested to me that he was about to mace me, handcuff me or shoot me. Any one of these things would have brought the Hot Nasties big show at the Calgary Stampede to a crashing halt, but—*man!*—what an amazing finish it would be. I kept playing. The cop kept glaring. The "rioters" kept "rioting."

It was July 13, 1980, and the Hot Nasties—along with quite a few punks and a dozen or so cops—were onstage at the Calgary Stampede. The nice people at the Calgary Stampede had invited us to play, I suppose, because they were interested in letting suburban moms and dads take a peek at this wacky new punk thing that everyone was talking about. We didn't ask what their motivation was, frankly. When the earnest, cowboy-hatted organizers offered us a chance to spread discord and dissent in the middle of the family-friendly annual event that makes Calgary, Alberta, Canada, world-famous—well, hell. We would have *paid* to stir up shit on that scale.

But, still. Having the dozen cops onstage with us probably made our point better than the scores of punks could. Our point being, punk wasn't about being comfortable, or complacent, or entertained. It was about pissed-off young people shaking things up, and having a bit of fun, and maybe changing a few attitudes (and redressing a few injustices) along the way.

The cop stepped closer, menacingly, apparently intending to signal how serious he was about arresting me for inviting punks onto the Stampede's stage to dance, and thereby, to wit and henceforth, causing a "riot," Your Honour. I stopped playing bass and waved to the rest of the Hot Nasties to cease and desist. Our song, a moderately popular three-chord rant called "Invasion of the Tribbles," ground to an inglorious stop.

"Okay, okay," I said into the microphone. Photos I have subsequently seen of that precise moment show me in my favourite biker jacket and a cowboy hat, the cop towering overhead, his back turned (rudely, I thought) to the one thousand or so folks in attendance. "I am going to be arrested for inciting a riot if you darn punks don't stop dancing and get off the stage." I paused and glanced at the cop, who seemed capable of murder at any moment. "You don't want me arrested, do you?" I asked the crowd.

A wild cheer went up.

"I thought so," I said. "But get off the friggin' stage anyway, okay?"

Alright, let's clear up a few things before this little punk show gets started, shall we?

Yes, I am in the first half of my forties. *Yes,* I live in a nice house and am happily married and have four great kids (all of whom love punk rock, by the way). *Yes,* I think I'm going to need reading glasses soon, and I am balding, and what isn't falling out is getting awfully grey. *Yes,* I am not nearly as politically radical as I once was—although there are plenty of rightist assholes who'd tell you that I have become a crazed Bolshevik as I have become older. *Yes,* I am a middle-class dad, and I sometimes wear ties. *Yes,* the writing of this book is probably some weird manifestation of the beginning of a mid-life crisis. *Yes,* I am, in effect, a boring old fart of the type that I used to malign, back when I wrote songs for the punk outfit calling itself the Hot Nasties. *Yes,* I have become that which I once sought to destroy.

Big fucking deal. *Piss off,* as a punk might say, if you don't approve. I still get excited by the music, and I still admire virtually every teenage punk I pass on the street—for their refusal to conform, for their guts, for their passion, for their commitment. I love punk, and—somewhere deep inside my geriatric chest—there is a sixteen-year-old in a black leather biker jacket, endlessly playing along to "Sheena Is a Punk Rocker." Spitting.

As you will shortly discover, I am about as subtle as a hand grenade in a bowl of porridge, and the same (hopefully) goes for this book. Given that this little tome is about punk, and given that I used to be one myself, subtlety seems ill-advised in any event. Punk has always been loud, noisy and fast, and anyone who knows me will tell you I'm that way too.

Nowadays, however, I stand at the back of the dark, dingy halls, with all the other old farts, singing along with the great punk tunes (new and less new) and laughing at the young punks down in front, jumping up and down, smashing into each other, diving off the stage and hoping like hell someone will catch them before they meet up with concrete. It's just so fucking great, this punk stuff, and I love it so much, I wanted to tell you why.

Oh, and there are a lot of swear words in this book. Punks swear a lot, and I've never lost the habit (ask my wife). When my kids get older, I'm going to get a fucking earful about this, believe me.

Okay, here's some biographical crap.

When I was fifteen, I belonged to the Non-Conformist News Agency. It was a non-existent political party that a few of us cooked up in our final year at St. Bonaventure Junior High School. We used the NCNA to cause all kinds of shit at St. Bonaventure: burning the school constitution at lunchtime, reading the *Communist Manifesto* in English class, demanding a day off to commemorate the shootings at Kent State University in 1970, running a fictional candidate named Herbie Schwartz for the student council elections (Herbie won, so a couple of us were forced to serve by the crypto-fascistic vice-principal, who called us "Marxist agitators"). And so on.

Growing up in Calgary, Alberta, in the seventies, I was (not entirely surprisingly) unlike many of my peers. To me, a weekend spent smoking dope and listening to Led Zep on headphones was a wasted forty-eight hours. If I was going to irritate my teachers and like-minded authority figures, there had to be a better way.

As things turned out, all of us in the NCNA loved nasty, gnarly rock 'n' roll—the raw stuff generated by early Who, Kinks and Stones (I had a soft spot for John Lennon's Beatles contributions, too). One of the guys got a guitar, then another guy got a bass, and then we met a guy in the Calgary Stampede Band who had a drum kit. So we decided to form a band, which we called the Social Blemishes. I was the lead screamer, but not the only one. Anyone who had a case of beer to contribute could commandeer the microphone for a while.

The Blems weren't actually a punk band at the start. Generally, we wrote songs that attacked people we didn't like, which meant we had lots of subject matter. And, while we wrote our own songs, it wasn't because we cherished creativity or anything like that; mostly, it was because we were too musically incompetent to figure out how to copy anyone else's stuff.

Along with my pals, Ras Pierre Schenk, Alan "Flesh" Macdonald and assorted other acne-afflicted miscreants who attended Bishop Carroll and Bishop Grandin high schools, I had read a little bit about punk rock in the Calgary newspapers. In the main, it seemed to involve throwing up on old ladies in airport waiting rooms, as the Sex Pistols were alleged to have done. That sounded pretty good to us, so we decided that the Social Blemishes was a punk band.

On January 28, 1977, I bought a copy of the first album by the Ramones, and—later that same day—I stood slack-jawed by my tinny hi-fi in my basement bedroom, my life forever transformed. Nothing would be the same after that.

The Blemishes practised our punkish sounds in Flesh's basement in southwest Calgary, tried to sound and look like the Ramones, spoke in fake English accents, saved up our money to buy biker jackets, needed a lot of late-night Slurpees, and started to attract a minute amount of attention. On December 21, 1977, the Blems opened for a boring rock outfit called Fosterchild at Bishop Carroll High School. When Flesh launched into a demonic version of "Heartbreak Hotel," a half-dozen teenage girls rushed the stage. We were hooked: maybe we would never get rich playing three-chord (sometimes one- or two-chord) raves, but actually meeting a real, live *girl* wasn't so bad. (Getting beaten up by jocks, however, we could do without. That happened more than we liked at the start.)

In time, the Blemishes became the Hot Nasties, a name we took from a porn movie. I was the bassist and lead singer, Ras Pierre

assumed the role of lead guitarist, Sane Wayne Ahern played rhythm guitar, and Tom Edwards kept the beat. Most of the songs were written by Pierre and me. One of them, "Invasion of the Tribbles," has apparently been called one of the top one hundred punk songs of all time by *Ugly Things* fanzine, which was fairly nice of them. In the local punk scene, we were loners, basically because I thought quite a few of the other bands were idiots, and I didn't hesitate to say so. As a result, we didn't get invited to a lot of parties.

Three of our songs, "I Am a Confused Teenager," "Secret of Immortality," and "Invasion of the Tribbles," came out on our own label, Social Blemish Records ("More Hits Than Zits!"), on an extended play single (EP) in 1980. A couple years ago, the EP sold for a while on the Internet for nearly $300 (U.S.!). Later, Flesh and three other guys started a band called the Sturgeons, and they too put out a single on Social Blemish. Somewhere in there, the Nasties got a shot at the big time when we opened for the British punk band 999, but the night ended in a massive brawl, with me at the centre of it. And, in 1980, the Hot Nasties issued an album-length collection of our songs. Some of our tunes were later covered, or adapted, by the likes of Moe Berg from Pursuit of Happiness, folk star James Keelaghan, and Nardwuar and the Evaporators (who did a rockin' cover of one infamous ditty Pierre and I wrote, called "Barney Rubble Is My Double"). Royalties, meanwhile, have remained elusive. Ditto groupies.

In 1994, a Montreal punk rock fan named Frank Manley issued a book and album about Canadian punk rock called (ironically enough, considering my later involvements) *Smash the State*. The album featured songs by the Hot Nasties, the Sturgeons and our Edmonton punk pals, the Rock 'n' Roll Bitches. And that was it for the Hot Nasties, unless you guys know something I don't.

These days, most of us are dads, and husbands, and pillars of society. But get a couple beers in us, and you'll see that the old NCNA ain't too fucking far from the surface. No sirree.

Okay, that's the end of the biographical part.

Research for *Fury's Hour* did not get off to a very good start. My attempt to interview the ex-Pistol Johnny Rotten, probably the most famous punk on the planet, nearly ended in fisticuffs. For quite a while, you see, I had been attempting to persuade Johnny to give me some time for a chat. I would write him, and email him, and call him, deploying every saccharine blandishment you can imagine; Johnny R., meanwhile, ignored me. When we finally met, I got a bit frustrated by his taciturnity and, well, I swore at him a little. He swore back, a little, and his bodyguard (actual name, swear to God: Rambo) looked like he was going to throw me through a wall, a lot. There's a possibility that Johnny Rotten and I will be great pals one day, but for now our relations remain somewhat less than cordial. So much for that interview.

But my encounter with Johnny was illustrative, and it got me thinking. Stalking back to my keyboard, cussing and huffing, I asked this question of no one in particular: What is it that all punks share, irrespective of race, religion, gender or partisan affiliation? Well, *anger,* of course. All punks are pissed off at something—at the music industry, for producing so much shite; at governments, for too often permitting bad situations to get worse; at their parents, for being parents; at George W. Bush, for being born; at corporations, for putting profit before people; at anyone in a position of relative power, for being powerful; at other young people for being racist or sexist or whatever. It's axiomatic: being punk means being pissed off.

The best place to start, therefore, is by looking at the unique and lasting contribution of the Sex Pistols to the adolescent anger industry. Along with producing some extraordinary punk rock music, and along with shaking up the popular culture, the Pistols were the temporal personification of fury. They persuaded young people to embrace anger—"anger is an energy," as Johnny Rotten would later famously chant—even though, irony of ironies, the Pistols aren't remembered for being terribly energetic about *anything,* least of all progressive social change. The Pistols, however much they failed on the socio-politico-economic indicators, succeeded at persuading kids (in Great Britain, North America and everywhere else) to rage against whatever it is that is holding them back. For that, they deserve our thanks as a society. And, to put a fine point on it, I deserve my interview.

With all of these punks running around feeling empowered and pissed off, what then? What are they supposed to *do* with that anger? The answer is found in one of the central—if not *the* central—punk concepts: Do It Yourself (DIY). Don't wait for someone to sign you to a record contract. Don't wait for someone to give you money to start up a fanzine. Don't wait for someone else to organize an anti-racism rally. Do It Yourself. To make my point, I rely upon the DIY insights of a cast of characters as diverse as Pearl Jam's Eddie Vedder, the Buzzcocks, the editor of the punk fanzine *Sniffin' Glue,* and a guy who worked nights and actually figured out how to put together a bestselling, full-length, illustrated punk book, DIY-style. They are all Do It Yourself pioneers. You can be one, too!

Punk anger is the motivator, DIY is the punk liberator: with both of those things in their scabby, tattooed fists, lots and lots of punks are getting increasingly preoccupied with politics—which can only be a good thing, given how screwed up the planet is. This part of the book, like the book itself, takes a bit of its name from the classic Clash song "Clampdown," in which Joe Strummer hollers, "Kick over the wall, 'cause governments will fall . . . How can you refuse it? Let fury have the hour, anger can be power! D'you know that you can use it?" To figure out what that means, I looked for inspiration in the direction of Joey Shithead of DOA, who has been at the forefront of punk activism for decades; Ian MacKaye, of the Teen Idles/Minor Threat/Fugazi, who kick-started an entire youth subculture with a single sulphurous punk song; the Slits and Bikini Kill, two punk bands who challenged the sexism latent in the punk movement—and manifest in the wider society—and made things arguably better in the process; and the kids of colour who changed racial attitudes and punk itself. Finally, I take a look at the political activity of the many, many punks and punk bands who valiantly organized to drive George W. Bush out of office (and who galvanized a lot of young voters along the way). They weren't successful, but they tried, and that's what counts most.

Now, like any youth subculture, punk is far from perfect. I admit it: punk ain't everything I crack it up to be. That's why I figured I had to shine a light into some of the darker corners of punk and take a hard look at one of the movement's greatest failures: how punk inadvertently encouraged violence and hate on both the far right and the far left. To that end, I profile Gerry Hannah, former bassist to Vancouver punk legends the Subhumans, who abandoned music to join the Squamish Five, a violent leftist cell that carried out a wave of terror in the early 1980s, maiming lots of innocent people in the process. I also profile George Burdi, the one-time lead singer of the punk/Oi! band RaHoWa (short for Racial Holy War) and the founder of the world's largest neo-Nazi rock record label, Resistance. For a few years, both of them were scary sociopaths— and both of them were briefly part of the punk underculture.

Before anyone gets the wrong impression, however, I wanted the book to acknowledge—and celebrate—the proposition that not all of punk needs to be sober, serious political activism, or even pissed off. So I call one of the chapters "Fuck Art, Let's Dance," which is taken from an old Stiff Records T-shirt I once owned, but which my disapproving mother threw out. This part of the book tells the story of the guys who literally invented punk rock, and made it all fun: Johnny, Joey and Tommy and Dee Dee Ramone. Along with Billy Idol, who made punk's image mainstream, I spend some time with the suburban punk-popsters who (to my occasional despair) dominate the scene now—bands such as Blink-182 and Good Charlotte. To ensure that art is given its due, though, I also invert Stiff Records' aphorism and briefly profile a few bands who in effect proclaimed "Fuck Dancing, Let's Do Art": Public Image Ltd., the Subway Sect and Wire. I end with a punk legend deciding whether poppy punks deserve to live or not. Personally, I think some of them deserve a firing squad, but that's just me.

The final few pages of the book try to refute the Sex Pistols' stated position in "God Save the Queen"—namely, that there is no future. Wrong! Wrong, wrong, wrong! There *is* a future! There are things worth *believing in!* There are things worth *living for!* This part of the book promotes the idea that true punks can, and should, work to get to the future—and, once there, make it better. Punk is about changing the world with music (or a fanzine, or a book, or a poem, or a political act) while remaining simultaneously rowdy and caustic and giving vent to every bit of adolescent (and post-adolescent) anger it can muster. Righteous anger, DIY, political activism—and even a little bit of dancing and artiness along the way—all come together to make up what punk was, is and can be: defiant, resistant and self-reliant. Anti-authority, youthful, loud, creative, independent, and totally unique. All of those things.

I end up saying that punk is alive and kicking, because it is. Punk, however much it failed at trying to change the world, deserves some credit for having tried to do so.

That's pretty much it, except for a few Top Ten lists at the end. I love those.

—

Punk was the search for real. It *is* the search for real.

If you're a teenager—and everyone is, at one time or another—you inevitably form the opinion that all things between heaven and earth are phony, and fake, and fraudulent. Your parents. Your teachers. Your governments. Your friends. Everything, in its essence, is without the slimmest amount of truth. It's all fucking bullshit.

When you are a young person, you inevitably tend to react to this news with disappointment, or anger, or both. You break things, you take drugs, you punch someone out, you join something. My best friend, Pierre, and I, we wrote a song. We called it "Secret of Immortality," and here are a couple lines from it:

> *Did you know that the grass is blue and the sky is green?*
> *They lied to you! This is the secret of immortality!*

I don't remember every little detail from my punk days, but I remember one night back in the spring of 1980. Our band was playing at the Union Hall on Seventeenth Avenue in our hometown of Calgary, and we were opening for Vancouver's DOA, the greatest punk band Canada has ever seen. "Secret of Immortality" was a peculiar little tune for a punk band to write—it was a bit slower and a bit quieter than the standard punk fare—but it took the position that there were no truths, basically, and that the only safe place left was the place inside your own head. Typical teenage paranoia, but our fans seemed to like the song a lot.

It was hot and sweaty in the Union Hall that night, with punks stacked in there like cordwood, and everyone was having a good time. No fights, no bikers, no raids by the cops. At one point in "Secret of Immortality," as Joey Shithead stood at the side of the stage and our band looked out over hundreds of dancing, slamming punks, I got to that line about the blue grass and the green sky. And when I sang the next bit—"They lied to you! This is the secret of immortality!"—four hundred punks suddenly screamed along, in unison, so angry and so loud that Joey stepped back, a bit startled, and looked at them. "THEY LIED TO YOU! THIS IS THE SECRET OF IMMORTALITY!"

As we kept playing to the end of the song, I wasn't quite sure what had just happened, either, but I was happy and immensely grateful that some words I had written in my room one night had actually been found to have some value by people I considered friends (or, at the very least, people who belonged to the same subculture as me). It was an amazing moment—and, like all amazing moments, I didn't figure out what it meant until later on. I remembered that amazing punk night, and I thought about it, and I think I figured it out.

Punk is about trying to scratch out some meaning in a big old world that seems pretty meaningless, most days. It's about being angry at being lied to, and smashing your fist against the doors behind which cower the liars, even if you know you're the one who is probably going to get hurt. Punk is about raging against all the powers that be, to try to make things better, if only for just an instant.

It's also about being yourself, and finding something that is *real*, and holding onto it as though your life depends on it.

Which, when you get right down to it, it does.

ANGER IS ENERGY
(or, we come to praise, and bury, the sex pistols)

Punk, if it means anything at all, is in its essence—in its scruffy, snotty, iconoclastic soul—about being young, pissed off and suspicious of anyone with money or power. Which is why it is fair to say this: if Johnny Rotten cared at all about punk, and if he believed a single word of the songs he made (in)famous, he'd piss off and retire.

But he won't. Not a fucking chance. Instead, Johnny Rotten, née John Joseph Lydon, slouches at the podium at the Holiday Inn on King Street West in Toronto, Ontario, the very personification of everything punk is not. Old, cynical and more preoccupied with lucre than he would care to admit. A boring old fart, a champagne snob, holding forth on his humble beginnings. Lydon, or Rotten, or whatever it is that he now calls himself, sips on a bottle of mineral water, his bleached-blond head cocked to one side. He is no longer punk's Antichrist. He is punk's Antithesis.

"I come from the lowest kind of shit you can imagine," says Johnny, who is wearing a black designer T-shirt, baggy black pants and shiny new pair of black Adidas. He is nearly fifty, and he takes his step-grandchildren to Disneyland. But he sounds genuinely outraged. "Working-class British. And it's worse when you are Irish," adds Johnny, who is the eldest son of a crane driver from County Galway, but is present today with a bodyguard, a group of hangers-on and a small army of publicists. He gets plenty of questions from the audience about his first musical dalliance, the Sex Pistols, and a few queries about his long-time artsy-fartsy project, Public Image Ltd. But, mostly, Johnny prefers to talk about himself.

His audience of two hundred, assembled at the "keynote address" of the 2003 North by Northeast Music and Film Festival, applaud enthusiastically after his every utterance. They adore him. Encountering no dissent, Johnny warms to his poverty-and-suffering theme. "In this world, there are no handouts," he declares. "None. Read your fine print. It's all right there. Don't just leave it up to your manager. That's a major mistake. And I know that one, alright." More applause. More mineral water.

Looking on impassively from the sidelines is someone John Lydon does not identify: his big-shot Los Angeles manager, Larry Einbund, whose office is just a little bit west of Beverly Hills. They travelled to Toronto together—the pair of them and the bodyguard, Rambo. Johnny may say that the aspiring musicians present shouldn't "just leave it up to [their] manager," but—to put a fine point on it—he does. All interview requests must be vetted by Larry; on this trip to the Great White North, only major daily newspapers generally get the nod.

An older cameraman from CBC Television, one of the friendliest media people around, attempts to ask Johnny a question that has not been approved in advance by his manager. Johnny sneers at the man, who is a bit overweight, and calls him "fatty." The crowd erupts in derisive laughter; the man looks embarrassed. Johnny says, "You don't deserve an answer." He looks proud of himself.

It's been twenty-five years since an emaciated, feral Johnny Rotten snarled that he was the Antichrist in the Sex Pistols' astonishing "Anarchy in the U.K." John Lydon has had his own television and radio shows (all cancelled); he appears on talk shows to expound on his world view (he was a regular on the popular *Politically Incorrect,* now cancelled); and the website he favours sells his CDs, obscure Hollywood movies in which he has had bit parts, and his autobiography, *Rotten: No Irish, No Blacks, No Dogs.* Long ago, the book was remaindered—that is, sold off cheaply by his publisher—but Johnny has made certain that copies are available for sale at his "speech," for $20, including relevant taxes. It seems almost impossible that Johnny Rotten and John Lydon are the same person.

To say that Johnny Rotten, former Antichrist, has become John Lydon, utter hypocrite, would not go over well with his adoring audience on this day. But a hypocrite he is, without much doubt. He sneers at the United States of America, calling it "the new Russia." But he lives there, and has for many years. He declares that he doesn't have a record deal—"And I don't care," he sniffs—but later allows that he would like to be offered one while in Canada. He says there is "no point" in offering new Sex Pistols material, then takes care to remind everyone that the band is appearing in Toronto in a few weeks' time.

He repeatedly pronounces that he is above politics, and insists that we need to "break down these barriers that we keep fucking putting between us"—and then he appears to mock black people, suggesting that their music comes from "the jungle." (On that single occasion, the audience goes silent.) He goes on like that for forty-five minutes or so, then adjourns the proceedings to sign copies of his autobiography. The lineup stretches around the room.

Having been unsuccessful in persuading Larry Einbund to permit a twenty-minute interview, I step up. I tell the former Sex Pistol that I'm the sap who sent a bottle of champagne to his room, on the slender hope that such transparent flattery would result in an interview. "Oh, you're the one who sent that cheap shit," he sneers, apparently unimpressed by the $150 champagne sent his way.

I get pissed off. "Too bad, pal. You're the one staying at the cheap, shitty hotel."

Rambo glowers, looking ready for a bit of the old ultra-violence. The former Johnny Rotten signs another autograph, pauses, then says, "Well, you can't have your cheap, shitty interview, then."

The Antichrist permits his bodyguard to light his cigarette, then turns his attention to the next autograph-seeker.

Alright, fine. Big deal. So he's old, he's a mainstream misanthrope, and he's more interested in putting together a record deal than a revolution. In the rock 'n' roll pantheon, John Lydon is hardly alone in that regard. The former Johnny Rotten has become the embodiment of all that punk sought to change or, failing that, hoped to destroy; popular culture tends to have that effect on too many promising young radicals. So what?

Well, because it *matters*. Because, at one time, Johnny Rotten himself mattered, however much he denies it now. Because the Sex Pistols, in their day, were the most important rock 'n' roll band on the planet. Legendary rock critic Lester Bangs called their "Anarchy in the U.K." single "one of the greatest records ever made," and *Rolling Stone,* at around the same time, described the Sex Pistols as "the most incendiary rock 'n' roll band since the Rolling Stones and the Who." They may have "finished rock 'n' roll," declared rock essayist Greil Marcus, approvingly; they are "a new rock voice and a new rock attitude," wrote critic Robert Christgau. "The greatest youth frustration anthem ever released," wrote Tony Parsons and Julie Burchill in their amphetamine-fuelled seminal 1978 book

The Boy Looked at Johnny. "Just over three minutes of blind raging fury, pushing rock's perennial demonic possession stance to totally unprecedented extremes, a singularly unpretentious/working class de-mystification, a beautiful, blistering, nerve-bruising paean to anarchy as self-rule . . ."

With their records, their art, their words, their clothes and their methods, Johnny Rotten and the Sex Pistols electrified a slice of youth culture, shook up rock 'n' roll, and made it acceptable (advisable, even) to be angry. Angry about your parents, your teachers, your life—angry about everything. While they were admittedly more nihilistic than idealistic, even the truly idealistic punk bands—in particular, the Clash and Stiff Little Fingers— acknowledge the Sex Pistols as the ones who started it all.

The Pistols, and the punk movement they helped to create, were a specific rejection of everything rock 'n' roll had become in the 1970s—namely an arena-sized, apolitical, coke-addicted, utterly-disconnected-from-reality corporate game played by millionaires. Punk, and the Pistols, changed all of that. They were loud, loutish, pissed off. They were of the streets, and for the streets. Whether they acknowledged it or not, they wanted rock 'n' roll—or, if not rock 'n' roll, then something, *anything*—to matter. In three minutes of earthly existence—in the three minutes (and twenty seconds) it takes to hear "God Save the Queen" for the first time, for instance—the Pistols accomplished more than the Rolling Stones did in three decades.

Even if that's overstating things (okay, it probably is), and even if punk was merely what Sham 69's Jimmy Pursey says it was—namely, "just six months in the summer of 1977"—then the Sex Pistols figured prominently at the centre of that definition, too. In their surprisingly brief tenure, they were everything a rock 'n' roll band should be: they were utterly outside the dominant popular culture. They were in-solent. They wrote great tunes. And they frightened parents, teachers and the elderly.

Listen, for instance, to "Anarchy in the U.K.," the one song that made punk real and started a revolution. Thirty years on, "Anarchy" is an astonishing, amazing, arresting, awe-inspiring—and, most of all, *angry*—record. There had never been anything like "Anarchy in the U.K." before, and there has been very little like it since. It was issued for the first time as a 45 rpm single by EMI in November 1976, in a plain black sleeve, with "I Wanna Be Me" on the B-side.

The song was written in the Sex Pistols' cramped rehearsal space in London's pop mecca known as Denmark Street, a narrow thoroughfare off Charing Cross Road in the West End, crammed with music shops and record stores. Jimi Hendrix and the Beatles rehearsed at spaces on Denmark Street, Bob Marley bought his first guitar at a shop on Denmark Street, and David Bowie even lived there, for a time, in a camper van. The Sex Pistols rehearsed at Number Six, in a room secured for them by a £1,000 deposit put down by their manager, Malcolm McLaren. Guitarist Steve Jones lived there for much of 1976 and 1977; periodically, the others would crash there, too.

The original riff for "Anarchy"—as with most of the band's best material—came from Glen Matlock, the bassist; drummer Paul Cook says that Jones subsequently helped to "beef up" Matlock's melody, which they all felt had an anthemic feel to it. The tune got its debut, sans lyrics, one night early in July 1976. Apparently, on that same evening, Rotten was seen lurking in a corner at the Denmark Street space, uncharacteristically quiet, scribbling on a scrap of paper— while, he recalls, the rest of the band argued (something that happened often). Why a song about anarchy? Rotten's response, recorded by a British writer: "I mean, *why not* anarchy? It was probably something to do with what I was reading at the time. No other reason."

(Rotten was being truthful. Anarchy, as a political philosophy, wasn't ever as much of a preoccupation for the Pistols as some of their fans would have liked. But in the punk movement that was to come, "anarchy"—accompanied by the ubiquitous punk symbol, the circled "A"—was a rallying cry for many punks and punk bands, with the British group Crass being its most enduring advocate. For the rest of us, anarchy is a dumb political theory, of course, because it is wholly unobtainable. Stripped of its rhetoric, anarchy is little more than lawlessness and disorder. Illegal downloading of punk songs or spitting on a group of performers are good examples of lawlessness, or disorder, or both. Out of the hundreds of punks I have interviewed, however, not one of them likes to be gobbed at or have their music stolen. So much for anarchy.)

Just as the group was packing it in for the night, Rotten presented his bandmates with the words. Ten months later, writing in *New Musical Express* about the British "punk" group that was shaking up all of rock 'n' roll, Lester Bangs—the departed, but still undisputed rock critic King of Kings—wrote, "I must admit, that as a vet of this rock 'ritin' game, I was totally blown away by 'Anarchy in the U.K.' I'm a sucker for rage from way back—and the lyrics are good, too."

They were also, as things turned out, unlike any words anyone had ever heard before in a song destined for the pop charts. At the time, pop music was sinking in a pit of sanitized, homogenized dreck. On the British charts—and the North American ones, too—songs like ABBA's "Mamma Mia" and "Dancing Queen" dominated, along with Barbara Streisand, Rod Stewart, the Jacksons and metric tonnes of soulless disco dross. It was almost as if someone, somewhere, had determined that rock 'n' roll would embrace the mainstream: none of the lyrics were angry, or political, or shocking. Some pub rock was alright, and glam had a bit to offer, but for the most part, it was a horrible time for music, filled as it was with glossy, inoffensive tributes to "love" and the status quo.

So, for a group to actually record—and promote—a song about the Antichrist, anarchy, destroying the passerby and getting pissed was, everyone agreed, unprecedented. Listening to the song, even now, the anger is its most distinguishing characteristic; the anarchy stuff isn't: at no point, then or now, were the Sex Pistols honest-to-goodness anarchists. Notwithstanding that, the words were without precedent: *"I am an antichrist/ I am an anarchist/ Don't know what I want/ But I know how to get it/ I wanna destroy the passerby . . ."*

The opening seconds of "Anarchy"—Matlock's thundering chords and, above the din, Johnny Rotten's demonic, reedy, unforgettable cackle: "Right! Now! Ha ha ha ha! I am an ANTICHRIST-*ah!* I am an ANARCHIST-*ah!*"—can still send chills down your back, if you let it.

Hearing Rotten's lyrics for the first time at the rehearsal space on Denmark Street, Glen Matlock was—according to the other three—rather angry. "He thought it was an appalling idea for a song," Rotten later wrote. "I proved him right." Matlock's melody had been transformed by Rotten's words, and vice versa. Said Cook, "'Anarchy' was a classic example of everything working together perfectly." It *was* perfect. It was the beginning of the first revolution rock 'n' roll had experienced in years—and, some say, ever.

Back in the early to mid-seventies, as now, there was plenty for young Britons to be pissed off about. Middle Eastern wars had spurred a fuel crisis; there was inflation, recession, massive unemployment and escalating labour strife that culminated in an unprecedented loan to Britain from the International Monetary Fund. Public spending was forty-five percent of the national income. A strike by municipal workers had filled London's streets with garbage, and queues for unemployment benefits—"the dole"—were growing exponentially. Young people (Sex Pistols Johnny Rotten and Sid Vicious among them, as well as Joe Strummer and Paul Simonon of the Clash) were squatting in abandoned houses. The Irish Republican Army was continuing to export its terrorist bombing campaign to English soil. Race riots, police brutality and soccer hooliganism were commonplace. And it was sickeningly hot in the summer of 1976, hotter than it had been at any time since the summer of 1940.

For the many young people disinterested in politics, there was little solace to be found in rock 'n' roll, and lots to loathe. In their outrageous (but wonderful) punk polemic, *The Boy Looked at Johnny,* Julie Burchill and Tony Parsons dismiss the popular music genres of the time:

Hip Easy Listening was an insipid aural palliative for and by jaundiced hippies of all ages and social standing . . . Disco Fodder was mechanical, mindless, sanitized soul, in which Uncle Tom sported an Afro to provide the staple dancing ration of the nation's youth whose lives were similarly mass-produced; it was the perfect backdrop for a slipshod education running the line to the factory, office or dole. Disco was the opiate of the prole—agent of social order, it featured no polemics beyond get down and boogie, party, party . . . the epic Teutonic aesthetic, Heavy Metal, was brutally ham-fisted renderings of blues-based white rock—a totally moronic downered wipe-out which complimented the Seventies teenage leisure activities of arson and alcoholism.

The grinding misery of those years, politically (in Britain) and musically (in Britain and the United States), made the punk explosion feel inevitable. Said Paul Cook to one interviewer at the time, "We wanted to shake things up. We grew up with three-day weeks and power cuts, sitting with candles. Corrugated iron everywhere, like a war was happening. Nobody considered the future, really." There was no future, as Johnny Rotten would howl in "God Save the Queen," and lots of young people agreed.

Ask any Sex Pistol, however, and he will undescore one point: too much ink has been spilled about the socio-economic significance of the band, and punk itself. Too much of it is bullshit. Rotten/Lydon, to his credit, has always been consistent about this. In a recent (and scathing) statement that could easily apply to any book that attempts to analyze punk—including this one—the Sex Pistols' front man sneered, "No matter what you've done, and all the right reasons you've put into it, and all the effort and the energy, there will always be a journalist who will misinterpret your personal motivations." Pause. "I'll give you an example. There's a book called

England's Dreaming by Jon Savage. Um, I was extremely annoyed by that book. That was written by a man who wasn't there at the time, had fuck all to do with anything, and yet became the spokesperson of punk . . . If I don't know what the fuck my own life is about, who the hell appointed this upper class twat to say it for me? You know what I mean?"

Well, yes, I, we, do. It is impossible—and wrong, even—to attempt to impose order on something as deliberately disordered as punk. But I think it's fair to attempt to figure out the *meaning* of something as genuinely important as punk. So fuck you, Johnny.

To paraphrase a lyric Lydon later recorded in the Public Image Ltd. era (in the hit single "Rise"), punk was about anger. "Anger is an energy, anger is an energy, anger is an energy," he chanted, over and over. Anger is energy because it overcomes youthful lethargy, and cynicism, and hopelessness. It gets one off one's ass.

In the summer of 2003, encountering him in the flesh for the first time, and just prior to our little verbal scuffle, I was selected to ask Johnny Rotten a question. So I asked him why, and if, anger is still energy. Scathing and contemptuous, he spat out his five-second answer at me: "*Why? Why* is anger an energy? Because it motivates you! Is love not an energy too? *Duh!*" He is a proper asshole, but he is right: punk is anger, and anger is (often) good.

It motivates you.

It's improbable in the extreme: four British lowlifes, barely out of their teens, scrabble together a rock band, and—despite poverty, criminal records, spotty education and relative musical inaptitude—figure out a way to provoke, and channel, the anger of millions of kids. Politicians and political parties everywhere acknowledge their continuing inability to capture the attention of young people, and get them to vote. Teachers try, and regularly fail, to stir the passion of students for literature or some other part of the accepted curriculum. How, then, did the Sex Pistols inflame an influential slice of the youth culture? Were they just one of a long line of smartly packaged pop music rebellions that tricked people—like Elvis's hips, or the Beatles' hair, or Woodstock's anti-war anthems? Were they an unplanned sociological roll of the dice, an aberration, one that had not been seen before, nor has been since? Or did they just have a lot of great tunes?

When it is first suggested to him that the Sex Pistols fell apart when he left the band—because he, more than any of the others, was the Pistol who created those great tunes—Glen Matlock is cagey. (He doesn't bite on the sociological or pop culture manipulation theories, either.) The man who wrote nearly every one of the Sex Pistols' songs—the good ones, anyway—is now back with the band, and he isn't eager to pick any fights with his mates. The Pistols have just concluded two weeks of gigging across North America, from East Coast to West, and this time the band didn't fall to pieces. Unlike the first tour, in January 1978, when they did, spectacularly.

The Sex Pistols' first bassist—the band's only bassist, really—is backstage in Toronto, smoking a cigarette and looking off into the middle distance. "C'mon, Glen," I say. "Sid Vicious wasn't about music. He was about PR. He was about shock value. There was no substance to what he did, you know that. When you left, it was the end of the Pistols. I mean, you need a musical base, even in the Sex Pistols, right? And you were it."

"I don't know if that's for me to say, but . . ." Matlock shrugs. He pauses for a long while, and then grins. "Okay, you're right. Sid, yeah. Basically he was a likeable dude with a good haircut. Not the sharpest tool in the box." He muses about Sid a bit. "John was enough of a front man, you know. When Sid came in, there were two front men, and they started fighting. And, on top of that, he couldn't play a bloody note."

Following the Pistols' breakup, Matlock adds, "I became relatively friendly with Sid, and we did a couple of gigs, and Sid was actually a good rock 'n' roll singer . . . It's all sad, really."

This is true. The two Sex Pistols bassists hooked up in the

summer of 1978 in a Maida Vale pub, Matlock recalls, near where Vicious lived with Nancy Spungen. They decided to play together in a kind of punk-style supergroup, featuring Matlock on bass, Rich Kids guitarist Steve New, and the Damned's Rat Scabies. They called themselves Vicious White Kids and played a single gig in August 1978, at the Electric Ballroom; fatefully, Vicious and Spungen left for New York City a few days later, never to return. Eight weeks later, Spungen would be dead—stabbed to death by Sid Vicious. By February 1979, Vicious would be dead, too, from a heroin overdose.

That's Sid. Any of the Sex Pistols will remark upon Sid's celebrated musical incompetence, and his vacuity. But mixed in with the critique is a sadness to which Sex Pistols are not supposed to be susceptible. You can sense that they quietly wonder, occasionally, whether the death of Sid (and Nancy, and Sid's mother, who also killed herself with a heroin overdose, in 1996) was in any way preventable. While they do not admit it, all of the Sex Pistols probably know that Sid Vicious's hateful brand of punk killed Nancy Spungen and Sid Vicious—and very nearly punk itself. (That was certainly Joey Ramone's view: in an interview with me, he contended that the shock and sensationalism that followed Spungen's murder made life exceedingly difficult for his and other bands for quite some time.)

In the case of Johnny Rotten, however, Matlock is slightly more forthcoming. Their disdain for each other throughout 1976 and 1977 is the stuff of music legend. In his 1994 autobiography *Rotten,* for instance, the Sex Pistols' front man admits to wishing that Matlock would "drop dead." Said he, "That's right, Glen. Drop dead. Unfortunately for him, he doesn't seem to think I meant it. I fucking well did. Continuously."

Reminded about that now, Glen Matlock is low-key but candid. "You know, well, John and myself are like oil and water, and we'll both admit that." On musical influences (Rotten: "I could never relate to Elvis Presley or the Beatles. Ever." Matlock: "I cut my teeth on the Beatles and American rock 'n' roll records."). On musical approach (Rotten: "These difficulties arose when they tried to change me into a Bay City Roller sort—being nice and singing these daft old songs, which of course I would not do." Matlock: "The way Malcolm was preaching it, we were his puppets, and John was a bit of an asshole at that stage. I just wasn't interested, you know?"). On musical roles (Rotten: "I knew [the rest of the band] couldn't write songs." Matlock: "[Rotten] was just the lyricist. That's it."). And so on.

Anger may indeed be an energy, but the angry Rotten–Matlock battles—sometimes onstage, with fists—were by early 1977 becoming a significant problem for their manager and fellow bandmates. Throughout the ill-fated Anarchy in the U.K. tour in December 1976, the relationship between Matlock and Rotten— never great to begin with—degenerated dramatically. By the end of 1976, the bassist's position in the band had become, as he admits now, "untenable." In March of the following year, Matlock says, "Malcolm called me up and said, 'Oh, look, we're going to have a meeting, you know, will you come to this meeting?' So I went to meet Steve and Paul and Malcolm at this café in Covent Garden, and they said to me, 'Look, we know you don't get on with John, can't you just pretend to like him?' And I said, 'Well, no, I can't pretend that I like him. He drives me bloody mad, you know?' He [was] a prima donna."

When the Sex Pistols reunited for a worldwide tour in 1996, they were questioned often about their willingness to regroup when the two principals—Glen Matlock, who wrote the music, and John Lydon, who wrote the words—had so obviously despised each other in the early days. Lydon, characteristically, attributed the reunion tour to a desire for money (appropriately enough, the tour was dubbed Filthy Lucre). Matlock is less cynical, but he freely acknowledges that the anger that forged and propelled them twenty-five years ago is mostly gone. It's about something else now, but not necessarily money.

"It's *fun*. I still think it's a lot of fun," he says. "I still think we knock the shit out of most bands that are out there today. There are a lot of great songs there, you know, which were hardly ever played around the world. And, you know, when we go and play these days, there's twenty thousand people who turn up in some places. So it's kind of a worthwhile cause, you know?" He pauses. "So there you go. I think we still have it. A lot of people in rock just never had it in the first place."

Matlock generally likes Steve Jones and Paul Cook, and all of them—to a one—despise their former manager, McLaren. Matlock explains, "John was the last one to get on the boat, you know? At the start, he always thought it was Steve, Paul and me against him, but that wasn't the case. Steve and Paul were kind of like, um, Fred Flintstone and Barney Rubble. Then there was me and there was John, so I suppose there was some balance there. But Malcolm started up a lot of arguments, and there was a lot of politics involved . . ." He trails off.

So what about McLaren, then? Was he really as bad as they all now say?

"What a schmuck." Matlock struggles to find something non-critical to say about the man who, loathed or not, invented the concept (if not the fact) of the Sex Pistols. "What I would say now is that the Pistols wouldn't have happened without any of the people who were involved. Including *him*." Matlock seems reluctant to utter McLaren's name. "He played his part, I suppose, and he did keep everyone on their toes all the time, alright. But he didn't actually deliver anything. Which isn't how he likes to pitch it, is it?"

Matlock, as Matlock freely admits, has always been the odd man out in the Sex Pistols. In the flesh, he is genial and completely unpretentious, and he admits that he still enjoys pop music. At the time of the Pistols' debut, in 1976 or so, his willingness to listen to other genres of music enraged Rotten. Now, as then, Matlock doesn't care. "We were all totally different, you know. Totally. John, myself, Steve, Paul, we all have totally different kinds of influences. I gave it a bit of depth with the tunes, I suppose. The whole thing is . . . you've got to have good tunes, basically. So there you go. It was something for John to hang his lyrics on."

Glen Matlock wrote the music for all of the Sex Pistols' hit singles, save one, and in the case of "Pretty Vacant," he wrote the words, too. "God Save the Queen," the incendiary Sex Pistols single that ultimately captured the number one spot on the British pop charts, was composed by Matlock on a piano, no less, as the band loitered during a demo-recording session at their Denmark Street space in late July 1976. Only "Holidays in the Sun," released in the summer of 1977, featured a Sid Vicious songwriting credit; tellingly (with Matlock by then gone to his own group, the Rich Kids), the song's melody was plagiarized, note for note, from the Jam's "In the City" hit single. As *Trouser Press* succinctly put it, "[The Pistols] swiped the riff."

Matlock was born in August 1956, an only child. His father built trucks; his mother was a clerk with a British utility. Quiet, shy, Matlock grew up in and around Kensal Rise, in London's North West. His principal interest, from the start, was music. "When I was growing up, in the middle of the 1960s, the BBC was, like, really straight and boring," he remembers. "And all these pirate radio stations sprang up and were broadcasting just right outside our coastal waters, in the North Sea and the English Channel, and it all coincided with the baby boom. You know, the Beatles and the Stones, and the Yardbirds and the Kinks and the Who, in their heyday, coming through the radio. And that is what I was listening to.

"A lot of my musical influences remain the same, and I hearken back to that. And I think the Pistols got a hell of a lot out of all of that. We didn't necessarily copy all of that. But we definitely had that kind of sensibility, you know?"

Matlock met Jones and Cook, famously, in Malcolm McLaren and Vivienne Westwood's controversial Sex clothing shop at 430 King's Road, where Matlock worked part-time on Saturdays. Sex was located on the street level of what was, in those days, a seedy four-storey Victorian building; it is now called Vivienne Westwood's World's End and is surrounded by a trendy Italian restaurant across the street, pricey bookshops and an upscale haute couture scene. In the window, Westwood has placed a clock that spins backwards.

Back in the early days, McLaren was a former art student and Westwood was an aspiring fashion designer. Boyfriend and girlfriend, of sorts, the pair opened their shop in 1971, first dubbing it Let It Rock. Disdainful of hippie culture, they were mightily impressed by the violent Paris student riots of 1968 and the Situationist International (SI) themes of the day. Situationists aggressively mocked and parodied the mass media and attempted to thwart the popular culture by twisting it—an approach that would later greatly influence McLaren's approach to the Sex Pistols. Like most Situationist fans, McLaren and Westwood disliked the hedonistic "love and peace" stylings of the hippies. Their little King's Road shop soon attracted a steady clientele of Teddy boys, drawn by Westwood's retro clothing.

The second wave of Teddy boy culture propelled McLaren (the marketer) and Westwood (the fashion maven) to a surprising degree of success. McLaren demonstrated an ability to attract media attention, and Let It Rock was soon getting mentions in British newspapers, and even in *Rolling Stone*. Ringo Starr and David Essex came by to shop. Restless, always dissatisfied, McLaren and Westwood discarded the retro Teddy boy look in 1972, started pushing a hard biker look, with lots of studded leather and chains, and changed the store's name to Too Fast to Live, Too Young to Die. Soon, even Iggy Pop—in London to record *Raw Power,* which some claim (incorrectly) is the first punk album—came in to look around. (McLaren wrote Iggy off as an untidy hippie, which is not entirely inaccurate.)

In the summer of 1973, McLaren and Westwood were asked to display some of their clothing designs at a fashion show in New York City. While there, McLaren met the New York Dolls' Sylvain Sylvain, who had a fondness for fashion. McLaren established an immediate rapport with the shambolic, noisy, cross-dressing Dolls.

"We like to look sixteen and bored shitless," lead singer David Johansen told *Rolling Stone* in the fall of 1972. McLaren loved the group, then just weeks away from releasing their controversial first album. Its cover would feature the Dolls sprawled on a couch, wearing platform heels and lots of lipstick; many maintain, still, that it is one of the best rock 'n' roll albums ever.

When the Dolls travelled to England to play, in early 1974, McLaren went everywhere they went. They were everything he thought a rock 'n' roll group should be—androgynous, shocking, filthy, loud. Most of all, the Dolls were new: they hadn't been done before, by anyone. McLaren changed the shop's name again—to Sex. It advertised itself with large, spongy pink letters out front and walls inside covered with a low-cost, grey, spongy-rubber material. Slogans were spray-painted here and there, like "Does passion end in fashion?" McLaren and Westwood started to sell the leather and rubber wear favoured by the S&M crowd (and often worn by the New York Dolls), along with other less pricey items, such as bizarre-looking T-shirts designed by Westwood out of two pieces of fabric awkwardly stitched together.

Matlock came to work at McLaren's shop in the summer of 1973 to fill in for Westwood and McLaren while the couple were exhibiting their clothes in New York City and hanging out with the New York Dolls. It was there that Matlock first encountered Steve Jones, a dropout and skinhead who was the son of a boxer and a hairdresser. Jones's best pal, Paul Cook, was the son of a carpenter and was a steady, easygoing sort; when he met Jones at age fourteen, his school grades went into a spiral from which they would not recover. Within a year, Jones had moved out of his family's home and was living with Cook's. Around the same time, Jones and Cook befriended an aspiring young guitarist who bore the decidedly uncool name Warwick Nightingale. The three decided to form a band.

Because they lacked any money to purchase instruments, Jones, the singer, put his burglary skills to work: he "nicked" equipment, as he put it. Instruments, and stuff that could be fenced, were pilfered from the mansions and gigs of the Rolling Stones' Ron Wood and Keith Richards and from Rod Stewart. In July 1973, Jones and gang walked into the Hammersmith Odeon, where David Bowie was to play, and stole a PA system and microphones worth tens of thousands of pounds. They simply snipped the wires and walked out with the gear.

The group started to practise in a furniture shop near the end of the King's Road. They adopted the name the Strand, after a Roxy Music song. But they needed a manager. Malcolm McLaren was their choice: he knew the New York Dolls, for one thing, and he let them (and other London delinquents) hang out at his shop. McLaren declined a number of times, as his part-time employee Glen Matlock—then a student at St. Martin's School of Art—looked on, keeping quiet. Worn down by Jones's persistence, however, McLaren eventually went to see the group perform. Jones sang, badly, while Nightingale played guitar and Cook drums. They had no bassist, no stage presence and no musical ability. But McLaren was intrigued by their determination and suggested they give Glen Matlock an audition. Hearing how well he could play, the Strand hired Matlock on the spot.

McLaren set the Strand to practising, relentlessly, under the direction of his sidekick, Bernie Rhodes, who shared McLaren's enthusiasm for the Situationists. While they did so, McLaren travelled again to New York to offer his services as manager to the New York Dolls. The group was falling apart, largely due to the fact that Johnny Thunders and Jerry Nolan were heroin addicts. Displaying the lack of judgment for which he would later become infamous, McLaren decked out the Dolls in red vinyl clothes, placed them before a hammer and sickle backdrop, and pushed the *Communist Manifesto* as a marketing strategy. It was the effective end of the group: Malcolm McLaren would shortly kill off the New York Dolls, just as he would help to kill off the Sex Pistols. He returned to London in May 1975, dejected and dispirited, carrying a single souvenir—Sylvain Sylvain's white Les Paul guitar. McLaren should have stayed in New York City awhile longer: in and around the same time frame, acts such as Television were starting to generate excitement at a New York bar, CBGB's. One of Television's founders, Richard Hell, favoured spiked hair, ripped clothing and a gaunt, dissolute look—a look one of the local fanzines called "punk."

Back in London, McLaren was impressed by the Strand's sound: they had come far under Rhodes's tutelage. Changes were necessary, however. Jones was a terrible lead singer, and Nightingale was too withdrawn and conservative. McLaren quietly loaned Jones Sylvain Sylvain's guitar and encouraged him to play. Within a short time, Jones discovered he had a talent for guitar. Warwick Nightingale, the forgotten Sex Pistol, was out.

With Steve Jones now exclusively playing guitar, the group needed a singer. McLaren and Rhodes considered Sylvain Sylvain, and even a young Glasgow musician, Midge Ure (who would later achieve fame as the founder of Ultravox). Neither worked out.

Also hanging around Sex in those days was a gang that was known, sometimes, as the Johns, because all of its members were named John. One was John Simon Ritchie, who would come to be known as Sid Vicious (named after his friend Lydon's pet hamster). Another was John Wardle—or, as he would be dubbed one drunken night, Jah Wobble—future bassist for Public Image Ltd. A third member was John Grey, a schoolteacher-to-be. John "Rambo"—the Arsenal football thug, bodyguard and jewellery designer—would come around periodically, particularly when there was the possibility of a fight. And the fifth member was John Lydon, soon to be known as Johnny Rotten.

Rhodes spotted something in Lydon—a creative, rebellious spark, coupled with an undeniable wit. He urged McLaren to get the Finsbury Park teenager to audition. Rhodes asked Lydon one evening in August 1975 if he could sing. Lydon—at that stage still terribly shy, which he masked with a sharp tongue and, occasionally, his fists—snapped, "What? What do you mean? What for? No! Only out of tune and, anyway, I play the violin." McLaren was interested. He asked Lydon to come by for an audition at Sex.

Sporting ripped clothing and safety pins, Lydon displayed teeth that were literally, well, rotten. (Thus the name later given to him by Steve Jones.) Lydon impressed his tiny audience that night. Holding a shower attachment as a substitute for a microphone, he twisted and lurched like he was being electrocuted by the old Wurlitzer McLaren kept in Sex. Lydon improvised lyrics. He screamed. He pretended to vomit. He was hired.

At the first rehearsal of the group that would become known as the Sex Pistols, above a pub called the Crunchie Frog in Rotherhithe, none of the band showed up. Except Lydon, who was furious. When Glen Matlock eventually phoned to apologize, Lydon told him he would "kill him with a hammer."

"Right, I thought," says Matlock, sighing. "Here we go."

The Antichrist has forgotten the words.

He's become enough of a rock star—a *professional entertainer,* of the type he once railed against—that it isn't immediately obvious to any of the thousands in attendance on this particular August evening. He hides it well. Swigging on a magnum of champagne, modelling a cigarette, glaring at those in front (the ones who have paid more than forty bucks a ticket and will therefore serve as the evening's prescribed ruling class, Her Majesty being unavailable), Johnny Rotten has actually forgotten the words to "God Save the Queen." But no one seems to notice.

It's pretty fucking odd. The set list, after all, comprises no more than fourteen songs, and the tunes themselves are about thirty years old. How could he have forgotten the words? Everyone else present—a peculiar mix of nostalgia freaks, teenagers, metal heads and aging punks decked out in spanking new NEVER MIND THE BOLLOCKS T-shirts ($50), Sex Pistols sweatshirts ($75, inclusive of partial swastika on the front) and underwear ($30, two styles, and both bearing the band's copyrighted logo)—seems to know what to sing. Johnny Rotten, looking increasingly irritated, doesn't.

Before a young punk can step forward to offer his or her services, Rotten's bad mood gets worse. At the commencement of "No Feelings," the fourth song in the set, Johnny spits, with evident relish, into the crowd. Almost immediately, he and the rest of the Sex Pistols are showered with garbage, beer and a veritable wall of gob. Jones and Matlock hustle away from the edge of the stage, closer to the enormous stitched backdrop made up of bits of flag and regal lions. Rotten, inexplicably, stays put. (Punk rock historians know that such a decision, in such circumstances, is risky. At one early punk festival, Damned drummer Rat Scabies spat in Siouxsie Sioux's eye, hastening a case of conjunctivitis; on another occasion, Clash front man Joe Strummer attributed a bout of hepatitis to a wad of spit that landed in his open mouth.)

I note that Rotten is looking down, squinting. On the ground, between his microphone stand and a bank of monitors, is a three-ring binder, filled with laminated pages—presumably to protect them from such phlegm assaults. The binder contains Sex Pistols lyrics.

Binder or no binder, by the time the band gets around to "God Save the Queen," Johnny is forgetting the words a lot. He looks intently at Matlock, perhaps for inspiration. If Matlock notices, he gives no indication. He keeps playing bass, bouncing back and forth to Rotten's right. A steaming geyser of human saliva is now cascading down on the stage and Johnny Rotten. The place is slick with it.

Looking suddenly weary, Rotten carefully places his microphone stand near Cook's drum kit. He is regarded with concern by his money manager, Larry Einbund, and by Rambo, the bodyguard. Rotten then addresses the crowd, some of whom are lunging at him to better place the next wad of gob. Rotten snarls, "Canada, I hope you enjoy your fucking socialism, because it is fucking you up the arse!" He then stalks offstage, followed shortly by Jones, Matlock and Cook. Einbund scurries after him; so does

Rambo, who scoops up the binder of lyrics along the way. No one is quite sure what socialism has to do with anything, but one thing is clear: Johnny Rotten is livid.

Backstage (where I have been smuggled in by a friend), Rotten is handed a towel to wipe off the sweat and saliva. His money manager and bodyguard flit around him, nodding sympathetically as he rails about the crowd. The rest of the Sex Pistols regard him with unconcern, or not at all.

When Rotten returns to the stage, Paul Cook commences the signature intro to the Stooges' "No Fun." The Sex Pistols lead singer balances atop one of the monitors and calls the ticket holders in the first few rows "posh cunts." He says something else, too, but nobody can really make it out. No one cares.

It wasn't always thus: at one time, the Pistols were the best live act in rock 'n' roll. One of the better Sex Pistols performances—one of the performances that ultimately served to shake up rock 'n' roll—came on August 29, 1976, at Screen on the Green, a theatre in Islington, London. An independent cinema house, Screen on the Green had a

big red neon sign out front, and a gritty, grimy feel inside. Also on the bill, for the admission price of £1, were the Clash, for their third gig, plus the Buzzcocks, who had put on their first-ever public performance in June of that year, supporting the Sex Pistols in Manchester. In between acts, there were screenings of Kenneth Anger's cultish short films *Kustom Kar Kommandos* and *Scorpio Rising*.

The idea for the gig had been Malcolm McLaren's. He was assisted by two art school friends, one of whom, Jamie Reid, designed the handbills. (Reid also created the band's sleeve designs for "Pretty Vacant," "Anarchy in the U.K.," "God Save the Queen" and "Holidays in the Sun," as well as the album cover for *Never Mind the Bollocks, Here's the Sex Pistols.*) McLaren's objective was to pull together the burgeoning punk scene for the first time. By showcasing the Pistols, the Clash and the Buzzcocks, McLaren hoped to demonstrate to the media and record company A & R men—many of whom were in attendance that night—that the punk scene was no passing fad.

Malcolm McLaren, for reasons known only to him, decided the entire affair should kick off at midnight and continue until dawn. A "Midnight Special," he billed it. Matlock laughs, recalling the scene at the Screen on the Green. Before the gig, McLaren had a nasty fight with Bernie Rhodes, his former disciple and now the manager of the Clash. McLaren punished Rhodes by ordering that the PA volume be turned down for the Clash's set. The inter-punk rivalry didn't stop there. Says Matlock, "We said that the Clash could build the stage. And they said, 'Okay, we'll provide a stage.' We said, no, not *provide* it, you've got to *build* it!" And they did. Bassist Paul Simonon later recalled, "We weren't very good that night because we'd been up very early unloading the scaffolding and building the stage."

Matlock describes the Screen on the Green gig as pure angry chaos—and, therefore, exactly right. The Buzzcocks opened the night's proceedings, with Howard Devoto snarling about "orgasm addicts," as 350 or so wildly garbed punks milled about, rubbing shoulders with the likes of famous record producer Chris Spedding and future famous punk musicians such as Steve Severin, Siouxsie Sioux and Billy Idol. Siouxsie, dressed in high-end leather and bondage gear, had her breasts on full public display, while a tabloid photographer madly snapped away. Bits of Anger's films were projected on the screen, genitalia flashes intact, as David Bowie songs were played. The air reeked of amyl nitrate.

The Sex Pistols took to the stage after a lacklustre performance by the Clash. Johnny Rotten—as he often did—mocked the audience, and the incongruously hippie feel to McLaren's event. "Should I say all the trendy fings like peace and love, maaaaan? Are you having a good time, maaaan? Believe it: this ain't the Summer of Love!"

It wasn't, not in the least. The Pistols launched into their set with a ferocious rendition of "Anarchy," then still new. That was followed by "I Wanna Be Me," "Seventeen" and "New York," among other Pistols staples. Covers played by the band, for which Rotten made up his own lyrics, included the Monkees' take on "I'm Not Your Stepping Stone" and the Who's "Substitute."

At one point, Rotten—leaning too far and too fast into his microphone stand—smashed his two front teeth out. There was blood and spit everywhere. Enraged, Rotten ordered the fans in the front rows to look for his teeth, as his anger pushed the rest of the Pistols to an extraordinary performance. Rotten was intense, ferocious; he howled at the centre of the Pistols' aural maelstrom, which sounded like a hurricane slamming into a Mack truck at 200 mph. Matlock remembers, "John was down in the front row, looking for the teeth. It was pure pandemonium. We were starting on our way, you know?" It all ended, gloriously, with the Pistols' manic take on the Stooges' "No Fun."

On that night, when the Pistols were still young, poor and pissed off, the furious foursome put on a show that was described by *New Musical Express*'s Charles Shaar Murray as "loud, clean and tight." He added, "The first thirty seconds of [the Sex Pistols'] set blew out all the boring, amateurish artsy-fartsy mock-decadence that preceded it purely by virtue of its tautness, directness and utter realism."

Nick Mobbs, the head of A & R at EMI Records, was there that night. "The Screen on the Green gig gave me this incredible feeling in the stomach. I think I'll remember it until the day I die. It reminded me of when I was a fan, back when I had nothing to do with the business. And yet, at the same time, my head was saying: 'They're not very good.' And, although I knew that wasn't the major consideration, I would lie awake all that night thinking about it, wondering whether it was something EMI could handle." As things turned out, they couldn't.

On the rock 'n' roll calendar, the Screen on the Green gig should have been no more than that—a gig. Another performance by yet another naughty rock 'n' roll group. But Screen on the Green, and the Pistols themselves, amounted to considerably more than that. For the first time in a long time, a band was writing and performing songs that weren't designed to make people feel *hopeful* about hard times—the Pistols were writing and performing songs that were calculated to make their audience feel *fucking pissed off.* And, if the songs *weren't* pissing you off—well, the Sex Pistols didn't fucking care. That, too, made them unique.

In *New Musical Express,* in February 1976, Steve Jones declared that he and his bandmates weren't into music: "We're into chaos." And that, certainly, was true enough. But most of all, more than anything else, the Pistols were into furious, resplendent, spit-flecked *anger:* it was what they did best, onstage or in a studio. Anger was their forte. Recognizing that there were lots of other kids like them—with no jobs, no education, no hope and no future, but plenty of anger as a result—the Sex Pistols made the punk manifesto all *about* anger. It worked.

From Glen Matlock's perspective—and everyone else's—the next key Sex Pistols performance came less than a month later, on September 20 and 21, 1976, at the 100 Club, located (naturally) at 100 Oxford Street, a former jazz venue, between Oxford Circus and Tottenham Court Road. It was the first punk "festival" anywhere, ever.

On the first night, the Pistols, the Clash, the Subway Sect and Siouxsie and the Banshees were slated to play; on the second, the festival featured the Damned, Chris Spedding and the Vibrators, the Buzzcocks and France's Stinky Toys. The opening night lineup of more than six hundred punks stretched along two city blocks. The tiny London punk scene was exploding. The founding members of the "scene" stared at punks they had never met before: waiting in the lineup future Stiff Records artist Johnny Moped; members-to-be of the youthful punk combo Eater; the Pogues' Shane MacGowan; Gaye Advert and TV Smith of the Adverts; the Pretenders' future founder Chrissie Hynde; and soon-to-be Sex Pistol Sid Vicious—who, in an ominous portent of what was to come, was apprehended carrying a knife he ostensibly planned to use on the female lead singer of the Stinky Toys.

The 100 Club Punk Rock Festival marks a delineation between the beginning and end of punk, at least for the Sex Pistols. The first night was what punk had been, and could be—with brilliant performances, no violence and the promise of a real rock revolution. The second night was Sid Vicious's night. The talentless, abusive junkie who effectively doomed the band threw a pint glass at the Damned during a cover version of the Stooges' "1970," smashing it on the club's central pillar near the front. A shard of glass struck a young female fan in the eye, blinding her. Vicious was swiftly pulled out of the crowd by police and, a week later, was locked up at the Ashford Remand Centre until trial. When it ultimately took place, the case ended without a conviction.

Another change, indicated by the Sex Pistols' performance on the first night of the 100 Club Punk Rock Festival, was that the band had moved from an obscure socio-musical cult to an imminent mass-market phenomenon. The club was packed with punks and punk fans, some of whom had travelled from the farthest corners of England to see the Pistols perform. In the early days, Rotten had seemed indifferent, or shy—or both—while onstage. At the Punk Rock Festival, however, Rotten was clearly in charge. Decked out in a Vivienne Westwood black bondage suit covered with zippers, safety pins, chains and crucifixes, Rotten was bound around his knees and chest.

According to those lucky enough to be present, the rest of the band had a greater presence than before, too—in the case of Jones, almost bordering on cock-rock swagger. Jones had an impressive guitar style, although he still (like most real punks) disdained fancy minor chords, sticking to the basics. The rhythm section—Cook and Matlock—was impressively tight, a virtual machine that made few mistakes.

Matlock recalls that the band had played at the 100 Club "two or three times" before the Punk Rock Festival, and usually before very few people. "By the end," he says, "we were packing them in. It was kind of madness, those days, and we were well on our way by the time the Punk Rock Festival took place. [100 Club manager] Ron Watts thought we were funny, and he gave us those gigs at the 100 Club. He thought there was something to this band of reprobates."

The Manchester reprobates known as the Buzzcocks remember their performance at the Punk Rock Festival—and the days preceding and following it—as life transforming. Lead guitarist Steve Diggle and lead singer Pete Shelley, who together remain the centre of the Buzzcocks, credit the Sex Pistols with giving them the opportunity to play for the first time—leading, ultimately, to nine Top Ten singles, and three Top Forty albums. The fury embodied by the Sex Pistols was a wonder to behold in those days, Diggle says. Few other bands were as angry onstage. Their

rage, he says, was a response to the gloom and despair of those days in the U.K. And it was precisely what the popular culture needed: a swift, hard kick in the arse.

Years later, when I interviewed him at a Buzzcocks show, Diggle said, "That's when I think the punk rock atom was split, you know, because all of the major music papers were going to be there that night. And the Sex Pistols were, even then, very savvy and glamorous and exciting. It was this angry rock sound, pouring off the stage—but, at the same time, they didn't care. They didn't give a fuck. It was like, you know, they're not just there to entertain you. *You're here to learn something.* It was something fucking magic happening. Time stood still, and you had to sort of question your whole life, or at least your whole way of looking at music. Suddenly, it was direct and in your face, you know?"

Not everyone who went to see the Sex Pistols—not everyone who fell under their demon spell—did so because they were angry. For many of the millions of British (then North American) kids who would become devoted followers of the band, there were plenty of other reasons to be there. Curiosity. Boredom. Controversy. Even the fact—Glen Matlock believes this to be partly true—that the pre–Sid Vicious Sex Pistols were an amazing rock 'n' roll band. They had great songs, they were riveting live performers, and their album, *Never Mind the Bollocks,* was one of the most exciting LPs anyone had heard in a long time.

But fury—about one's life, about the world, about rock 'n' roll— was a defining characteristic for many of the early converts to the punk movement. The Pistols, and Johnny Rotten in particular, denied that they sought to generate strong feelings about anything, really. Rotten was (and largely still is) unwilling to lead any particular parade. But the Pistols—on the basis of one album, just a few live shows and even fewer singles—unleashed a bona fide mini-revolution. All over Britain (and then Europe, and then North America, and then everywhere else), punk bands started to sprout up, independent record labels formed, fanzines were published, and teenagers were spotted everywhere with colourful punk clothes and colourful punk haircuts.

The curious thing about it all, so many years later, is that the Sex Pistols had no manifesto to foist upon the planet. They didn't promote left-wing revolution (as the Clash briefly did), or rightist jingoism (as Sham 69 or the Angelic Upstarts did, sort of), or feminism (as X-Ray Spex or the Slits did), or gay rights (as the Tom Robinson Band did), or art (as Wire did), or even dumb fun (as the Ramones did, gloriously). Apart from a vague call to anarchy in the first single and a half-hearted contention that Britain was "a fascist regime" in "God Save the Queen," the Sex Pistols weren't very political at all. No philosophical or ideological fervour gripped them: they were not left wing, not right wing, not anything. Just unbelievably pissed off.

Think about it: with the most meagre of tools—and a bit of stolen musical equipment—they prompted a rebellion with no name. That's not easy to do: even the most successful revolutionaries are usually capable of providing a *reason* for their revolution. Not the Sex Pistols. If you were to ask them if they were angry, their answer would be, Yes. If you were to ask them what it was all about, they would say, Nothing.

Creating an entire subculture, a new one, based upon nothing—nothing apart from (seemingly) impotent, directionless teenage rage? That is a big achievement, *maaaan.*

Getting ticked off about an aging John Lydon on the lecture circuit—or the Sex Pistols themselves as a punk nostalgia act—isn't such a big deal, perhaps. It isn't anything to get *angry* about. The Sex Pistols never claimed to be the leaders of a new rock revolution or some outré political movement for teenage outcasts. They were just a bunch of punks.

Glen Matlock has the last, best, word: "You know, the whole Pistols thing was, all things considered, a series of accidents. Not in terms of what we were singing, necessarily, but just in terms of being in the right place at the wrong time, or the wrong place at the right time, or whatever. And turning it to our advantage."

And so they did.

Get pissed! Destroy!

DIY
(or, doing it yourself is doing it right)

Eddie Vedder, the lead singer of Pearl Jam, is explaining his love for punk rock, generally, and the Buzzcocks, who are opening for his band, specifically. "It was the tunes," he says, grinning. "It was the Buzzcocks' melodies. For a suburban punk like me, who started out with the Sex Pistols, the Buzzcocks were . . . They did it all on their own, you know?"

He's backstage, it's summertime, and thousands of people are lining up to see his band. He is wearing dark wraparound shades, brown sneakers and a green army fatigue jacket over an ancient Ramones T-shirt. Beside him, beaming, is his pal, Buzzcocks' lead guitarist, Steve Diggle. Diggle says nothing, clearly delighted just to listen to Vedder talk about punk rock and DIY—the Do It Yourself culture that is the very heart of the punk movement. And that the Buzzcocks championed, on a punk record, before anyone else. In a few minutes—just before the Buzzcocks commence their blistering opening set, and as a pre-concert warm-up—Vedder will slip onstage to sing the Beatles' "You've Got to Hide Your Love Away," solo, accompanying himself on harmonica and acoustic guitar.

Growing up in La Mesa, California, a suburb of San Diego, Vedder was a punk and a surfer. Restless, smart, ambitious, he played in local garage bands, knew lots of people and collected punk records (including all of the Buzzcocks singles). While pumping gas on the graveyard shift, Vedder played in punk bands with names such as the Butts, Bad Radio and Surf and Destroy. He was a DIY disciple from the outset: for Bad Radio, Vedder acted as promoter, manager, booker—and even designed the group's gig flyers. Like all true DIY disciples, Eddie Vedder the punk rocker wasn't particularly interested in getting signed by a record label—he was interested in Doing It Himself, and thereby maintaining artistic control and integrity.

One night in the fall of 1989, Vedder skipped out on his paying job at a local Chevron station and went to see Joe Strummer perform

at a San Diego alternative club called the Bacchanal. Backstage, Vedder passed some time chatting with Strummer, who was performing a series of club dates in preparation for the recording of a solo album, his first. Significantly, Vedder also met Jack Irons, former drummer for the Red Hot Chili Peppers, who, on that evening, was keeping time for Strummer. The pair hit it off. In the following year, Irons would send Vedder a tape of music by a Seattle band in need of a singer. Vedder returned the tape, with his singing and lyrics on top. Pearl Jam was the result.

"I loved the Sex Pistols, and the Damned, and I loved these guys," Eddie Vedder says, pointing a finger at Diggle. "I had all of their singles in a box at home. I'd take them out and look at the sleeves for hours . . . they were wonderful."

What made them so wonderful?

"Because they did it themselves," says Vedder. "They didn't wait for someone to do it for them. They did it themselves.

"That's real punk rock."

Of all the theories that make up the philosophy of punk, none is as important as Do It Yourself. At the beginning, as now, it was the one thing that distinguished punk from other types of rock 'n' roll and other youth subcultures. Don't wait for someone else to give you permission. Don't wait for someone else to offer you a contract. Don't wait for an invitation. Be independent—*and just Do It Yourself.*

Listen to this stirring declaration from Joel, a Minneapolis punk, found in *Profane Existence* fanzine in the fall of 1991: "The driving ethic behind the most sincere punk efforts is DIY—Do It Yourself. We don't need to rely on rich businessmen to organize our fun for their profit—we can do it ourselves for no profit. We punks can organize gigs, organize and attend demos, put out records, publish books and fanzines, set up mail order distributions for our products, run record stores, distribute literature, encourage boycotts, and participate in political activities. We do all of these things and we do them well. Can any other youth-based counterculture of the Eighties and Nineties claim so much?"

The answer, mainly, is no: the DIY ethos remains one of punk's singular achievements. Punk music is different from the mainstream, as are punk fashions and styles. But they are not so different that they are incapable of being assimilated by mainstream rock 'n' roll or commercial youth culture. DIY was always different. It was a defining characteristic of punk from the outset, and it has remained that way. It hasn't been co-opted or compromised. Do It Yourself, and change yourself. Change everything.

Punks despised rock stars. They were mostly disinterested in musical ability. They hated the fact that there was distance—literally and figuratively—between the performer and the audience. To join a punk band, all you really needed was some sort of an instrument and a desire to play. Technical competence and a fondness for the hierarchies found in other types of rock 'n' roll were anathema in punk. So, too, was a willingness to go along with the rules and regulations promulgated by corporate interests: thus, when the Clash entered into a long-term contract with CBS Records for £100,000 in January 1977, Mark Perry of the first British punk fanzine, *Sniffin' Glue,* declared, "Punk died the day the Clash signed to CBS."

As much as he dislikes the suggestion, Mark Perry himself was the embodiment of punk's DIY spirit. Born in Britain in 1957, the first rock 'n' roll show Perry saw, at fourteen, was a Beach Boys performance at the Royal Festival Hall. He lived in a council flat with his parents in South East London. By 1974, the year he left school, he was a glam rock aficionado, "stumbling about on silver stack-heeled boots, purple loon pants, a stripy tank top, brown satin jacket and topped off with shoulder-length hair."

Recalling those days, Perry declares, "Rock music wasn't crap before punk, but I'd always had this feeling that there was a gap between us, the fans, and them, the bands, that you couldn't cross. It was like a special club . . . and the only way to become a member was to sit for years alone in your bedroom learning how to play the guitar. People in bands seemed somehow special, in so much as I thought [of] myself as ordinary." In late 1975, Perry noted a change: bands like Dr. Feelgood, Eddie and the Hot Rods, and the Kursaal Flyers— all pub-rock stalwarts—started to attract a following. Pub rock, as Perry admits, was really just revved-up rhythm and blues, but it was decidedly better than the shite then clogging the British airwaves.

And then, in May 1976, Perry read in *New Musical Express* about an American band called the Ramones. The group had a brutal, simple, loud rock sound, but they were unlike anything that anyone had ever seen. In the review, Nick Kent quoted approvingly from a November 1975 stateside assessment of the band by his *NME* colleague Charles Shaar Murray: "They're simultaneously so funny, such a cartoon vision of rock 'n' roll, and so genuinely tight and powerful, that they will enchant anyone who fell in love with rock 'n' roll for the right reasons." While clearly reluctant to sound faddish, Kent confessed that he was impressed: "The Ramones don't say much," he wrote. "They're pretty vacant. But they rock out with a vengeance."

"[I] couldn't wait to hear it," Perry remembers. Once in possession of the album, he returned home from his dead-end banking job and hurriedly placed the Ramones' eponymous first waxing on his turntable. He was blown away by what he heard. Banking suddenly didn't seem very interesting anymore.

On July 4, 1976, for the first time in Britain, the Ramones unleashed their sound at the Roundhouse in North London's Chalk Farm. Despite the fact that Da Brudders Ramone—as they were called by all who loved them—were sandwiched between the Mersey Beat–loving Flamin' Groovies and local misogyny-rockers the Stranglers, the show electrified the then-nascent U.K. punk rock scene. In an epochal DIY moment, the Ramones brief performance at the Roundhouse, before an estimated two thousand fans, inspired a score of British punks to form their own bands on the spot. Backstage, the Clash—who hadn't yet played in public—lined up to meet the Ramones like a posse of star-struck teens. So, too, did the Sex Pistols' Johnny Rotten and his sidekick Sid Vicious, who were handed bottles of beer—in which, DeeDee later claimed, the Ramones had pissed. Meanwhile, milling about near the Roundhouse stage, Mark Perry met Brian James, a guitarist formerly with London SS, just starting out with something called the Damned.

In the days following the seminal Ramones Roundhouse gig, Perry searched, in vain, for a magazine about this exciting new phenomenon. He couldn't find anything, anywhere, in London.

Punk magazine was put out by friends of the Ramones in New York, but there was nothing by and for British punks. An acquaintance suggested that Perry start his own magazine. Partly inspired by the title of a Ramones song from their first album, the bank clerk went home and typed up the beginnings of a fanzine he called *Sniffin' Glue and Other Rock 'n' Roll Habits.* He wanted his publication to look and read like punk music itself—raw, rude and wholly DIY.

The first edition was written using a typewriter Perry's parents had given him for Christmas when he was ten years old. The headlines and graphics, if they could be called that, were scrawled by Perry using a thick felt marker. Says Perry, "It celebrated the DIY ethic, but was also representative of the very best that I could do." The first edition, all eight pages of it, featured reviews of the Ramones' performances at the Roundhouse and the following night at Dingwalls, plus assessments of records by the Runaways and Television, as well as Eddie and the Hot Rods. In his maiden editorial, Perry wrote, "I hope you enjoy sniffin' our little

contribution to the punk culture . . . I just hope we can keep it together!" As it turned out, he did, for about a year.

Perry and his girlfriend printed up about fifty copies of the fanzine on a Xerox machine at the office where she worked, then took the resulting publication to one of Perry's regular haunts, the Rock On record stall in Newport Court in Soho. Rock On agreed to sell *Sniffin' Glue*—and gave Perry money to print up fifty more. The first print run sold out quickly, to Perry's utter amazement. In no time at all, *Sniffin' Glue* would become a fixture of the local scene—ultimately selling an astounding fifteen thousand copies of its final edition. Establishment rock critic and novelist Nick Hornby says Perry "is, without question, one of the most important figures in punk history, a vastly unappreciated groundbreaker . . .

the seminal *Sniffin' Glue* fanzine largely determined the direction of the U.K. punk movement." True enough: it provided a blueprint for punk's early days, describing where shows were taking place, who was worth listening to and what was punk—and what wasn't.

John Cooper Clarke, sometime Manchester punk musician— and often called by some "the poet laureate of the British punk movement"—takes the position that *Sniffin' Glue* was an unprecedented event in the still-incomplete history of punk rock. "*Sniffin' Glue* became the chosen rag of the Blank Generation," he writes. "First of the fanzines, it featured the more realistic rock scene . . . with its cheapskate house style, and semi-literate enthusiasm, it conveyed there was a piss-or-get-off-the-pot urgency about the whole production." Meanwhile, *NME* declared that Perry's publication was "the nastiest, funniest and healthiest selection of the alternative music press in the history of rock 'n' roll and other habits." (It wasn't perfect however: *Sniffin' Glue,* and Perry, were occasionally sexist. More than once, the magazine and its founder declared that punk was no place for women.)

Perry modestly dismisses the plaudits from *NME,* Clarke and Hornby. But it is a fact—despite its maleness, his *Sniffin' Glue* was tremendously important, and not simply because it was unafraid to bash bands, or poke fun, or breathlessly wax enthusiastic about the latest acned, skinny group of shouters to appear on the scene. *Sniffin' Glue* was important because it *existed.* It was a perfect reflection of what it chronicled—a punk movement that owed everything (at the start, at least) to a desire to Do It Yourself. *Sniffin' Glue* shouldn't have happened, but it did.

Following distribution of the first issue on newsstands and in a few record shops in July 1976, Perry was telephoned by Ed Hollis, the manager of Eddie and the Hot Rods, who told him, "We've seen your fanzine, and we really like it." Hollis asked Perry if he wanted to ride in the band's van to a gig in Hastings. Perry was flattered and surprised, to say the least. Also along for the ride to Hastings—which resulted in a gushing review in the second edition of *Sniffin' Glue*—

were big-time rock journalists Jonh Ingham and Caroline Coon, later girlfriend to the Clash's Paul Simonon (and briefly, disastrously, the band's manager). It was Coon who took Perry under her wing and brought him to his first Sex Pistols gig, in late July at the 100 Club.

Years later, slouching in a Hackney rehearsal space called Audio Underground, Mark Perry grins, recalling his *Sniffin' Glue* days. He's in this nondescript place, sandwiched between a reggae shop and a convenience store, in what he acknowledges is a "tough area"—to practise with members of the latest incarnation of Alternative TV. Perry formed the band in March 1977; their first single, "Love Lies Limp," was a flexidisk included in the twelfth and final issue of *Sniffin' Glue*.

Perry doesn't look all that different from the way he did in the late seventies—he has a youthful manner, with a friendly, open face and an easy smile. Gathered with his bandmates to practise for a punk rock festival in Germany, Perry repeatedly scoffs at the notion that he is a punk/DIY icon. "That's bullshit," he says.

There isn't much doubt that Perry still despises imperial posturings in rock 'n' roll, or popular culture generally—and it is also clear that he believes the best way to do almost anything is to do it oneself. Asked for one piece of practical advice for punks starting out, he laughs. "Well, really, practical advice is what I recently gave to this guitarist, who wanted to be in a band and he was asking me about guitars. And I said to him that if he wanted to be in a band, it's a really sad thing, but no one ever really hires a band if they have to go around picking them up. Especially if they live miles away. So I said to him, 'Forget about the guitar and get your driver's licence. Because otherwise, no one is ever going to help you get a gig if they have to go pick you up!'" Much laughter ensues. (In a separate interview, by the way, Pete Shelley of the Buzzcocks gives exactly the same advice—learn how to drive!)

So that is what the DIY ethos is all about, when it is distilled down to its base elements? Getting a driver's licence?

"No, no," Perry says, laughing some more. "Most of all, I think it's important to read a lot. There's a lot of music out there that is quite often really good. But then, when you read some of the lyrics, you almost . . ." He rolls his eyes. "You want DIY? You've got to get literature in your head, so that you can get a good vocabulary going, and so you can develop some good ideas. You need good ideas. And then you just act on them."

Perry accepts that punk—conceived to be unorthodox— became the proponent of various orthodoxies itself, in fashion, idiom, sound, politics. He deplores the fact that the early DIY disciples made it tougher, deliberately or not, for the next generation of punks to be independent and do it themselves. "Some punks quickly set up their own cliques, back in 1977," he says. "They pulled up the ladder so that others couldn't get up to where they were. For me, Do It Yourself meant encouraging others, and it meant not feeling threatened by anyone or anything."

Perry was happy that *Sniffin' Glue* gave way to a score of other punk fanzines, with names like *Bondage* and *London's Outrage*. One such "competitor" was *Sideburns,* which liked the Stranglers, and which provided the best punk DIY exhortation of all. In December 1976, *Sideburns* ran a feature with the typewritten title "Playin' in the band . . . first and last in a series" over rough diagrams for the guitar chords A, E and G and scrawled instructions: "This is a chord. This is another. This is a third." At the bottom, underlined, is the command, "NOW FORM A BAND." That, Perry agrees, is truly DIY, and the very spirit of punk.

Before the advent of the Internet, fanzines such as *Sniffin' Glue* and *Sideburns* represented the principal means by which punks could communicate with one another. Most of the fanzines were produced like Perry's: photocopied, stapled together by hand and lacking much in the way of grammar, spelling or copyright protection. Typically, punks were (and are) suspicious of the mainstream media. So, not long after Perry's fanzine hit the streets in Soho, hundreds of fanzines started to appear wherever punks had organized themselves into a "scene"—in Britain, in Europe, in Canada and the United

States. That may not sound like a significant achievement now, with Internet-based networks and weblogs found everywhere. But it is, actually—an extraordinary one. With little money, no resources and no distribution networks, a few hundred punks actually conceived, and created, an alternative media that still functions around the planet. Who else has done that, ever, without corporate support? Who? No one.

More than anywhere else, fanzines flourished in the United States—seething just below the surface in what is arguably the most conservative democracy in the world. There, zines with names like *Flipside, Slash* and *Profane Existence* sold hundreds of copies. The most successful, by far—and the one, fittingly, that has become the target of many punks' ire for its aggressive promotion of a particular philosophy of punk—is MAXIMUMROCKNROLL. *MRR,* as it is known, was founded in San Francisco in 1982, and achieved success with "scene reports" contributed by punks from all corners of the globe (among them, from the start, the Dead Kennedys' lead singer, Jello Biafra). For much of its early existence, the zine boosted progressive views— something that still irritates even progressive punks, because *MRR* was so single-minded in communicating its politics.

Some 250 issues after its debut, the magazine's beginnings can be traced back to 1977 and a Berkeley punk rock radio show at station KPFA, hosted by Tim Yohannon. A sixties student activist at Rutgers and a member of the Communist Party, Yohannon regarded punk as the beginnings of an international, anti-capitalist, pro-peace movement. He left the radio program to devote himself to *MRR* full-time. From the very first issue, there can be little doubt that he used *MRR* to promote his world view. Many opposed his ideological rigidity, arguing that the punk scene was first about music, not politics. But Yohannon refused to waver, while donating *MRR* profits to some four dozen other fanzines and creating an all-ages punk perfomance venue called the Gilman Street Project in North Berkeley.

MRR first appeared as a newsprint booklet in *Not So Quiet on the Western Front,* a compilation LP released on Jello Biafra's label,

Alternative Tentacles. Yohannon would continue as editor of *MRR* until his death from lymphatic cancer in April 1998, at fifty-two. The zine he founded would attract punk readers and supporters in Europe, Asia, South America, Australia—and even in Iceland, Saudi Arabia, Israel and Micronesia. Like *Sniffin' Glue,* which partly inspired it, *MRR* helped to shape and promote a generation of punks.

The common theme of *Sniffin' Glue, MRR* and virtually every other punk fanzine, Mark Perry says, is that it is essential that young people should read, and listen, and learn for themselves—but also that they should try and change things, even if they repeatedly fail. He arrived at this point of view very early on—in the fifth edition of *Sniffin' Glue,* in fact, published in November 1976. There, Perry comes closest to defining the DIY ethic. After slagging mainstream music weeklies for invading the territory of punk pioneers ("Leave our music to us, if anything needs to be written, us kids will do it. We don't need any boring old fart to do it for us!"), Perry writes, "All you kids out there who read 'SG,' don't be satisfied with what *we* write. Go out and start your own fanzines or send reviews to the established papers. Let's really get on their nerves, flood the market with punk writing!"

That, truly, was DIY: don't listen to those who are advising you to Do It Yourself. Don't even listen to the DIY trailblazers! Just DIY.

Thinking back on those days now, Perry says the DIY punk value system ultimately faltered when punk bands started appearing on Top of the Pops, when the Clash signed to CBS and, particularly, when Perry himself permitted corporate advertising in *Sniffin' Glue* (the first being an EMI display ad for the Sex Pistols' "Anarchy in the U.K." single and tour—in the same fifth edition that contained Perry railing against what he called the "establishment rags"). When those things happened, Perry felt that punk was well on its way to becoming part of the popular culture, the most grievous sin of all. What's more, Perry says, he simply lost interest in *Sniffin' Glue.* So he moved on, forming his band—still functioning—called Alternative TV.

DIY is irrefutable proof of the hope that punk embodies—and it disproves the nihilism and cynicism of, say, the Sex Pistols' Johnny Rotten. Without getting too corny about it, DIY encourages youth to find their own way and to believe in themselves, without funding, without anyone's help, without permission, without limits. Just DIY—the method that punk, more than any other musical genre or subculture, pioneered in London and New York in 1976 and 1977.

But Mark Perry is not taking any credit. When it's suggested that his DIY credentials are impeccable (and that *Sniffin' Glue* was as unique as everyone says it was), he scowls. "Look," he says, "I'm sure there were fanzines in the fifties or sixties, and around when Dylan came along, printed up on those old machines . . . my little magazine wasn't a big deal. I just decided to do something on my own, that's all."

Perry looks at his watch; he has to go and practise with Alternative TV. Before he takes off, I ask if punk had a soul and, if so, if it lost its soul when it got big—as it is now, with bands such as Green Day or Blink-182. Did punk die in 1977, as many believe, and as he has claimed once or twice himself? Perry muses about that for a bit, as the members of ATV jam without him, one floor below. Finally, he says, "Punk's not dead. It's just lying low a bit. You know, it's right where it should be: it's underground. I mean, the Do It Yourself type of thing, where you just stick to it, and get up there and have a good time, you know—like, that's all over the place.

"Just doing it yourself—that isn't dead. If anything, it's stronger now than it ever was."

The Clash weren't really DIY, because—as Perry and plenty of others noted, derisively—signing to one of the biggest record labels in the world wasn't a very fucking punk thing to do, was it? So, too, the Sex Pistols: under Malcolm McLaren's Machiavellian tutelage, the self-professed anarchists were quite content to be courted, and signed, by the likes of EMI, A&M and Virgin. In fact, following one staged contract-inking ceremony with A&M outside Buckingham Palace in March 1977, the Pistols swilled champagne and played the role of naughty Rock Stars for the assembled press corps. It was bloody awful, even if it was meant to be funny or ironic (or something).

As the Pistols did, punk bands that submitted to the attentions of major record labels often regretted it. In the summer of 1981, to cite one notorious example, California hardcore pioneers Black Flag recorded their first album, *Damaged,* and agreed to let a small label, Unicorn, distribute it. Media conglomerate MCA became interested, however, and signed the band. When MCA's bright lights heard *Damaged,* they refused to release it, calling it "anti-parent." Unicorn, meanwhile, refused to pay Black Flag, and successfully sought an injunction preventing them from releasing any records on their own. The expensive, litigious mess occupied Black Flag for years, and provided plenty of punks with a cautionary tale about the dangers of *not* doing it yourself.

Plenty of other punk/punkish bands disposed of their DIY credentials without the briefest of hesitations, however: the Ramones, the Jam, Richard Hell and the Voidoids, the Stranglers, Siouxsie and the Banshees, Talking Heads, 999, Generation X, Sham 69, Wire, Television—all of them signed to corporate labels at the moment a record contract presented itself. It seemed that punk, the movement that was supposed to oppose and change the system, was willing to become part of it if lucre was involved. As the Clash's Joe Strummer wrote in "White Man in Hammersmith Palais": "The new groups are not concerned/ With what there is to be learned/ They got Burton suits, ha you think it's funny/ Turning rebellion into money." Twenty-four years later, Strummer and Co. sold the rights to "London Calling" to Jaguar, for use in a commercial advertising an "entry level" luxury sedan—and, before that, in 1991, they permitted "Should I Stay or Should I Go?" to become the soundtrack for a Levi's campaign (and, in 2005, a soundtrack for a Pontiac ad). Rebellion for money, money for rebellion; no one seemed to be immune. Except the Buzzcocks.

The Buzzcocks were not about rebellion, either, but—at the start, at least—there was no purer manifestation of DIY than the Manchester punk combo. In their first incarnation, the Buzzcocks comprised John Maher on drums, Steve Diggle on bass, Pete Shelley on guitar and Howard Devoto on vocals. Devoto and Shelley were born Howard Trafford and Peter McNeish, and were students at the Bolton Institute of Technology. They changed their names to Devoto and Shelley following a fabled sojourn to London in late February 1976 because "Trafford" and "McNeish" weren't terribly punk-sounding. In London, the pair saw the Sex Pistols twice, at High Wycombe's College of Further Education and Welwyn Garden City. Inspired, they rushed back home to Manchester to form their own punk group. Bassist Diggle was recruited through a classified ad tucked inside the pages of the *New Manchester Review.* Maher, age sixteen, was found via another classified, placed by a friend in *Melody Maker;* he would later come to be regarded as one of the best drummers in rock 'n' roll, though he had been playing for only a few weeks when he hooked up with the Buzzcocks. Their name was a pun—for a vibrator.

Diggle describes how the Buzzcocks ended their set following their legendary opening for the Sex Pistols at the Lesser Free Trade Hall in Manchester on July 20, 1976: "We ran through the audience straight up to the bar. [The audience] couldn't understand it yet. They thought it was weird because they were so used to seeing bands finish their set and disappear into the dressing room. We felt we were a part of them . . . The natural thing to do afterwards was to go and drink with them and watch the Pistols."

Afterwards, Diggle recalls, "I walked from the Free Trade Hall and stood in the bus queue with all the kids I'd been at the gig with and stood at the bar with. [By then] I could tell that they had all got it, they understood what it was all about and what we and the Pistols were trying to do. The message was Do It Yourself! . . . I can't emphasize how important it was for those kids at that time, how important it was for music . . . Here were bands that were saying: 'Get up off your arse. Express yourself. You too can do it.' They were all relating to it. The barrier . . . between the ordinary kid on the street and the musician on the stage [was gone]."

As the Buzzcocks continued to gig in and around Manchester (picking up a loyal following along the way, among them Mark Perry in distant London), Howard Devoto quietly suggested what Steve Diggle calls "a pretty radical thing to do"—that they should set up their own record label and put out their own album. The name they had previously cooked up for their management team—New Hormones—could also serve as the moniker for the record label.

Devoto's idea *was* radical. In the history of rock 'n' roll up to that point, every act—no matter how revolutionary and anti-establishment they might be—had sought to get "signed" by a record label. The notion that one would, or could, circumvent that process was unheard of. To create your own record label was to admit that you were unpopular—and non-viable commercially.

The Buzzcocks were intrigued by Devoto's proposal. At the drug rehabilitation centre that served as their rehearsal space on Lower Mosely Street in Manchester, the Buzzcocks each chose a song to be included on the record—which was to be an EP, or extended play single, containing three or four tunes. Diggle selected "Breakdown," the others, "Time's Up," "Friends of Mine" and the unforgettable "Boredom."

The band hired a local character named Martin Hannett—or, as he was sometimes known, Martin Zero—to produce the EP. Hannett was a native of Manchester's North Side who had immersed himself in the city's rock scene. Working a day job in a chemistry lab, Hannett was a proverbial jack of all trades, toiling part-time as a soundman, writing for the *Manchester Review,* playing some bass and forming his own music promotions company. He told the Buzzcocks he was a producer, which he wasn't.

Diggle recalls, "To be honest, I don't think he'd ever recorded anything in his life. He was an eccentric electronics boffin who drove the studio's engineer mad. Every time the engineer got the sound just right, Martin would lean across and fuck it up. He must have done it a hundred times until the engineer gave up and let him mix it his way. That's why we ended up with the poxy tinny sound." Hannett went on to record and produce celebrated records for A Certain Ratio, John Cooper Clarke, Durutti Column, Happy Mondays, New Order, Devoto's Magazine, Orchestral Manoeuvres in the Dark, Psychedelic Furs, the Stone Roses, U2—and Joy Division, whose Ian Curtis witnessed, and was inspired by, the Sex Pistols/Buzzcocks gig at the Lesser Free Trade Hall in Manchester in July 1976.

Shelley's father provided the band with £250 to pay for the recording session, while a fan and friend who assisted on the New Hormones managerial venture loaned them £100 out of her university tuition fund to pay for the pressing of the disk, to be called *Spiral Scratch*. Another friend made use of his Polaroid camera to snap shots of the Buzzcocks near Piccadilly Gardens for the record's cover.

A firm near London pressed one thousand copies of the record for £500. Diggle says, "I couldn't believe it was so easy. It sounds stupid now, but I couldn't get my head around the fact that we would have our own record . . . The excitement was unbelievable." Diggle and Devoto travelled to London to pick up the vinyl. Back in Devoto's kitchen, the band stayed up all night, drinking wine and carefully placing the records in the *Spiral Scratch* sleeves. The record was officially released on January 29, 1977.

They would have laughed at the suggestion that it would eventually sell sixteen thousand copies. Or that, when it was re-

released in 1979 by Virgin Records, the EP would rise to number thirty-one on the U.K. charts. Or that *Melody Maker* would advise its scores of readers to immediately rush out and buy it—because "they're running out quickly." Or that Mark Perry, in *Sniffin' Glue,* would write, "Buy it, if you don't you shouldn't be reading this mag." Or that *NME* would come to describe it as "tinny, amateurish, neurotic, untogether, out of tune, ridiculously short and . . . a life-altering cultural event in the lives of thousands." Back in February 1977, the Buzzcocks sold their perfect, life-altering little record for just £1—or, occasionally, they gave it away.

The record's highlight, in the view of most, is "Boredom." On it, Devoto snarls, "You know me, I'm acting dumb/ You know the scene, very humdrum/ Boredom, Boredom/ I'm living in this, uh, movie, but it doesn't move me/ I'm the man that's waiting for the phone to ring/ Hear it ring-a-ding-a-fucking-ding." The tune became a bit of an anthem for the nascent punk movement, which regularly professed to be bored with everything. It was sarcastic and electric, with lyrics taken from a notebook in which Devoto scrawled surrealistic fragments of words. The song's guitar "solo" was Shelley playing two notes, over and over. It was only the third punk record to be issued in the United Kingdom—after the Damned's "New Rose" and the Pistols' "Anarchy" a week later—but *Spiral Scratch* was the first to be entirely self-financed, self-produced and self-made. If people didn't know what DIY was before, they did now. The Buzzcocks had shown them.

Nearly thirty years later, Shelley and Diggle—plus a couple of other guys who are relative newcomers to the band (former members John Maher and Steve Garvey are now, respectively, a well-to-do race car aficionado and a suburban dad)—muse about the significance of the first DIY punk record. Diggle looks like he always did, though his onstage Townshend-style leaps and bounds are less frequent these days. Shelley is a bit larger than he used to be, with bleached hair and a bemused expression—particularly when Diggle is in the vicinity.

Diggle suggests that the band's willingness to put out their own record—to do it on their own—was nearly as radical as the record itself. It was their sense of independence that attracted many early fans, he says. "That kind of approach gave it an urgency, you know. And I think the audience responded to that. I think they realized that we didn't own anything either, that we were like them. There were a million young people on the dole back then, and there was nothing happening musically. The soil was fertile for punk and the Do It Yourself thing to happen. And we still meet people who have achieved a lot of things in their lives, and they say to us, 'If it wasn't for punk, I wouldn't have achieved this. I wouldn't be who I am today.' Did we change things? I don't know. But I'd say people got something out of it."

Shelley nods at his old friend's obvious understatement. Punk, he says, was all about "enfranchising people to be creative . . . It was about coming from nowhere, and trying to get somewhere." The record industry, the fashion industry, the media, the politicians—all, he says, were on the outside of punk looking in. "It was all supposed to be spectacular failure. But it ended up being very liberating."

Even when Howard Devoto left the band—suddenly, in February 1977, pompously declaring that "what was once unhealthily fresh is now a clean old hat"—the Buzzcocks persevered. Devoto told Shelley and Diggle he had achieved all of his goals for the band: namely, making a record and opening for the Sex Pistols. He wanted to return to school to finish his degree. Not much later, Devoto would form the post-punk group Magazine, but would never achieve the sort of success or acclaim enjoyed by the Buzzcocks. (He has remained friendly with his former bandmates, however, and has even done some experimental recordings with Shelley.)

Shelley and Diggle decided to soldier on without Devoto. Shelley became the vocalist, Diggle switched from bass to lead guitar, and Steve Garvey was recruited to play bass. They became a punk rock hit machine—an odd combination of the Sex Pistols' prickly attitude and the Beatles' songwriting ability.

Sans Devoto, the Buzzcocks recorded thirteen extraordinary singles, half of them major hits in Britain, as well as three acclaimed albums: *Another Music in a Different Kitchen, Love Bites* and *A Different Kind of Tension.* All were released through United Artists, after the band signed with the label in August 1977. But Diggle and Shelley remain understandably proud of what they achieved with *Spiral Scratch,* well before attracting the attention of a major record label.

Says Shelley, "Everybody thought, to put out a record, you had to go through a record company. But record companies are just like other manufacturers. They're nothing special. We just changed the emphasis from them to us. That's all. We wanted artistic control. We thought, if we do it ourselves, nobody can tell us what we can and can't do. We can do whatever we want."

Exactly.

If Mark Perry's *Sniffin' Glue* was the most important punk DIY fanzine, and the Buzzcocks' *Spiral Scratch* the most important punk DIY record, then Craig O'Hara's *The Philosophy of Punk: More Than Noise!* is the most important punk DIY book. In fact, it may be the *only* punk DIY book; it's certainly the only one that is an international bestseller and is regularly reprinted.

From his retreat in the mountains of rural West Virginia (where he moved following a decade in San Francisco, having concluded that the cost of living there was simply too high for someone trying to eke out an existence as an anarchist publisher of books), O'Hara is dismissive about his achievement. When pressed, he merely admits that *The Philosophy of Punk* represents only his own point of view. He is aware that his anti-corporate, anti-police, anti-government pronouncements aren't shared by everyone, including even some punks. He's also aware that punk has experienced more than a few spectacular failures over the years. But he's unapologetic. "There's no doubt I'm putting a positive spin on something that I thought was rather positive at the time," he says, on the line from one of the "two shacks" where he works and lives, alone. "I don't think punk has changed things like an election does, or like political parties do. But it has changed the lives of lots of people."

While a student at Boston University in the early 1990s, O'Hara—a rural Pennsylvania native who had followed the U.S. punk scene for a decade—jokingly referred to himself as OPOC: Only Punk on Campus. Then, in 1991, he became deeply angered and ultimately radicalized by the Persian Gulf War: "The war politicized *a lot* of people." In the following year, he completed *The Philosophy of Punk*—printed on 5.5-by-8.5-inch sheets at MailBoxes Etc. in Yocumtown, Pennsylvania. Lacking any means to bind it, O'Hara drilled the pages with two holes and clipped them together with binder rings. The edition eventually sold more than three thousand copies.

The second edition—upgraded slightly, with dozens of photographs of lesser-known U.S. punk bands and no binder rings in evidence—was printed at a Kinko's in San Francisco, where O'Hara had relocated (for three years he worked nights at Kinko's: "I was copying bank statements for corporations all night long, I figured I might as well make a few copies for my book . . ."). That edition sold more than three thousand copies, mainly through word of mouth.

O'Hara handed over responsibility for the third edition to a radical workers' collective, AK Press, which sold many thousands more (O'Hara still works with AK). Along the way, there have been German, French, Turkish, Russian and even Lithuanian translations of the book, selling more than a thousand copies in the latter case. Early on, a Chinese translation was created for Hong Kong punks. It, too, sold well. Greek and Brazilian versions will soon be hitting the market. "It's selling pretty good," O'Hara says. When he wrote *The Philosophy of Punk,* Craig O'Hara didn't expect such an extraordinary response for a DIY book that extolled DIY. He didn't expect *anyone* to read it, in fact. "I didn't even plan on it becoming a book. My intention wasn't to write something a lot of people would read. It was just something I was doing for myself . . . I happened to be in school at the time, and you have write papers all the time when you are in school. I was of the view that, if you're going to have to spend a lot of time working on something, it might as well be something you enjoy, or something you're interested in. I'm not interested in things that happened in the 1700s or the 1800s. However, I was then involved in something—the punk scene, or movement, or whatever you want to call it—and there weren't any fucking books about it. Punk was it, for me. So I figured, what the fuck. I'm gonna write this book."

The Philosophy of Punk isn't glossy, it isn't subtle—it isn't even completely comprehensible, in some parts. But it is ambitious, rebellious and independent, and it represents the first attempt to define punk's raison d'être (and concludes that punk must be radical and oppositional or it is not punk). Lithuania's state censor, O'Hara notes with understandable pride, called it "a vile, rebellious, offensive document." MAXIMUMROCKNROLL, now the leading punk fanzine in the world, declared that *The Philosophy of Punk* represents "the highest ideals that [punk] aspired to obtain."

The book's nine chapters tackle a myriad of punk-related issues, among them: misrepresentations of punk by the media; the differences between punks and skinheads; fanzines; anarchism; gender (from sexism to feminism and gay and lesbian rights); environmental concerns; the Straight Edge movement; and, most of all, DIY, which pervades the book's 170 pages.

Along with its disdain for mainstream society and its trappings—something that has been *de rigueur* with most punks since the early 1980s—*The Philosophy of Punk* is characterized by an unshakeable optimism about youth and the future. It gently urges punks to embrace a lifestyle that safeguards the environment and is tolerant of racial, religious and gender differences; it is highly suspicious of virtually anything produced by corporations, capitalism and the mass media. O'Hara's conviction—unshaken after more than a decade—is that punk is a youth movement that favours rebellion and change, and one that can represent "a formidable voice of opposition."

Even now, O'Hara gets excited discussing DIY. "It's a stepping stone to being able to think for yourself, and to being critical about the things that are around you in society. If you never made your own fanzine or book or record, then how would you know to question the shit that you pick up at the store or in the media or whatever? Once you start doing it yourself, you start to question how things are presented to you. What punk and the DIY thing enabled people to do is to question all of it—everything.

"And as far as I'm concerned, the questions and the answers that the punks came up with were pretty fucking good."

In his book, O'Hara takes the position that the earliest punk scenes opposed the commercialization of youth culture—and, particularly, the notion that anyone was more important than anyone else. In the punk music context, this meant (and means) that audiences were as important as the people up onstage. Everyone is equal: no bosses, no boundaries, no VIPs. DIY adherents, O'Hara writes, want to "break down the traditional star/audience boundaries. Anyone could be the 'star' or no one could be!"

He argues that co-operation, not competition, is (or should be) the prevailing approach in punk circles. Bands, for example, lend each other equipment, divide gig profits fairly, collaboratively organize gigs and promotional campaigns and even offer one another a floor to crash on. O'Hara—like many of the punk theorists who followed in his wake—is understandably skeptical about punks who move from independent ventures to corporate ones. Is it really possible to "keep a radical, uncompromising political stance whilst working for a major label whose job it is to sell records to a mass audience"? The answer, almost always, is no, O'Hara writes, noting that the music industry wants to make money using radical rhetoric, but rarely tolerates radicalism when it jeopardizes profits. (Ask the Clash.) Compromising your ideals doesn't have to happen if you aren't rubbing elbows with people who require you to compromise.

That, perhaps more than anything else, is the beauty of DIY: it removes the temptation to sell out.

Nowadays, O'Hara says, he doesn't listen to punk as much as he used to. Living in the wilds of West Virginia, it can take hours to drive to a show featuring a band he likes. And, he says, he's not as young as he used to be. He laughs. "Punk is a youth movement," he says. "That's one of the things that makes it so magical, so worthwhile and so valuable—because it affects people when they *are* young. They're young and confused, but they're a hell of a lot more optimistic about what can be done."

But if even O'Hara admits he hardly ever listens to punk anymore, can it honestly be said that punk, and DIY, are still a going concern?

O'Hara snorts. "When people say punk is dead, it's just usually because they're not young anymore. They realize how truly the world does indeed suck, and it's hard for them to be optimistic. I'm older now, too, and I don't think anymore that punk can change the world. But there are a lot of fifteen- and sixteen-year-old boys and girls out there, a lot of them, who have just been turned on to this original and independent way of thinking for themselves. And maybe *they* will change the world, one day, you know?

"Punk's not dead," he says, by way of conclusion. "I don't think it ever will be. For millions of people worldwide, it's definitely not dead. That's why you are not ever going to get me to say that punk, and the Do It Yourself spirit, is dead.

"Punk lives!"

FURY'S HOUR
(or, talk minus action equals zero)

It's mathematics, basically. Most of the people who were punk rock pioneers—the ones who discovered it in the mid- to late 1970s, in London or New York or somewhere else—are getting pretty old. If you figure they were in their late teens or early twenties when they first heard "Anarchy in the U.K." and "Blitzkrieg Bop," then most of them are now closer to fifty than forty. And, for a subculture that was entirely by, for and about youth, that presents quite the philosophical dilemma. Mortgages and kids are somewhat irreconcilable with a furious punk's manifesto, aren't they?

Joey Shithead, the former Joey Keithley, the founder and front man of seminal Vancouver punk outfit DOA, is sitting with me in the corner of a big, noisy Irish pub somewhere, not so long ago. Like the rest of us, Joey Shithead ain't as young as he used to be, and he's manifesting symptoms of decidedly unpunk behaviour. He's settled down and gotten married, has three kids, has run for political office, has acted on different TV shows—and has even played the occasional folkie-style acoustic show ("I got the hang of it," he grunts). Joey Shithead has been around, and he looks it. His features are gaunt, just as they were in the old days, but now age seems to be the reason, not the malnutrition and sleep deprivation one associates with a truly cool punk rock lifestyle. His eyes have a sad, knowing look to them, and a wariness, too. He's *wise*, even. And yet, and yet: a conversation with Joey Shithead makes it clear that he's still a punk.

"One final thing," I say to him. "We're all joking around because we're kind of old farts now, and it's hard to be angry all the time when you're an old fart. So here's the question: Does punk equal young? Do we have to be young to do it?"

Joey Shithead and I both know that plenty of people *think* that "old punk" is an oxymoron, because we thought the same fucking thing, way back when we were teenagers, and back when we convinced ourselves that we wouldn't be alive by the age of twenty, let alone thirty or forty. Or *fifty*, for the love of God. Punk is young, right? So, if you're as old as your parents were when you started ripping up your clothes and scrawling "I HATE" all over everything, then it's game over, right? You might as well be dead, because you sure as hell aren't a punk rocker anymore. Right?

"No," says Joey, finally. "I don't think it really has anything to do with that."

"Come on," I say. "Did you really think that when you were twenty? It *was* about being young, wasn't it?"

"Um," says Joey Shithead, finally, definitively. "No. I had thought punk was about causing shit. I was just someone who was plain causing shit by causing trouble. But the activism stuff that I'm into now . . . that's how I cause shit now. Musically, philosophically, it's the same; it's not about age. So it wasn't just about being young. It's about the spirit of rebellion—about thinking for yourself, about being your own boss, about doing what is right.

"It's about kicking the establishment in the groin as hard as possible, repeatedly," he laughs.

And that, more or less, is the mission around which Joey Shithead has structured the last thirty or so years of his life. To drive home the point, and to ensure that no one misunderstands, he had T-shirts made up that are sold at every DOA show. On one side is the band's logo. And on the other is this: TALK MINUS ACTION EQUALS ZERO.

So, if punk is an attitude and not just music, and if punks are a furious, non-conformist bunch of people and not just a freakish subculture, then Joey Shithead's maxim best captures the pith and the substance of it all. Punk is about being *angry* about something (like politics, like parents, like pop music) and *doing something* on your own (with a band, with a fanzine, with a book, with grassroots organizing) to fix it. It's not about waiting for someone else to solve the problem for you, or being impotent with rage, forever and a day. It's words plus action. To do anything less is to be like everyone else.

Over the course of a lengthy chat in the pub (and over the course of his punk rock lifetime, of course), it becomes evident that there are a number of ways in which Joey Shithead—and lots of other punks—have endeavoured to do what is right. As fanzine writer Lucy Toothpaste wrote in 1977, "Punk isn't gonna change the world. But punks might, one of these days."

This chapter contains stories about punks trying to change the world—stories about taking punk's anger on the one hand, and its Do It Yourself spirit on the other, and combining them to improve the planet. Because, even so long after punk got started, it's still all about doing what the Clash sang about in "Clampdown," way back in the fall of 1979, when DOA opened for them at the Pacific National Exhibition in Vancouver: "Kick over the wall, cause governments to fall/ How can you refuse it?/ Let fury have the hour, anger can be power!/ D'ya know that you can use it?"

These punks used it.

Ian MacKaye, one of the smartest punks on the planet, *ever,* sounds irritated. I've just suggested to the lead singer of Fugazi—and the founder of the Teen Idles and Minor Threat—that punk did *not* change the world. Reached at the Washington, D.C., offices of Dischord Records, the punk record label he helped create in January 1981, MacKaye can barely contain his annoyance.

"It depends on what your definition of the world is, doesn't it? But c'mon! Punk *had* a cultural impact," he insists. "It may not necessarily be the same impact that politics has, or it may not necessarily be Joey Keithley who is getting all the accolades, but punk as a culture . . . it's *had* an impact. It hasn't necessarily been all positive, sure. But my God! It's certainly seemed to affect parts of [youth] culture, hasn't it?

"In my mind, there is always too much of an obsession with the result. When you have a kid who says he or she wants to change the world, I think what's important is *not* whether all of the world has changed. What's important is that people *desire* change, and they want to *work* toward that. They feel they have their own power, and they feel what they do can actually have an effect on things."

He's past forty now, but Ian MacKaye still speaks in a reedy, excitable voice, sentences running together, twenty different ideas being expressed at once. He's still suffused with passion and conviction, and he doesn't like small talk or bullshit. This is the same voice that, in the late 1970s, changed the face and direction of punk. Back then, the scene received its marching orders from a few druggy cynics across the Atlantic in London, or another group of arty, druggy cynics up in New York City (or even, as some suspected, the satanic, cynical forces of the music industry, located in both places). Until 1979 or thereabouts, it was a small number of people in those two cities who determined What Is Punk and What Is Not Punk. And then, in 1979 or so, along came a scrappy, pissed-off D.C. teenager who helped to dispense with that kind of garbage for good.

From the outset, Ian MacKaye was a punk like few others—an oddball in an oddball subculture. After seeing a Cramps show in January 1979 with his high school friend Jeff Nelson, MacKaye was transformed. He went home and shaved his hair off with a dog trimmer. "This is the world I think I can breathe in," he would later say. "This is what I need."

Now, every punk has a story like that. All punks remember where they were when they heard one of the Sex Pistols singles for the first time, or the first Ramones album, or just about any of the early Clash stuff. And when MacKaye and Nelson formed a punk band called the Teen Idles—well, plenty of punks did kind of thing, too. But MacKaye's gang was different with a *difference*. The nascent D.C. punk combo took on society's conventions (which every punk band did) but also punk's own conventions (which no punk band ever did, really). In one memorable Teen Idles tune called "Fleeting Fury," MacKaye and his pals eviscerated bands like the Clash and the Sex Pistols for selling out, for becoming rock stars. "The clothes you wear have lost their sting," the song goes. "So's the fury in the songs you sing!" So much for the clampdown.

Lots of punks like to assert, or at least believe, that they are non-conformists simply by virtue of their non-conformist approach to fashion, or music, or whatever. But punks can be just as conservative, in their own way, as the society from which they have removed themselves: for instance, nothing could be more punk than showing up to a punk show in a suit and tie, with a neat haircut—but no one ever did that. Punks dressed like all of the other punks, usually. Behaved and talked like them, too.

Ian MacKaye was unique because he wasn't afraid to attack his fellow punks and the orthodoxies that had started to spread, virus-like, within the punk scene. Like about drugs and booze.

Early on, the Teen Idles—and its successor wrecking crew, the brilliant, perfect punk band called Minor Threat—were openly disdainful of the intoxication culture that pervaded punk, and every other rock 'n' roll genre extant. Back in those days, of course, a lot of rock musicians (and a big portion of their audiences) couldn't imagine a performance where you weren't completely fucked up on something. Things got so bad, in fact, that drugs and drug use became the ruling aesthetic of the day. Sure, the hippies loved their status drugs (cf. Eric Clapton's moronic hit "Cocaine"), but the punks had *their* pharmaceuticals of choice, too—most often cheap drugs designed to stoke aggression (cf. Johnny Rotten snarling that speed "is all I need" on "Seventeen," or the Ramones harmonizing "now I wanna sniff some glue" on their first album, tongue admittedly in cheek). A lot of it was very boring and depressing.

So thought Ian MacKaye, anyway. The issue of drugs—and booze, too—came into sharp focus in the fall of 1980 at a gig at the infamous punk venue called the Mabuhay Gardens in San Francisco. Previously a Filipino supper club, the Mabuhay—along with the Deaf Club, Club Foot and 330 Grove Street—were the West Coast headquarters for hardcore bands. The youthful Teen Idles were permitted entry only after their hands were inscribed with large "X" marks, signalling that they were underage. That was an important innovation, because many of the Teen Idles' fans—and the band members themselves—were under the legal drinking age. As MacKaye later put it, the fact that he wasn't going to buy alcohol made him unwelcome at shows. "It was fucked," says MacKaye, succinctly. "It was totally the wrong thing . . . Kids should see shows, and alcohol should not be the deciding factor."

So, at the very last performance of the Teen Idles on November 6, 1980, at the 9:30 Club in Washington, MacKaye told the management to put "X" marks on the hands of all punk minors; kick out any one of them caught drinking alcohol, he told them. It was a good idea. The show, as they say, went on.

For their next musical project, MacKaye and Nelson already had a name: Minor Threat. As in minors who were no threat at all. The name fit for another reason: Ian MacKaye was irrevocably straight, and not just because he was a minor who was obliged to be straight by prevailing drinking laws. MacKaye did not drink, and he did not take drugs, and he did not smoke. Period. "I was just not into it," he says. So, despite the abuse he received from his peers, and despite the impact it had on his social life, MacKaye did not merely Just Say No—he did so with a vengeance. There are a lot of theories about what prompted a stubborn seventeen-year-old from Washington, D.C., to turn his abstinence into a thriving international sub-subculture: that he had a family member who was an alcoholic; or that one of his pre-punk icons, Ted Nugent, was anti-drug; or that he never forgot nor forgave being denied access to a Stiff Little Fingers show because he was underage. No one knows for sure, and MacKaye isn't really saying. Besides, it doesn't matter. He did it, and it came to be hugely important. It changed the world, in fact, in a good way.

Minor Threat's debut was auspicious enough: the D.C. punks immediately saw that the new band was angrier than the Teen Idles, and faster and louder, too. But one of their first recordings—a forty-three-second rant MacKaye wrote, called "Straight Edge"—caused a sensation. The song is a brutal, blistering slice of punk power, delivered with ferocious conviction—and it ultimately improved the lives of thousands of kids across North America and Europe:

> *I'm a person, just like you*
> *But I've got better things to do*
> *Than sit around and fuck my head*
> *Hang out with the living dead*
> *Snort white shit up my nose*
> *Pass out at the shows*
> *I don't even think about speed*
> *That's something I just don't need*

I've got the straight edge
I'm a person, just like you
But I've got better things to do
Than sit around and smoke dope
'Cause I know I can cope
Laugh at the thought of sniffing glue
Always gonna keep in touch
Never want to use a crutch
I've got the straight edge

Out of that would come an entire youth movement, and dozens upon dozens of new punk bands, too: 7 Seconds in Nevada, DYS and SSD in Boston and the Necros in Michigan; later, Agnostic Front, Gorilla Biscuits, Insted, Dishonor, Judge, No for an Answer, Uniform Choice, Warzone, Supertouch, Hard Stance, Free Will, Outspoken and Youth of Today, from all over North America.

The telltale "X" symbol MacKaye devised, meanwhile, would become the signifying element of the Straight Edge scene around the world; even now, the Straight Edge "X" can be found on gig posters everywhere (and on the backs of kids' hands) indicating that "all ages" are welcome, but that booze, drugs and tobacco aren't. Straight Edge would even spawn sub-subcultures, like krishnacore (Straight Edge punk practised by adherents of Hare Krishna) and vegancore (Straight Edge punk favoured by vegans—who don't eat meat, fish, dairy products, eggs or any other animal product). Youth of Today, for example, wrote a song promoting the vegan lifestyle and urged their followers to take a "morally straight" position on animals. In "Free at Last," the band sang, "This world is filled with competition and greed/ A disgusting way of life, but we'll try to break . . ./ Free! Free at last!/ From the animals in the slaughterhouse, to the drugs on the streets/ They'll pollute our minds, our bodies."

Even people like Hilly Kristal, the owner of CBGB's in New York City—the bar where the Ramones, the Voidoids, the Dictators and punk itself got started—were impressed. Hardcore flourished at Kristal's CBGB's. "Hardcore was basically much faster and louder and more aggressive [than traditional punk]," Kristal tells me in an interview at CBGB's. He was also impressed, he says, by Straight Edge and its insistence on a near-ascetic lifestyle. "It was very interesting, I have to say."

Craig O'Hara has thought and written a great deal about Straight Edge. O'Hara believes that the early days of the movement were extraordinarily important and life-affirming. Says O'Hara, "[By] spreading a positive and personal message, the Straight Edge movement quickly spread to Boston and most of the East Coast. The message was simple: you do not have to drink alcohol, smoke or indulge in any mind-altering drugs to have a good time. Straight Edge caught on fast with suburban teens who were feeling peer pressure [about intoxicants and tobacco] and were rejecting it . . . [Straight Edge] offered a hardcore alternative to both straight society and the English 'drunk punk' we couldn't identify with. The new intensity and conviction of this music brought back to life a punk scene that had begun to stagnate with political sloganeering and 'party time' attitudes."

However, as O'Hara and others note, Straight Edge eventually started to attract "jock" types and alienated even the likes of Ian MacKaye. Racist skinheads were flocking to Straight Edge shows in droves—attracted, Wisconsin cultural studies professor Stacy Thompson has written, by Straight Edge's "fascination with moral and bodily 'purity' that served as an analog for racist notions about 'pure' blood and 'pure' races." And, as one former Straight Edger wrote in a widely circulated essay, Straight Edge has too often become "teenagers drunk on machismo, puritanism, and dogma. All this empty grunting about 'strength' and 'oath' and 'truth' and 'brotherhood' and 'honour' (and any other vacant gibberish that wouldn't sound out of place in a Baptist tent meeting) is a lot of hot air that only serves to cover up what is essentially another trend for kids who want someone to tell them what to believe." In some places, Straight Edge became even worse than that: in 1998, for example, two Salt Lake City Straight Edge "hard edge" types were convicted of murdering a young person who disagreed with their abstemious lifestyle.

Beth Lahickey agrees that Straight Edge, while once a positive force, has occasionally lost its way. She was a junior high school student in Connecticut when she stumbled across Straight Edge in 1985. It changed her life. Later a published poet and an employee of a Straight Edge record label in Seattle, Lahickey wrote *All Ages: Reflections on Straight Edge* in 1997. In the book, she chronicles the lives of many of the key figures in the Straight Edge movement, including MacKaye. While it was certainly a way of life, Lahickey believes that Straight Edge was also, first and foremost, an extension of punk rock: "Straight Edge means different things to different people. While some may simply appreciate the 'substance free' philosophy that it embodies, others may take it to the extreme. The Straight Edge philosophy is expounded through powerful music . . . [and the] Straight Edge kids loved these bands."

They loved Ian MacKay's Minor Threat in particular. Between 1981 and 1983, the band played sold-out shows all over the United

States and Canada, attracting tens of thousands of intense, clear-headed young fans through little more than leafleting, word of mouth or hard-to-get records issued by the band's respected DIY label, Dischord. In their way, Minor Threat—ably assisted at the start by their roadie, MacKaye's close friend Henry Garfield, later better known as Henry Rollins, lead screamer for Black Flag—were to the Straight Edge movement what the Sex Pistols and the Ramones had been to punk itself. They started it.

Not everyone was impressed, of course. In March 1981, Lester Bangs declared that MacKaye and Minor Threat were "muscleheads from Washington." Typically, MacKaye concluded that a musclehead was a person with a large brain, and urged his followers to "flex your head" on Minor Threat's speed-of-sound cover of Wire's "12XU." To ensure that no one missed his point, Dischord released a seminal D.C. hardcore compilation called *Flex Your Head*. Even big wheels like Lester Bangs did not intimidate Ian MacKaye.

For the many kids who loved punk but hated drugs and alcohol and tobacco, Straight Edge (and Ian MacKaye) made it cool to resist peer or societal pressure to get fucked up. Straight Edge (and Ian MacKaye) may have dissuaded a kid, somewhere, sometime, from becoming an addict—and, probably, saved his or her life. And if saving someone's life isn't changing the world, then what is?

Being a contrarian from way back, Ian MacKaye isn't accepting any of the accolades regularly dropped at his doorstep, of course. But on the key issue—namely, whether it is possible for a punk to do something that has a significant and lasting and positive impact on the lives of many others—MacKaye is resolute. "I think too often people will just study the end result and say that things didn't change. But that is really such a cynical way of doing things!"

He is getting worked up and says to me, "Because punk changed *you*, didn't it? It affected *you*, in your life. Even if you've gotten away from punk, ultimately it changed you, it *did* have an effect on you. I guess some people might say that is just life—you know, that's what happens to every human being in their life." He pauses. "The only difference is, I think there is a certain proactiveness that is not solely unique to punk, but is seriously celebrated by punk."

Asked if he has anything else to say on the subject, Ian MacKaye laughs out loud. "Hell, man! Of course! I'm just getting fucking *warmed up!*"

—

Punk wanted to destroy rock 'n' roll. It wanted to smash it to bits—
every self-indulgent drum and guitar solo, every synthesizer, every
costume change, every overpriced ticket, every stupid lyric about
metaphysical bullshit, every hippie haircut, every honorific
bestowed on another overpaid musician, every phony love-and-
peace sermon recycled from Woodstock, every pompous Studio 54
rock star millionaire, every fawning focus-grouped profile in *Rolling
Stone,* every performance by coked-up arseholes standing motionless
on a stage that is so far away they resemble ants. All of it. Smash it
to fucking bits, and then start over again.

In respect of some of those things, punk was successful. Rock 'n'
roll songs became shorter, again, and a lot of bands went back to a
sound that was raw and therefore more real. Twenty-minute guitar
solos became the exception, not the rule. Hair got shorter.
Buckingham Palace, briefly, found fewer takers for medals.
Rhapsodies about peace and love got supplanted, at least
temporarily, by the gritty reality of hate and war. Gig venues
became smaller. Guitars were being heard more, synthesizers less.
Musicians wore clothes that real people wore, or clothes that didn't
cost a real person's annual salary. And bands started writing lyrics
about things they knew, taken from the lives they actually lived and
not some distant, surreal, fantasy bullshit world inhabited by druids
and hobbits.

Hallelujah! Praise the Lord! But, after all that achievement,
there was still work to do—particularly of the socio-economic variety.
Having learned that pissed-off punks could change the face of
popular music, and having learned that punk's DIY spirit could
change the way a lot of people approached the impediments to their
ambition, and having learned that punk could change the way that
people actually live their day-to-day lives, it was only natural and
normal that punks should turn their attention to politics. Politics was,
after all, the subject matter of a lot of songs by a lot of British bands,
such as the Clash, Sham 69, Stiff Little Fingers, the Tom Robinson
Band, X-Ray Spex—and, later on, pissed-off North American punks

such as Minor Threat, Bad Brains, DOA, the Dead Kennedys, Black Flag, Rancid, Anti-Flag, Pennywise, Bad Religion and NOFX. Singing about politics, and social change, was good. Doing something to bring about actual political and social change was better.

It's impossible to point to a single instance where a single punk, or a few punks, changed entire political systems; but, again, the same is true of most people who devote their entire lives to politics. Not too many of *them* have changed the course of human history, either. Punks have had a modest impact on some fronts, however. Because punk has always been essentially leftist in its political orientation (leftist because punk is anti-authority and the authorities in the Western world almost always lean to the right), its influence has been most readily felt with respect to issues that have been regarded as traditional preoccupations of the left: women's rights, anti-racism, anti-capitalism and political enfranchisement. On those issues, punks *have* changed things, a bit.

Ari Up, the former lead singer of the Slits, will deny that her band changed very much, if anything. But the fact is that they did. *She* did.

That rock 'n' roll (and the world) is rife with sexism and misogyny is so obvious it barely merits saying. Men mostly run politics, and they mostly run rock 'n' roll, too. Women are the exception, not the rule: as Simon Frith noted in *On Record: Rock, Pop and the Written Word,* "rock is a male form . . . the music business is male-run; popular musicians, writers, creators, technicians, engineers and producers are mostly men." Everyone knows that, but not everyone is pissed off enough to try to change it. (And it's not insignificant, if you accept that most males and females take significant gender cues from popular culture.)

At the conclusion of the hippie-era "sexual revolution," some women suspected the whole thing had been a con—a pretext by which men could more easily bed women. "Up until then," Germaine Greer wrote, in a wonderfully vivid put-down, "women had been represented . . . principally [as] wispy bare-breasted flower children and the pneumatic creations of Robert Crumb. The Sixties were the heyday of male display; the most successful Sixties women were scented, decorative and slender, voluptuously dressed in diaphanous chiffons, old embroideries, baubles, bangles, beads and boots, and spoke in blurred voices—if at all."

The seventies, however, weren't much better. Whatever gender idealism had existed in the sixties gave way to no idealism at all. Bimbo culture was celebrated on *Charlie's Angels* and in lots of other places, notably in discos; reproductive rights were still being denied; surveys showed that most *educated* men believed a woman's place was in the home; wage discrimination was rampant; and women continued to be grossly under-represented in politics, media, professions and cultural industries. Says British feminist columnist Polly Toynbee, "There is a dangerous mythology among young women of good intent who imagine there was once a glorious feminist moment, lost somewhere in the mists of time back in the early seventies. They look at [today's society] then they sigh for an imaginary yesterday [in the seventies] that never was . . . The truth is, it wasn't like that then. There was no 'movement.' There were some dazzling feminist stars . . . but there was no 'movement.' There was precious little unity. There were, to be honest, precious few women involved at all."

Punk did what it could. Vivienne Westwood, for one, declared war on the disco era's stupid fashion standards, and the sexualization of women that went with it. Her designs, sold mainly at Sex and (later) at Seditionaries, were characterized by a lot of zippers, rubber, studs, buckles and bondage gear—along with ripped, safety-pinned T-shirts covered with provocative slogans. The objective, Westwood later claimed, was to "seduce [women] into revolt." Lucy O'Brien, the British author of *She Bop: The Definitive History of Women in Rock, Pop and Soul* and a former member of the punk group the Catholic Girls, has written that punk was ideally suited for feminist women who despised the sexism inherent in rock 'n' roll. "One of the attractions of punk was having an outlet for political outrage, that disaffection with the status quo which was cemented by the early years of a Conservative government hostile towards dissent, and a leader, Margaret Thatcher, who took great pride in disassociating herself from 'shrill feminism,'" O'Brien wrote in a 1999 essay titled *The Woman Punk Made Me.* "For women, this revolt was present not just in words, but music that deliberately veered away from standard rock 'n' roll time." In other words, punk didn't just sound different, it looked at most contentious issues differently, too.

Enter the Slits. In May 1976, feminist and artist Patti Smith arrived in London to perform a few shows at London's Roundhouse and immediately became an inspiration for the burgeoning punk movement, although she was not entirely a punk herself. A fourteen-year-old girl named Arianna Forster was in attendance at one of Smith's shows; so was Paloma Romero. The pair met and, with little effort, became friends. Paloma (later christened Palmolive as a joke by the Clash's Paul Simonon) was living at the time in a London squat with Joe Strummer, who was in the process of creating the Clash. Palmolive wanted to form an all-girl punk band. Arianna, a.k.a. Ari Up, was much younger than anyone else in the British punk scene, but was clearly very smart: when Palmolive asked her to be the band's lead singer, Ari Up immediately said yes.

As charismatic as she was beautiful, Ari Up came from what she calls a "bohemian" family. Her mother, Nora Forster, was the daughter of a wealthy newspaper proprietor and had been a friend of Jimi Hendrix, a paramour of famous rock producer and musician Chris Spedding, and—much later, after the pair were introduced by her daughter—the wife of Johnny Rotten. Nora's flat in Shepherd's Bush was a crash pad for many bands over the years, the Sex Pistols among them. (Legend has it that Hendrix complained about his inability to write songs when he stayed there, while a younger Ari practised piano in the next room.)

At the start, the Slits also included guitarist Kate Korus and Suzi Gutsy; Korus soon departed for the Mo-dettes, and Gutsy for the Flicks. Their spots in the Slits' lineup were filled by Viv Albertine on guitar (formerly part of the Flowers of Romance, with Sid Vicious) and Tessa Pollitt (formerly of the Castrators) on bass. They played their first gig in March 1977 at the Harlesdan Coliseum. After that— and some say due, in no small measure, to Palmolive's relationship with Joe Strummer—the Slits secured a berth (along with the Buzzcocks and the Subway Sect) on the Clash's fabled White Riot tour in May 1977. It was, by all accounts, an extraordinary series of gigs: at the May 7 performance at the Rainbow in London, two hundred seats at the front of venue were ripped out and tossed onto the stage.

Despite their presence on the tour, or perhaps because of it, the Slits were unable to get a record out or even secure a recording contract in 1977 and 1978. They played whatever gigs they could on the pub circuit. One August 1977 gig at the Vortex caught the attention of *Rolling Stone,* which sniffed, "Any current American audience would reward [them] with a shower of bottles. The guitarist stops in the middle of the fourth song to announce, 'Fuckin' shit! Listen to this!' and plays an ungodly out-of-tune chord that no one else had even noticed in the cacophony. The singer, apparently the only one with pitch, has to tune her guitar for her. 'Fuckin' shit!' explains the singer, plucking the strings. 'We never said we were musicians.'" *NME* called them "shambolic and puerile, with just a hint of something special [to] make these silly displays so frustrating." Despite all of that, the Slits were not without their fans: a year-end *ZigZag* poll awarded them the title of Number One Best Unsigned Group.

The all-female lineup sometimes resulted in extraordinary reactions. Pollitt would later recall one involving Ari Up around the time of the Sex Pistols' August 1976 gig at Screen on the Green in Islington, where a man approached the Slits—who were well known, but had yet to play in public. "In the foyer, this guy came up to us, came up behind Ari Up and said, 'So you're the Slits? Well, here's a slit for you,' and he just shoved a knife into her backside. Sliced her butt, quite literally, right there. Luckily for Ari, she was wearing so many layers of clothes, the damage was limited. It just seemed to others that we were asking for it. The vibe towards us was, 'know your place, woman!' It seemed that we couldn't go anywhere without getting a reaction from people. The attitude was that we were asking for it, but we certainly weren't asking anyone to come up behind us with a knife."

The band's perseverance in the face of such anger and hate gradually transformed them into feminist punk icons, even though it was music, not politics, that first attracted them to punk. They didn't need to make speeches or hand out leaflets on street corners; the Slits became "political" simply by existing. They stood out in other ways, too. Compared to most punk bands, who were already starting to sound derivative by 1978, the Slits' sound was unusual—it combined reggae and dub and sharp, angular rhythms in a way that the others would not, or could not. The band's lyrics, meanwhile, toyed with gender politics in a way that was clever and understated, as in the wonderful "Typical Girls":

> *Don't create, don't rebel, have intuition . . . Typical girls*
> *Get upset too quickly . . . Typical girls*
> *Are so confusing . . . Typical girls*
> *You can always tell . . . Typical girls*
> *Are unpredictable . . . Typical girls*
> *Try to be . . . Typical girls*
> *Who invented typical girls?*

The epicentre of the group was Ari Up–extraordinary for what the Slits were doing, extraordinary for her determination to play (whether men approved or not), extraordinary for starting it all at the age of *fourteen*. Asked now how frightening it was, at fourteen, to perform at occasionally violent punk gigs, or to occasionally encounter violent men with knives, Ari Up is genuinely blasé. Reached at her New York home, Up says stepping onto a stage when barely out of childhood was no big deal. "It wasn't scary. It was relieving. I didn't join to follow the punk movement—I was there for the birth of it. You're not really worried when you give birth to something incredible like that.

"Being fourteen, you don't think about being fourteen when you're fourteen. You just think about breaking out, breaking loose. And you do it."

That's not true, of course. Very few fourteen-year-olds would consider doing what Ari Up did, let alone go off and do it. The band, and Ari, unleashed reactions that the older male punk bands simply did not. Throughout the Clash White Riot tour, as she strode about in a pair of Queen's Jubilee panties stretched over her trousers, Ari Up was spat upon by people passing her on the street, refused service in restaurants, denied hotel rooms that had been booked in advance by the Clash management, and targeted with violence. But she kept at it (on one occasion, squatting onstage and pissing in front of the horrified, mainly male, punk audience).

The Slits were unprecedented, actually, because they adamantly refused to go along with the cultural conventions that had not been seriously questioned by any female rock 'n' roller prior to 1977. Now, of course, it's pretty commonplace, with a significant number of female performers on rock 'n' roll charts and pushing for social and political reform; back then, it wasn't, at all. Writing in the fanzine *The Jolt*, outspoken punk feminist Lucy Toothpaste depressingly summed up a depressing situation:

> It's not really surprising if girls are still a bit uncertain about how to bust into rock. The very fact that rock, the so-called rebel culture, has always been completely male-dominated–[it] just goes to show once more that there's

one person more oppressed than a teenage boy, and it's a teenage girl. Girls have been so squashed that we haven't even dared [to] complain. And now we've woken up at last, we haven't just got to cope with the total lack of encouragement, but also with the gawking and the sniggering of the male music establishment.

Any girl band immediately attracts attention just 'cos they stick out like a sore thumb, they can't be judged on their own merits, so they're bound to be self-conscious. But NOW'S the time for us to get going. It doesn't matter if we don't know how to play guitar yet . . .

Punk's early promise did not extend to women as readily as it should have, however. For all of the female punks—Poly Styrene in X-Ray Spex, the Raincoats, Pauline Murray in Penetration—it was tough going. In early 1978, for instance, Blondie's record company ran a large display ad featuring Debbie Harry in a skimpy dress—below the words: WOULDN'T YOU LIKE TO RIP HER TO SHREDS? (Harry, no noted feminist, and certainly no punk, was moved to say in *NME* that she was "furious" about the ad.) With the notable exceptions of Caroline Coon in *Melody Maker* and Julie Burchill in *NME,* the mainstream media, meanwhile, were uniformly awful—focusing on the clothing of female punk performers or subjecting them to critical standards they did not extend to male punks. The punk fanzines, which should have known better, didn't: "I love those visual come-ons that draw me to the stage, lusting for the Slits and loving being manipulated so easily," wrote one male in *Ripped and Torn.* And then there was this review from *Viva la Resistance:* "The Slits came on and ravaged their way through a brilliant set. By the way, Arianna has a super pair of legs." It was enough to make one want to quit.

But Ari Up and the Slits wouldn't. If anything, they became more determined to shake things up. Whether they acknowledge it or not, Ari Up and the Slits challenged the prevalent sexism of popular music and the society of which it was part: they *deliberately* dressed in rags, they *deliberately* refused to comb their hair, and they *deliberately* refused to behave like any of the female performers that had gone before them. None of that was particularly new, some might argue: Mama Cass and Janis Joplin, to cite just a couple of examples, hadn't been supermodels or paragons of virtue, either. But neither of them—nor any other female star, for that matter— had been as deliberately provocative and oppositional as the Slits; ultimately, the Slits were the first to refuse to play along with the male-run, male-dominated game, punk or otherwise.

If punk was rebellion, then the Slits were a rebellion *within* punk itself. The reason, obviously, was that they were women—*punk women*—who were flipping the finger at society in a way no one had done before. Even many years later, they remain important to feminists because they demonstrated a way to break free of a lot of social conventions, particularly those relating to femininity.

The Slits and another female band with a great name, the Castrators (in which Pollitt had briefly played), were, as early as January 1977, the targets of a *News of the World* feature headlined: "Here Come the Punkesses." The teaser read, "Fasten your seatbelts! The all-girl rock shockers who make those Sex Pistols look like choir boys are ready to land!" The story, like most of the subsequent stories, seemed to convey a higher degree of detestation for female punks than for male punks. ("The media really hated us," recalls Ari Up.) Female punks tore up the rulebook for women in rock 'n' roll, and they paid a price for it.

"We weren't just outcasts," says Ari Up. "We were worse than that. It was more like a witch hunt. We weren't just verbally attacked [as the other punk bands were]—we were physically attacked. It got to the point where it was actually physically dangerous for us to be in that band."

Ari Up is unconvinced, however, about the political import of the Slits. For the last twenty years, she has been bombarded with an endless number of questions, and theories, about the feminism of the

Slits and the path the band blazed for the likes of Hole, Liz Phair, P.J. Harvey, Exene Cervenka of X, Bikini Kill, the Donnas, Babes in Toyland, Lydia Lunch, the Au Pairs, Le Tigre, Nina Hagen, the GoGos and a score of others. "It was like trying to do the impossible," she says. "[In music], everything was managed and put together by men. But we were the first real girl band that played our own music. We played our instruments, and put it all together ourselves, and danced to our own fiddle.

"When we asked Viv to join the band, she felt very apprehensive. She told us, 'Oh, it's been done before, I don't want to be part of a gimmick.' But we told her we didn't want to be political or feminist about anything, we just wanted to be us. We just wanted to be unconditional females, without anyone—not even a female movement—telling us how to be female."

In late 1978, the unconditional females were finally offered a recording contract by Island Records—by which time many lesser male punk bands were already working on their second or third LP. The Slits' first album—really their only album—was the seminal *Cut*. Recorded at Farm Ridge Studios with reggae producer Dennis Bovell, *Cut* is arguably one of the most creative and innovative records to be put out by anyone (punk or rock 'n' roller) in the past three decades. Unlike the vast majority of punk bands, who—in and around 1978—were to be seen lurching towards heavy metal, the Slits struck out on an entirely different course: fusing punk and dub and reggae in a way that the Clash or the Ruts or Stiff Little Fingers might have hoped to, but didn't.

Typically, most reviews were preoccupied with the album's cover, which featured a cavorting, grinning Ari, Viv and Tessa apparently naked and smeared with mud. The dean of the rock 'n' roll critics, Robert Christgau, was smitten by the record's sounds, and not just the cover art:

> For once a white reggae style that rivals its models for weirdness and formal imagination. The choppy lyrics and

playful, quavering, chant-like vocals are a tribute to reggae's inspired amateurism rather than a facsimile, and the spacey rhythms and recording techniques are exploited to solve the great problem of female rock bands, which is how to make yourself heard over all that noise. Ari Up's answer is to sing around it, which is lucky, because she'd be screeching for sure on top of the usual wall of chords . . . I sure hope they keep it up.

They didn't. The Slits broke up near the end of 1981, having never achieved the kind of commercial success enjoyed by male-dominated punk acts. The significance of what they did would sink in later. Ari Up—now dividing her time between motherhood, solo work, Jamaica and New York—remains puzzled by the anger the band unleashed. "I don't quite know what we did that was so offensive," she says over the phone line, as her son plays on a Game Boy nearby. "I really don't quite know . . . except, I suppose, that we were twenty years ahead of our time. We were acting like the females we were, which is like everyday females now. Females you see now on the street, the females of today, it's all okay. But when you do the same thing in a different time frame, like we did in England [twenty-five years ago], it's going to be very freaky for a lot of people."

The Slits shook things up. They and other female punks assisted the efforts of the Anti-Nazi League and Rock Against Racism in the late seventies and early eighties, and they were there for the creation of important early innovations such as Rock Against Sexism, in late 1978. (The umbrella group organized benefit concerts to raise money for rape crisis shelters and women's aid.) But the Slits' campaign to open up the culture (and the punk subculture) to women was not to be fully realized until some twenty years after their debut, and far, far from their London base, with Riot Grrl.

Riot Grrl (or Riot Girl, or Riot Grrrl: spellings vary) was a hardcore punk rock derivative known for its proud, positive militant feminist stance. It got its start in the grunge mecca of the U.S. Pacific Northwest in the summer of 1991 or so, and was an angry retort to punk's continuing male-cult machismo. The phrase itself was allegedly coined by Jen Smith of Bratmobile in the wake of rioting in the Mount Pleasant district of Washington, D.C., in May 1991. "We need to start a girl riot!" Smith wrote in a letter to a friend. By the time the International Pop Underground conference took place in Olympia, Washington, in August 1991, the phrase "riot grrl" had caught on. (The spelling of "Riot Grrl," meanwhile, was coined by the brilliant Bikini Kill drummer—and one-time Kurt Cobain girlfriend—Tobi Vail, who wanted to poke fun at militant feminists who spelled "women" as "womyn.") The whole movement, the Riot Grrls hoped, was "revolution girl-style now."

Like the Slits more than two decades earlier, the Riot Grrls sought to establish all-women (or women-led) bands, such as Bratmobile, Bikini Kill, 7 Year Bitch, 5 Days Late, L7, Tiger Trap, Babes in Toyland and Heavens to Betsy. And they mostly disdained the interest of male managers and the major record labels, preferring instead independent outfits such as Kill Rock Stars. They championed the DIY ethic more energetically than any punks that had gone before them, producing fanzines with names like *Sister Nobody, Chainsaw* and *Girl Germs* (crammed with articles about abortion, rape, eating disorders and feminist politics). They also encouraged young women to get onstage as soon as they could. While undeniably more political than the Slits, the Riot Grrls were all-female at the outset, as the Slits had been, and were determined to challenge or subvert male dominance in the punk subculture. They were assisted by the fact that most hardcore punk gigs of the era had become so violent—and dangerous—that many young women were refusing to attend.

"Taking the DIY ethos of punk that had inspired early female bands like the Slits, the Riot Grrls made music, but beyond that gave a subcultural network of emotional support to young women," wrote feminist Cressida Miles in *The Clubcultures Reader* shortly after the Riot Grrl scene exploded in 1991, capturing international attention. The scene was also arguably more pissed-off than any earlier punk variant had been, as the lyrics of "Calculated," by Heavens to Betsy attest:

I hate you with a passion
That will run for a million years
My fury is a force that is equal
To a billion of your tears

In Washington State—where the Riot Grrl movement probably preceded the Riot Grrl movement in Washington, D.C.—the preeminent Riot Grrl band was Bikini Kill. Formed by students Kathleen Hanna, Kathi Wilcox and Tobi Vail at Evergreen College, a liberal arts school in Olympia, Bikini Kill was also the name of a feminist fanzine the three created. Their eponymous first record was produced by none other than Ian MacKaye, who became an ardent fan and friend. Bikini Kill's songs were classic punk rock, but Bikini Kill was more strongly feminist than any previous punk band had been, regularly performing, for example, against a banner that read ABORTION ON DEMAND AND WITHOUT APOLOGY, or disseminating feminist literature at gigs, or even asking female members of the audience to step up to a microphone and talk politics. Men were sometimes directed to the back of the hall.

Bikini Kill's lyrics left no doubt about the band's intensity or commitment, as seen in "This Is Not a Test":

You don't make all the rules
I know what I'm gonna fuckin' do
Me and my girlfriends gonna push on through
We are gonna stomp on you, yeah!

Spin magazine called Hanna the "angriest girl of all," and that was probably true at the time. She grew up around Washington, D.C., and after high school moved to the Pacific Northwest to study. When she was low on money, she would perform in a strip club. Of those who challenged the contradiction—a lap-dancing feminist—Hanna would deadpan, "They don't get deconstruction." Hanna still flirts with galling contradictions: she has eschewed the honesty of punk for the trendy pop-discotheque art band Le Tigre. And she has seemingly given over control of her career to her manager—a man.

Tobi Vail, however, has remained true to Bikini Kill's principles. Vail—who, according to legend, was the inspiration for Kurt Cobain's "Smells Like Teen Spirit" (she used to wear the fragrance)—still lives in Olympia, busying herself with political organizations such as Bands Against Bush. While she acknowledges that the Slits were very important to Riot Grrl, Vail stresses that Bikini Kill's relative isolation in a smallish town in Washington State made finding new music difficult. In an interview she recalls, "We had to actively educate ourselves and our friends with the history of women in punk rock because that information was not easily accessible. Growing up in the seventies and eighties, it was easier to find information about Fleetwood Mac, Heart, Patti Smith, Chrissie Hynde, Joan Jett, the Go-Gos, Siouxsie Sioux and Debbie Harry. Being in Bikini Kill, we tried to share what we found out and encourage other females to start bands. As we found out about the early Rough Trade stuff, we became inspired by it, but it was hard to find [in record stores] . . . It was just not possible to find their records growing up in small Northwest towns, pre-Internet, pre–punk history books, pre–CD reissues."

Bikini Kill would sometimes use this lack of information about female-led bands to their advantage, revealing themselves to be accomplished manipulators of the mainstream media in the process. When *L.A. Weekly* interviewed the band for a report on the phenomenon, the publication was told that Riot Grrl chapters had sprung up in a number of U.S. cities, which they proceeded to name. It was bullshit; no such chapters existed. Young women who tried to locate the fictional Riot Grrl chapters were undeterred, however. Finding no Riot Grrl chapters in their hometowns, they went ahead and created them. In an eerily similar (but gender-reversed) portent of the cult film *Fight Club,* where male-only cells pop up around the country to challenge authority, Bikini Kill's interview hastened the birth of Riot Grrl fanzines and bands where there previously had been neither.

Riot Grrl, say the Riot Grrls themselves, helped them overcome eating disorders, speak up against oppression and deal with the fallout from sexual abuse. It was an alternative feminism that nurtured a feeling of community within the culture and, perhaps, society itself. In 1992, a weekend-long Riot Grrl convention took place in Washington, D.C. Women-only workshops discussed rape, racism, sexuality, domestic violence and fat oppression, while the Washington Peace Center featured Riot Grrl bands and performers all weekend. In 1994, two Riot Grrl conventions took place—in New York City and Philadelphia. Said one member of the biggest British Riot Grrl band, Huggy Bear, "I don't know why it caught on like it did, except that it was so much more of an exciting and alive idea of feminism than we were all coming across in books. It was imaginative and active, and it not only worked in theory, it also related to everyday life."

For that reason, punk also attracted a lot of gay and lesbian participation, right from the start. For a generation, gays and lesbians have been key members of the punk coalition—with the notable exception of early-eighties hardcore, which was suffused with homoeroticism in any event—and have influenced how punk sounded, looked and evolved. Out Punk, or Queercore, or Homo-core—as championed by the likes of Canadian Bruce LaBruce, Queerpunks.com, Pansy Division, Team Dresch, the Queers, Tribe 8 and Queeruptions in London, San Francisco, New York City and Berlin—was and is a thriving, proud punk sub-genre. And it is a fact that queer kids made up much more of the punk population than did, for instance, black kids.

Because Riot Grrl doesn't attract as much media attention as it used to, a lot of observers have concluded that the movement is dead—just another punk subculture that arrived in a blaze of media hype but had no staying power. That's false. In the case of the Riot Grrl phenomenon—a phenomenon that would not have happened without the Slits—the impact was worldwide: literally hundreds of Riot Grrl–style bands, fanzines and chapters could be found in every corner of the globe, from Canada to France to Australia to Britain. It was a perfect example of punk's power to change lives, and to persuade people to fight for positive change. Asked about Riot Grrl now—asked about the Slits now—so many years after Bikini Kill broke up, Tobi Vail says, "We listened to the Slits while we were in the group. We liked them a lot . . . Many people our age, or younger than us, didn't know they existed. We tried to help people, especially women and girls, find out about them, we made them Slits tapes and told people to listen to the Slits, to seek them out."

In her essay "The Woman Punk Made Me," Lucy O'Brien sums it up best: "What [has] survived . . . was punk's meaning for women. It reacted against, yet at the same time re-defined Sixties feminism, resurfacing in the Nineties with grunge and Riot Grrrl. [It] still has an impact on the way women operate, not just in music, but [in] culture generally. We still find it difficult to shake off the questioning rigour that the scene demanded, and maybe we don't want to.

"That's the women punk made us."

Why was punk—why is punk—so *white?*

While punk rock did many things, breaking the colour barrier was not one of them. Was there ever a genre of rock 'n' roll that was whiter? Was there ever a youth subculture that was whiter? Few punks like the answer, but they know the answer in their tiny, grimy hearts: no, on both counts. Go to a punk gig, anywhere, and you'll see what I mean.

Some might say that is an exaggeration. But not Tasha Shermer, a queer black feminist punk from Los Angeles who has written extensively on the subject. Her verdict: punk is white as snow, white as milk, white as a Klansman's sheet. And it sucks. In one widely distributed essay on the web, Shermer writes,

> To like punk should not be like joining a whites-only club. But when you get involved in the "scene," when you come in contact with other people who like punk, when you go to shows and do zines—you're stepping neck-deep in an institution steeped in racism. It's subtle. It's not like I'm going to go to a show and find myself swimming in white power skinhead girls testing out a tree to lynch me on. It's the kind of thing that [is] really hard to put a finger on, yet there nonetheless . . .
>
> I am ostracized by the black community and I am only partially accepted by the punk rock community as a token of punk's "fight against racism" . . . The idea of punk rock as some kind of beacon of open-mindedness is bullshit. Most white punk rockers like to consider themselves absolved of their privilege simply because they publicly denounce racism and don't attend weekly KKK meetings. Let me reiterate: *Just because you think racism is wrong does not mean you are not a racist.*

She's right, of course.

People of colour can be observed at punk shows. Some bands may even contain a member who isn't white. But, overwhelmingly, punk subculture and punk rock remains a white bastion. The fact that the majority of punks oppose racism, and fight it, doesn't obviate this pathetic state of affairs. In fact, it makes it worse—punks are supposed to *know better.* To invoke a cliché, punks haven't practised what they preach.

"Punks are niggers," Richard Hell told *New Musical Express* in October 1977—meaning, of course, that the early punks (like Hell) were ostracized and discriminated against in much the same fashion that blacks are. If that is true, then why did so few blacks feel a kinship with punk? Punks certainly wanted links with Rasta culture, what Dick Hebdige calls a "parallel white ethnicity" in *Subculture: The Meaning of Style.* And sure, Hebdige writes, punks played a big role in the development of things like Rock Against Racism, and they openly acknowledged the huge significance of reggae to the punk subculture. "But at another, deeper level," Hebdige writes, "the association [between white punks and black Rasta youth] seems to have been repressed, displaced on the part of the punks into the construction of a music which was emphatically white."

Some, like Clash deejay Barry "Scratch" Myers, go further. Myers, a reggae expert, opines that punk's oft-heard rallying cry— "Disco Sucks"—was "often a thinly veiled cover for deeper intolerance," given that black acts dominated the disco scene.

While the two solitudes regularly expressed affection for each other (Bob Marley with songs like "Punky Reggae Party," the Clash with dozens of songs they wrote or covered), the two solitudes largely remained that way—apart. Why? For starters, the musical forms were wildly different. Punk was angry, loud and fast; reggae sounded joyful, and it favoured gentler, slower melodies. Moreover, while both punk and reggae were musical genres about rebellion, the nature of the rebellion—and the rebels—was dramatically dissimilar. Joe Strummer adored reggae, for instance, but as much as he tried, he would always be the son of a diplomat who was made a Member of the British Empire, while the vast majority of British black kids who liked the Clash would always remain what they were: dirt poor, marginalized and discriminated against by those whose skin possessed the same hue as Joe Strummer's.

Most of all, Hebdige and others have written, punks and Rastas—however much they hoped to destroy history, were part of history. "At the heart of the punk subculture," writes Hebdige, "lies this frozen dialectic between black and white cultures—a dialectic which beyond a certain point is incapable of renewal, trapped, as it is, within its own history, imprisoned within its own irreducible antinomies." To some of us—to me, at least—that is semiotics as penned by Sid Vicious. It is too pessimistic. While punk still has a long, long way to go, it has improved upon its monochromous state since Hebdige wrote those words in 1979. Ask James Spooner.

Spooner is the first person, pretty much anywhere, to take a serious look at the issue of punk and persons of colour. In his award-winning sixty-six-minute documentary, *Afropunk: The Rock 'n' Roll Nigger Experience,* Spooner profiles a number of African-American kids who—despite the colour barrier that Tasha Shermer and others continue to decry—have successfully immersed themselves in the punk subculture.

Growing up between California and New York, Spooner was the product of a mixed-race relationship. He had a hard time fitting in. By the age of fourteen, in the early nineties, Spooner was sporting a mohawk and multiple facial piercings: he had become a punk, and a regular at punk shows in New York City and elsewhere.

By the time he had reached his twenties, Spooner no longer dyed his hair bright colours and the piercings were gone. But he was, he says, still "feeling lost and alienated." He belonged to two races, and two cultures, but he was part of neither. As all true punks do, Spooner decided to confront his dilemma and not simply pretend his sense of isolation was a passing phase. *Afropunk* was the way he did it: using his camera to follow the exploits of four black punks, Spooner learned something about himself, and punk, in the process. What he discovered, he says in an interview, is that punk rock was regarded as a white subculture by most blacks: "The black community is very conscious of blackness, and what it means to be black. When something has been claimed by white people, like punk, black people don't want to be part of it. We have a long history of being hurt by white people. So a lot of black people think punk is just white music. And, beyond that, they have these stereotypes of skinheads, and they see it all as just one thing."

Spooner, who can be fairly regarded as one of the leading thinkers (if not *the* leading thinker) on ethnocentricity in punk, says he was intrigued by the fact that there were other young blacks like him who embraced punk notwithstanding its all-encompassing whiteness, notwithstanding the fact that they were often the only black kids in a community hall filled with hundreds of whites.

As James Spooner and others note, people of colour—specifically people of African descent—have made a positive contribution far out of proportion to their numbers. Punk has been profoundly changed in three ways by black youth: one, by the things white punks have learned from black culture, specifically reggae and its derivatives such as ska and bluebeat; two, by the things black youth have taken from punk that have positively affected the development of rap and hip-hop; and three, by the massive impact of one punk band—the all-black Bad Brains—on the U.S. hardcore punk movement in the 1980s. In all of these ways, black culture and punk culture met, mixed and arguably produced something better than what had existed before.

The moment that punk started to benefit from reggae, and be influenced by it, is easily identified: the first week of June 1976, when Joe Strummer quit the 101ers and joined the Clash. Strummer, like Clash bassist Paul Simonon, adored reggae. Reggae had been part of Simonon's life for quite some time: long before the Clash existed, Simonon saw Jamaican singer Jimmy Cliff's wonderful 1972 film *The Harder They Come,* and was enthralled by it. As soon as he could, Simonon bought the soundtrack, as well as the related book and, much later, video. With its immortal roots reggae songs from the late sixties and early seventies—such as Desmond Dekker's "Shanty Town," the Melodians' "Rivers of Babylon" and the Maytals' extraordinary "Pressure Drop" (one of the greatest songs ever recorded, in any genre)—the soundtrack of *The Harder They Come* got heavy rotation at the Clash's rehearsal space. At any point in the Clash's existence, Paul Simonon's signature bass lines owed far more to reggae than to rock 'n' roll. (The first song Simonon ever wrote and recorded for the Clash was the pure reggae "Guns of Brixton," on *London Calling*).

Strummer's love of reggae predated Simonon's, going back to his days as a teenage boarder at the City of London Freemen's School (CLFS), where Strummer—then known as John Mellor, the name he was born with—spent nights listening to rockabilly and reggae tunes on his transistor radio, or reading about his favourite artists in *Melody Maker*. Strummer's interest in reggae was not restricted to Bob Marley, who had crossed over to the mainstream (and superstar status) circa 1973. He was also an early fan of Jamaica's more obscure dub and roots reggae sounds. Later on, he would play the occasional reggae number when busking in London's Underground.

Strummer and Simonon—with the support of Mick Jones, who was a fan of a wide variety of musical genres—decided to record one of their favourite warm-up tunes, "Police and Thieves," on the band's first album. Written by the brilliant Lee "Scratch" Perry and Junior Murvin, "Police and Thieves" marked the first time that any British punk band (all white) lovingly embraced the work of reggae artists (all black). At six minutes even, "Police and Thieves" was easily the longest song on the album. The Clash retained Perry to produce their third single, "Complete Control," widely considered one of their greatest achievements. Similarly, in the critically adored "White Man in Hammersmith Palais," the band sounds more reggae than punk.

The Clash's willingness to promote reggae would prove to be hugely significant: once the punk revolution got started in earnest, reggae rhythms (and songs) were recorded by scores of punk bands, among them the Ruts, the Slits and—later on—the ska revival pioneered by bands like the Specials, Madness and the Selecter. The Clash, more than any other punk band, broke the colour barrier for plenty of white kids who had yet to experience Bob Marley, and introduced them to a musical culture they otherwise would never have heard.

That is how punk learned, and benefited, from reggae and

black culture. But the education worked in the opposite direction, too. One evening in 1981, an Adelphi University student named Carleton Ridenhour travelled from Long Island to Manhattan to see a performance by deejay Kurtis Blow, a friend of the Clash who sometimes opened for them. On that night, Ridenhour watched as the many punks who were present threw tomatoes at Blow. When he later heard the Clash for the first time, Ridenhour—soon to be better known as Chuck D of Public Enemy, the greatest rap group ever—was blown away: "The Clash completely broke it that night. It was an awakening for a New York cat like me."

Chuck D read up on the Clash and became intrigued by their politics. At around the same time, his friend Bill Stepheny—one of the original members of Public Enemy—started playing Clash songs on his hip-hop radio show at Adelphi. Chuck D recalls that Stepheny made the punk sounds work within the context of hip-hop, which he thought would be difficult to do. "[It] opened up a lot of people's minds," Chuck D would later say. "[Stepheny] was instrumental in exposing a lot of hip-hop cats to what the Clash were doing . . . I had great respect for Joe Strummer."

Strummer proudly incorporated reggae and dub rhythms into his music in a way that was markedly different from what Elvis and others had done (namely, steal the black man's music, make lots of money and not pay any of it back). Chuck D says, "Strummer always paid homage to those who came before him. I admired [that]." The Public Enemy front man says punk's rebelliousness and politics influenced what would become Public Enemy, N.W.A. and other politicized rap groups. (Chuck D, for instance, was photographed more than once wearing a Minor Threat T-shirt.)

Before a lot of rap and hip-hop slid into the morass of misogyny, violence and crass materialism seen every day on MTV, Public Enemy caused many to suspect that hip-hop was black punk rock—or, perhaps more accurately, that punk rock was white hip-hop. In 1988, Chuck D and Public Enemy released *It Takes a Nation of Millions to Hold Us Back*. Awash in samples of everything from

Funkadelic to Isaac Hayes, bristling with Chuck D's anger, bouncing with Flavor Flav's humour, *ITANOMTHUB* is arguably one of the greatest punk albums, even though it is rarely categorized as such. Chuck D and his pals Flav (William Drayton), Terminator X (Norman Lee Rogers) and Professor Griff (Richard Griffin) were like the best of the best punks—the Clash, Sham 69, Stiff Little Fingers— in their collective desire to stir up anger and then channel it into positive political change.

When rap and punk are looked at from a distance, the characteristic that divides the two genres (race) is perhaps less significant than the characteristics that unite them (they're angry, political and—regrettably—overwhelmingly male). In the years that followed the release of *It Takes a Nation of Millions to Hold Us Back,* plenty of others followed Chuck D's lead and continued to build on the overlap between rap and punk: showcasing punk *and* rap acts at the influential and annual Vans Warped Tour, stealing from each genre's stylings (as the Beastie Boys do, and have done for years) and generally attempting to provoke a political awakening among voting-age youth of all colours (as seen during the lead-up to the 2004 presidential election in the United States).

Another way in which black youth changed the evolution of punk rock carries a name: Bad Brains. It's a name that thousands of punks still revere, more than two decades after the band made their debut in their hometown of Washington, D.C. They were, without much doubt, the single most influential American hardcore punk group—and, unlike all other hardcore punk groups, they were all black. Everyone from Black Flag to Minor Threat to Bikini Kill cites the Brains as a key influence; their first album was no less than "the best punk/hardcore album of all time," declared Adam Yauch of the Beastie Boys. "They were the bridge between punk and hardcore," says CBGB's Hilly Kristal, who can be said to know a thing or two about the punk movement.

In Ian MacKaye's case, the Minor Threat founder met the members of Bad Brains handing out leaflets in January 1979 at the

Cramps show in D.C., where MacKaye received his punk-rock awakening. In time, MacKaye and the Brains would become close friends, even sharing equipment and a practice space. At the Cramps gig, the members of Bad Brains were, according to MacKaye, "the coolest-looking, most heavy-looking dudes" in the place. For MacKaye, the Brains were without equal. "The Bad Brains," he says, "were really one of the great bands that existed of any time."

So what was so great about them? For starters, their ability to play fast. In the month that MacKaye met them at the Cramps show, the Brains had just released their first DIY single, "Pay to Cum," which is one of the fiercest, fastest songs ever etched on vinyl. The Bad Brains—H.R. on vocals, Dr. Know on guitar, Darryl Jenifer on bass and Earl Hudson on drums—were amazing musicians, playing tighter, and at higher velocities, than anyone else on the burgeoning hardcore punk scene. The foursome came together in the late 1970s to form a jazz-fusion combo they called Mind Power. When they heard Joe Strummer's take on "Police and Thieves" on the first Clash album, they were profoundly affected: not only did they become punks (and select a name for themselves that was taken from a Ramones song), but they also started on a path that led to their conversion to Rastafarianism.

The Bad Brains experienced prejudice and oppression in a way that white punks—who regularly wrote songs about prejudice and oppression—never would, or could. If punks were society's outsiders, the members of Bad Brains were outside all of *that*, too. As if to make that point, one of their best albums was titled *Banned in D.C.*—a testament to the difficulties they had in finding gig venues in their hometown. Frustrated by the experience, the band was ultimately forced to move to New York City to find venues that would let them put on shows. Their live performances were the stuff of legend, and their earliest recordings were hard to find (and therefore greatly prized by American punks). But throughout the eighties the Brains broke up and reunited many times—too many times—and lost a lot of momentum as a result. They remain, however, unique for being the first to truly break through punk's colour barrier—and for being the first, and best, black punk band.

James Spooner, who knows his stuff, says punk's values transcend race, or gender, or other things that traditionally divide society—and if they don't, Spooner says, they should. Spooner insists that more unites punk than divides it. "All punks, whatever their race, feel alone in their world," Spooner says. "Punk rock is a place where outsiders can get together and fit in. Punks share the same feelings of angst, the same kinds of politics, the same aesthetic. *That's* what counts."

Perhaps. But it still doesn't address the key question: *Why* is punk so white? Is it the music? Socio-economic factors? Latent racism? Or is it simply because white kids largely invented punk, and they kept it on their own side of the divide? Everyone seems to agree that the question is an important one, but no one knows the answer for sure.

One thing is certain, however: of all the theories, Billy Idol's is the most likely to produce a laugh. Interviewed a generation after the fact—after he was member of the Sex Pistols' Bromley Contingent retinue, after he founded the punk band Chelsea, or the punk-pop band Generation X—Idol reflects on punk's whiteness. While Idol is dismissed by a lot of punks for "selling out" to make it big (and he did make it big, mostly in the 1980s, thanks to MTV and the attention he paid to image), the fact is that Idol was one of the first British punks to embrace, and play, reggae-style dub. And to work extensively with black musicians and record songs written by black artists.

Looking a lot older than he used to, Idol comes closer to an answer than anybody else has: "Punk was the white reaction, in a way, to what was going on at that time," he says. "Whereas reggae was the [Rastafarian] reaction or rebellion."

While many of the political objectives may have been similar, Idol says, black kids and white kids ultimately did not remain apart due to ideology, or sociology, or economics. Now promoting an album and a new band after a decade-long absence from the music scene—an absence that was the direct consequence of drug abuse and an out-of-control lifestyle, he admits—Idol says that black kids never fully embraced punk because, in its essence, punk music just wasn't the kind of revolutionary soundtrack they were looking for. (It still isn't.) To Idol, it's simple. Black and white kids liked different music. Says Idol: "I mean, it's pretty wild, really. And it kind of shows you how fragmented people are. In my case, when I moved on to [a solo career], I very much used dance music, or the disco I'd been listening to. But that made me unique. I wanted to streamline the energy of punk and make it danceable." He taps a tabletop for emphasis. "Because one of the things about punk was that, um, you couldn't really have sex to it. Black music is sexier. It had a groove that punk didn't."

He laughs and claps his hands. "You can't fuck to punk very well, now, can you?"

It was a lot easier to like Alice Cooper when he bit the heads off chickens, or bats, or whatever.

Alice Cooper, née Vincent Furnier, is the fifty-six-year-old fellow who used to be a rock 'n' roll star, but who has more recently achieved distinction for golfing with former Republican presidents and attending NBA games with Republican senators. For years, he has acted as the worst kind of shill for said Republicans, and sneered at the efforts of Bruce Springsteen, REM, John Mellencamp and assorted other rockers to fundraise for efforts to unseat U.S. president George W. Bush. "To me, that's treason. I call it treason against rock 'n' roll because rock is the antithesis of politics. Rock should never be in bed with politics," he told the Canadian Press, with a straight face, prior to launching a fifteen-city Canadian tour in the summer of 2004.

Said Alice, "When I was a kid and my parents started talking about politics, I'd run to my room and put on the Rolling Stones as loud as I could. So when I see all these rock stars up there talking politics, it makes me sick . . . If you're listening to a rock star in order to get your information on who to vote for, you're a bigger moron than they are. Why are we rock stars? Because we're morons. We sleep all day, we play music at night and very rarely do we sit around reading the *Washington Journal*."

Alice's pithy observation got a lot of play in newspapers across North America. When some of us read what Alice said to the Canadian Press, however, we wanted to do to him what he allegedly used to do to chickens (he didn't actually ever deliberately kill a chicken, by the way: more than three decades ago, at a show in Toronto, he threw one into the audience, mistakenly thinking that chickens could fly, and the fans promptly tore the bird to pieces). But we shouldn't kill him just yet. After all, Alice—even if he is a self-described moron—has raised a legitimate issue: Should rock 'n' rollers ever comment on politics?

There was a time when quite a few of us thought they shouldn't. After all, rock stars have a tremendous ability to sway young minds; therefore, isn't it better that kids learn about important political choices in the traditional ways (reading newspapers, watching TV, falling asleep in social studies classes)? Should coke-addled, pot-bellied, self-indulgent, hedonistic rockers be permitted to pass along their ideological biases to millions of impressionable teenagers?

For quite some time, our collective answer to that question was no. And then some of us heard the first Clash album, circa 1977 or so. It was raw, it was loud, and it was fiercely political— about things that were largely beyond a North American's ken, such as Britain's system of "the dole," monarchists, aristocrats and racist subcultures. But here's the thing: the Brit fans adored that LP, and not simply for its sound. They loved it, they said, *because it was music that wasn't afraid to urge kids to get involved in politics and try to change the many things that suck.*

There: that last part is in italics to ensure that no one, not even poor old Alice Cooper, could miss the point—to wit, that rock 'n' roll fucking well matters, and not simply because it's fun to dance to.

But don't just take my word for it. Ask some musicians, particularly the punkish ones. Morons that they are, punks have some very insightful insights to pass along to Alice Cooper. Ask Jake Burns of Stiff Little Fingers, as I did: "You can do things to make your life better—that is what the Clash were putting forward, and that appealed to me. Particularly since I was growing up in Northern Ireland, and it didn't seem like there was anything that could make our lives better. And that really impressed the hell out of me."

That is the very best rebuttal of the words of the calculating old cynic named Alice Cooper: a political song gave some hope to a kid growing up in a place as bleak and as soul-destroying as Northern Ireland. And it gave him a desire to get involved somewhere, somehow, and make things better.

That's not being a moron, Alice. That's being smart. That's evidence that rock 'n' roll can change peoples' lives, in a demonstrably good way.

"Moronic," we'd say, is best defined as any formerly besotted, misanthropic, soulless aging rock star who is willing to campaign for George W. Bush and then turn around and attack rock stars who have the temerity to campaign for his Democratic opponents. Just like Alice.

As despicable as it is, as rotten as it is, Alice Cooper's side of the argument is the one that is winning. For now.

Rock 'n' roll's audience is mostly young, and young people mostly aren't voting. Despite the best efforts of a lot of musicians—

and, recently, a disproportionately large number of punk musicians—young people remain stubbornly uninterested in politics and political choices. The statistics tell the story.

Young people represent the largest block of unclaimed voters in the United States, Canada and most modern democratic states. Generally, out of all of the young people entitled to vote, as few as one in five regularly do so. *One in five!* In the United States, people aged eighteen to thirty represent twenty-five percent of the total voting population, but—according to Yale University's Department of Political Science, which is widely recognized as the expert on the depressing phenomenon—only a third of them actually bothered to cast a ballot in the 2000 presidential election. Had more of them done so, pretty much everyone agrees, George W. Bush would have been denied his narrow victory over the Democrats' Al Gore (not to discount the invaluable assistance provided by Bush's golf buddies on the U.S. Supreme Court, of course, or Florida's banana republic voting system).

In Canada, the story isn't the same—it's worse: in the 2000 federal election, from the eighteen- to twenty-four-year-old group, a pathetic twenty-two percent bothered to cast a ballot; had more of them voted in the 2004 federal contest (which saw the numbers go up, somewhat), rightist political parties—which were favourable to the war in Iraq and missile defence, and hostile towards gay marriage—would have been obliged to moderate their policies or lose support. In Britain, the situation is marginally better, but not dramatically so: there, thirty-nine percent of the country's eighteen- to twenty-four-year-olds voted in the 2001 general election.

It's a vicious circle, all of this. Political candidates routinely ignore young people because of their poor voter turnout; young people cite candidate indifference as one of the big reasons why they don't vote. With each election, a bad situation gets worse. (Some punks, or punkish fans, find the situation so distressing they throw themselves into political activism, or even run for office. Out west, where I lived and loved punk, it's not uncommon to see punk names on a ballot: I recall that David Mitchell, a member of British Columbia's legislature, was a member of a punk combo called the Shmorgs; Jello Biafra ran for mayor of San Francisco, coming fourth; DOA's Joey Shithead was a Green Party candidate; and, I confess, I ran unsuccessfully for Parliament against a rightist politician, in part because I objected to his inability to denounce a local Holocaust denier.)

As they studied the problem—a problem that, everyone should agree, has the potential to destroy democracy itself—the experts at Yale discovered a number of things about young people, and about the way young people regard politics. For example, young potential voters are much more interested in a candidate's position on the issues and much less interested in his or her partisan affiliation. And they like candidates who have been involved in issues at a community level, in a hands-on way. Young people care very little about a politician's appearance or style or manner, and a great deal about his or her record and experience and effectiveness.

According to the Yale experts, young voters—or those many, many young people on the cusp of voting for the first time—want a candidate's attention and respect, because they feel (rightly) that they have been left out of the political process. They know when they are being patronized. They feel the system does not take them or their issues seriously. They like candidates who are authentic, who listen, who show some kind of commitment. And they don't like fakes and phonies—they can spot those miles away.

None of this is particularly surprising. A lot of it seems like common sense, or the sorts of things that older voters want too. But the Yale studies have found that—when a candidate actually spends time with young people, face to face; when he or she is honestly and truly more preoccupied by community activism than by politics; when a campaign simply reminds young people about the importance of voting and helps them to do so—youth turnout can be boosted by as much as *eight percentage points*. Eight percent may not sound like a lot, but it is: an extra eight percent might have persuaded politicians such as Paul Martin (who can't make up his mind about anything) and George W. Bush (who won't change his mind about anything) to adopt more moderate policies or, better yet, retire. Eight percent, in fact, is far more than the margin of victory enjoyed by most winning politicians in most electoral contests. *It can make a difference.*

And that, of course, is why right-wing political interests are so nervous about serious efforts to mobilize young people to vote. They know that if such campaigns are successful, democracy itself will be changed. They know that if they don't discredit attempts to get the youth vote—as nasty old Alice Cooper has tried to do, more than once—then a lot of them will be looking for other work, very rapidly.

Which endeth the political science lesson, and brings us backeth to the punks. And Pennywise.

For the first little bit, and if you don't listen to any of Jim Lindberg's words whatsoever, Pennywise seems to resemble a lot of other West Coast punk outfits—they're all-male, they're muscular, and they favour lots of black T-shirts and ball caps. Onstage, they are impressively fast and tight. But in one key respect, Pennywise is decidedly unlike a lot of other successful California punk bands— such as the bored and boring millionaires in, say, Offspring, whose music has little or nothing to offer that can be considered even remotely political or progressive. The members of Pennywise are fiercely political, proudly liberal and completely unafraid to challenge the prevailing consensus in the United States of America, which is fiercely, proudly *illiberal.* Consequently, they've got balls to spare.

The band members—Lindberg on vocals, Fletcher Dragge on guitar, Randy Bradbury on bass and Byron McMackin on drums— are from Hermosa Beach, California, the same tiny town from which Black Flag sprang. Formed in 1988 with their original bassist, Jason

Thirsk, the band was unique right from the start. Their 1993 album, *Unknown Road,* sold hundreds of thousands of copies on the Epitaph label; not surprisingly, the majors rapidly converged on Hermosa Beach, offering Pennywise big-dollar recording contracts. The band declined. "We know when it feels wrong for us, and when it feels right," says Lindberg, an articulate, well-read father of three, who disdains what he calls "corpo" punk. "We've turned down a lot of corporate sponsorships in our time that could have brought us a lot of money. We turned down a lot of television shows, radio shows, different things that we didn't think were right for the band. Bands like Offspring get millions and millions in sales, and the 'sell out' issue [doesn't] ever stop being an issue for them."

In 1997, Pennywise's album *Full Circle* sold hundreds of thousands of copies—as did 1999's *Straight Ahead.* In 2000, they released a live album, plus the blistering *Land of the Free?,* which featured "Fuck Authority," the Pennywise song that remains most popular at the band's typically sold-out shows. But their pace and intensity eventually caught up with them. In the year that followed, Pennywise was buffeted by the sudden death of Dragge's father, and a lot of second thoughts about the band's direction that had apparently been lingering since the death of Thirsk (who committed suicide at the age of twenty-seven). It was a difficult time—and then 9/11 happened.

For Pennywise, as for many other people, the murders at the World Trade Center and the Pentagon were galvanizing events—but for different reasons. Immediately following the attacks, a lot of people were seen rallying around ultranationalist themes, demanding an overwhelming military counterattack and manifesting a disturbing willingness to suppress dissent. It was a difficult, dangerous time. Instead of aping the jingoism that was seemingly everywhere in the aftermath of September 11, Pennywise (courageously, whether you agree with them or not) publicly urged caution. On their post-9/11 album *Out of the Ashes*—the title a specific reference to the events of that terrible day—the band also revealed the depth of their disdain for George W. Bush's America, in the furious, combustible "God Save the USA":

God you must be kidding me, thought this was supposed to be
The home of the brave and the free for you and me
But now there's something wrong, shit's been going on too
long.
Never gonna change, there's no way, so I say:
What's the CIA? And the NRA?
They're all the same—just the names are changed.
Fuck—there's no excuse—any way you lose.
It's all a joke in the good old USA.

All we need is more factories pumping filth into the sky.
Corporate greed and perverted priests, it's the story of our
lives.
And apathy's the national disease and there is no end in sight.
God save the USA—blame the president and say your prayers
tonight.

The irony of liberty is no one here is truly free;
When elections are stolen by greed, the G.O.P.
So watch the nightly news, find out how you are getting
screwed.
Whatcha gonna do? There's no use, so I say
Fuck the industry, the aristocracy.
They're all the same—just the names are changed.

In an essay he published on a popular punk website, Lindberg leaves no doubt about the band's post-9/11 views: "In the flag-waving, red, white and blue tidal wave of patriotic fervour that has grown in the wake of 9/11, anyone who dares to question the motives of the right-wing conservative agenda will be ridiculed with the same sort of vicious persecution this country suffered during the McCarthy era. Any person . . . urging restraint against American aggression overseas—or warning of the backlash that will undoubtedly occur—[is] labelled a traitor and communist. If they are allowed to speak at all."

Lots of people think Lindberg is right. Witnessing the vilification of the Dixie Chicks when they spoke up against George W. Bush and his illegal war against Iraq—or even poor old Linda Ronstadt, for the love of God, who did no more than praise Michael Moore's anti-Bush film *Farenheit 9/11* in front of an audience in Las Vegas—plenty of musicians have remained silent, or muted their criticism. Pennywise, however, was re-energized, and resolved to get back to work. "The important thing to remember," Lindberg writes in his essay, "is that White House officials are concerned with [something] crucial to their survival and the implementation of their policies . . . the potentially adverse reaction from pissed off people who might suddenly decide they'd heard enough and either (a) vote them out of office, or (b) coalesce into a group with numbers large enough to stage effective protests, boycotts and demonstrations.

"They can do whatever they want if we remain mildly content and apathetic."

And for that reason, Lindberg says, Punk Voter was born. Following the 2000 presidential election—which, in case anyone has forgotten, Al Gore actually *won*—lots of people were upset. One of those, says Lindberg, was his friend Fat Mike Burkett, bassist for the legendary punk combo NOFX. Like many other punks, Lindberg's friend had been politically minded, although not necessarily politically active. The disputed election result enraged Fat Mike and plenty of others. The San Francisco Bay–area headquarters of NOFX's Fat Wreck Chords label soon started hosting meetings of punks to discuss what to do. The key, Lindberg says, was getting more young people to vote—because, had they done so in greater numbers in 2000, George W. Bush would not have been able to seize the White House.

Attempts to persuade young people to vote had been tried before; Punk Voter was more than that. Not only did Punk Voter want more young people to vote, it also wanted those same young people to vote *against* Bush. Punk Voter was not simply another inoffensive, feel-good campaign by and about the establishment, as had been the case with Live Aid in 1985 or No Nukes in 1979; it was pissed-off, militant and decidedly partisan. *Punk,* in other words. The owners of the two biggest punk/alternative labels in the world— Brett Gurewitz of Epitaph and former Dead Kennedys singer Jello Biafra, now of Alternative Tentacles—offered to help sponsor both Punk Voter and its supporting tours. In the end, Fat Mike's effort would be supported by more than a hundred punk bands, among them Anti-Flag, Bad Religion, Blink-182, Circle Jerks, the Donnas, Dropkick Murphys, Less Than Jake, Lunachicks, Mudhoney, New Found Glory, No Use for a Name, Rancid, Social Distortion and Sum 41. And, as noted, Pennywise.

In his essay, and in a lengthy discussion with me in the Pennywise tour bus prior to the 2004 U.S. presidential election, Lindberg notes that right-wingers—and particularly conservative religious organizations—are particularly effective at getting out their vote. Holding a bottle of Gatorade with one hand, jabbing the air with the other, Lindberg says that if young people do not start to vote in greater numbers, they will be facing an emboldened right wing that will reveal itself to be more and more extreme—by reintroducing conscription to bolster Bush's war in Iraq, or making abortion illegal, among other things.

Lindberg says, "I'm constantly amazed when I talk to people who have the opinion that it doesn't matter if you don't vote. That kind of attitude is hurting us. We need to get past that, and that's why a lot of bands are putting more politics in their music . . . There's a [rising] level of indignation about what is going on in the world right now. Hopefully we will spur more people to go to the polls."

To do that, Punk Voter focuses its efforts on education and registration (in the United States, unlike in many other democracies, citizens must fill out a prescribed form in order to be permitted to vote). At Pennywise gigs—and at gigs by the other bands associated with the Punk Voter effort—young people are provided with information about how to vote, and are encouraged to do so (against George W. Bush). Throughout the Vans Warped Tour, voter registration booths were on-site, staffed by volunteers; in some cities, hundreds of people were registered by Punk Voter. The U.S. voter registration form is also offered as a download on the Punk Voter website.

Punk Voter has even hired legal counsel and a Washington lobbyist to assist it in manoeuvring through the Byzantine corridors of power. Their lobbyist, Scott Goodstein, is a lawyer and a former D.C. punk who has represented trade unions on Capitol Hill. Goodstein has also advised Punk Voter on assorted legal difficulties—such as when high schools attempted to prevent students from wearing Punk Voter's NOT MY PRESIDENT T-shirts in class. And, naturally, Punk Voter has so far issued two low-cost compilation CDs on Fat Wreck Chords titled *Rock Against Bush;* Pennywise's "God Save the USA" is found on volume one. Proceeds from the sale of the CDs—which quickly became America's number one indie sellers—go to Punk Voter's advertising campaigns against Bush and to promote youth voter participation. On its website, which attracts thousands of visitors on a daily basis, Punk Voter describes what it calls "Objective One":

> *To activate punks and other disenfranchised young people to participate in elections.* In the 2000 election, Bush "won" Florida by only 537 votes. Two million registered voters in Florida did NOT vote in that election. If only 600 of those had voted for Gore, our country would be in a very

different position. Additionally, only thirty-eight percent of young people (18–29) voted in the 2000 presidential election. This is not only sad; it is pathetic. Besides the multitude of local issues in every election in which a hundred votes can decide an issue, the 2000 presidential election showed us that ANYONE, especially young people, CAN make a huge difference. Apathy can be fatal. As concerned members of the punk rock community, we need to become ACTIVE in the election process. Voting is the crucial first step. We know that you care, now show it. Don't let history repeat itself.

Fair enough; impressive words. But words minus action equals zero, as Joey Shithead has said. Who else in the community has stepped up, in a big way, to support Punk Voter's "Objective One"? Has anyone actually had an impact? To the despair of many punks, George W. Bush was ultimately re-elected. But even though he was pessimistic about the odds, Bad Religion's Brett Gurewitz—one of the most influential names in punk for the past two decades—threw his considerable weight behind the anti-Bush effort. And, in punk circles, that matters.

Many hardcore punk bands rocketed out of the Southern California scene in the early 1980s, but Bad Religion has survived the longest, with the most fanatical base to show for it. For more than two decades, the band has offered a variety of melodic sounds, all demonstrating a capacity for pissed-off, political punk rock. Along the way, Bad Religion has been a germinal influence for hundreds of punk bands.

Formed in the suburbs around Los Angeles in 1980, Bad Religion's starting lineup comprised high school pals Brett Gurewitz on guitar and Greg Graffin on vocals. An early convert to DIY, Gurewitz set up a record company to release the band's records, calling the company Epitaph. Following the 1983 release of their debut record, *Into the Unknown,* Bad Religion captured the attention of the surging international hardcore scene—but Gurewitz was forced to absent himself from the band for a while to deal with a substance abuse problem (a demon Gurewitz has been forced to confront more than once). That left Graffin as the band's only original member. At different times, Graffin was joined by former Circle Jerks guitarist Greg Hetson and Minor Threat guitarist Brian Baker. Once clean, Gurewitz returned to the Bad Religion lineup.

Gurewitz drifted away again, disillusioned (like many others) when Bad Religion signed to major label Atlantic Records in 1994. He thereafter devoted himself full-time to Epitaph, which was experiencing extraordinary growth. When Atlantic dropped Bad Religion in 2000, Gurevitz lured his old friends back to the fold at Epitaph. Then, in the summer of 2001, after being away for most of a decade, Gurewitz rejoined the group. His involvement in Bad Religion hasn't been full-time since then—Epitaph preoccupies too many of his working hours for that, he says—but he still considers himself a member of the group.

Bad Religion, he says, formed two decades ago in a social and political atmosphere not unlike the current one: with rightist organizations asserting their control over the agendas of governments and entire countries. Conservatism, he says, is in the ascendancy; liberals everywhere seem to be losing the battle. Says Gurewitz, "Well, you know, it's not something that has happened overnight. It's something that has been happening little by little over a long period of time. That's something that Bad Religion was railing against in the early eighties—when we made up the name Bad Religion. It was in response to Jerry Falwell and Jimmy Swaggart and the rise of televangelism. But in the last two decades that stuff didn't go away. It just went a little more underground, and it's been swelling and growing and organizing. And now we have this huge, huge faction of fundamentalists and conservative Christians in the United States . . . And it's frightening to me."

As a consequence, Gurewitz says, it wasn't difficult to agree to donate a song or a video to Punk Voter's fundraising efforts. The fact that he had been friends with NOFX's Fat Mike for twenty years made the decision even easier, he adds: "We have the same, or similar, world views."

Ascertaining Brett Gurewitz's world view isn't difficult; just ask him. He is irritated (very irritated) by the suggestion, made by some of his own label's artists, that conservative governments like that of George W. Bush are "good" for punk rock—that they give punks something to rebel against. "Was the Vietnam War *good* for anything?" Gurewitz asks, without waiting for an answer. "Was it *good* because we had the sixties revolution as a result? I don't think the Vietnam War was good for *anything,* and I don't think George Bush is good for anything either. I just can't bring myself to say that! He's been terrible for the poor! He's been terrible for minorities! He's been terrible for science and enlightenment! He's been terrible for the planet! He's been terrible for the infirm! He's been terrible for the poor, did I mention that?" Gurewitz gives a dark laugh. "He's just terrible! He's a scourge! You know, he's good for cronyism and elitism, that's what he's good for!"

Gurewitz pauses, but not for long. I find myself wishing I could take the question back, but it is too late for that. He continues, "So some people say: 'Hey, Reagan was great for punk rock. Best thing that ever happened to punk rock. And, now that George Bush stole the election from Al Gore, it's going to be the best thing that happened to punk rock since Reagan.'" He sounds like he wants to spit. "Yeah, I've heard *that.* I think it's a *snide* thing to say. Punk rock just isn't that important, you know? It's like saying, well, you know, heroin addiction is great for the common cold because heroin is analgesic. So I'm never going to have a runny nose now! So, yeah, I guess that's true. But it's an odd way of looking at things, you know?"

I know, I know. And it probably *is* snide. As his dogs yip around his heels, and as an Epitaph band gathers in his Los Angeles home for a photo shoot, Gurewitz admits that he is feeling very pessimistic these days. The forces of conservatism—the reactionaries, whose policies have been ineffectually unchallenged since the terrible events of September 11—are everywhere, he says, and he wonders whether something like Punk Voter can have any impact at all. "I see a lot of nationalism and a lot of xenophobia now," he says. "I see a lot of homogenization taking place in the mass media . . . it's as if the world view of millions of Americans comes daily from the administration's talking points, which in turn comes straight from the Pentagon. In the United States, I see almost this aversion to enlightenment, and a return to traditional values . . . all of these things are happening, and they combine to make a potent brew. That's why Bush is so popular, despite the evidence."

He sighs. "If it sounds like I'm rather pessimistic, it's because I am. I don't know how to change it. I just made a record called *The Empire Strikes First,* okay? And you'd be surprised how many kids come up to me and say, 'What's the empire? What do you mean by that?'" Gurewitz shakes his head.

The album, like Gurewitz himself, leaves no doubt about its politics. In track after pounding track, Bad Religion doesn't so much play songs as it delivers an indictment against conservatives, generally, and George W. Bush, in particular. When the album was released, the *Los Angeles Times* wrote, "The veteran punk band's thirteenth album doesn't disappoint, unleashing the kind of un-bridled fury that used to define punk before it was co-opted for sneaker commercials and lust-struck teens with the hots for their neighbor's Mom . . . even if some songs unfold more like political manifestos than songs, Bad Religion has succeeded in expressing its outrage more eloquently while sustaining its musical muscle over the years." It is, in fact, one of the best punk albums ever produced.

Reminded about that—and reminded that the 2000 presidential contest ultimately came down to only a few hundred votes in a single state, and that the 2004 competition saw the popular vote split almost exactly 50/50—Gurewitz relents, and tries to sound a little less bleak about the future. "*Yeah,*" he says, exhaling. "I do think punk is making some kind of a positive impact. It just feels like a ripple in the middle of a typhoon, you know?" He rallies. "Punk Voter is bigger than just one record or one song. What Punk Voter has done is really, really great. It has gone out and harnessed a potent force. It has grabbed all these disparate forces, people who all share a feeling, and pulled them all together to be greater than the sum of all of their parts . . . And that's a real, beautiful punk thing. It's going to have an effect.

"It's going to change things."

IF THE KIDS ARE UNITED
(or, we shall never be divided)

Way back in July 1978, Sham 69 had a Top Ten hit song in Britain called "If the Kids Are United." Here are a few of the words, which every real punk has engraved on his or her heart, or should:

Just take a look around you
What do you see
Kids with feelings like you and me
Understand him, he'll understand you
For you are him, and he is you

If the kids are united then we'll never be divided
If the kids are united then we'll never be divided

More than two decades after he sang that remarkable song, taking time for an interview in London, Sham's singer Jimmy Pursey agrees: the thing to keep in mind about extremism is that, for a lot of people, it all starts with the best of intentions. Nobody starts out as a hater; they become one. "I think some people, *on purpose,* just don't *want* to understand other people," says Pursey. "That leads to insanity."

Later on, I thought about what Pursey had said. Most people, it is true, do not set out to find a girl to kick in the face with a steel-toed boot as she cowers on a city street, because she opposes racism and couldn't get away fast enough. Most people don't participate in plots to plant a massive bomb that blows apart a young man whose only crime is working a low-paying job as a security guard. Most people do not plan on doing those sorts of things, however much they are angry about immigration or the arms race. But some do; some did, in fact.

When a young person (a punk, let's say) exchanges complexity, nuance and patience for the arrogance and conceit of bumper sticker ideologies promoting radical, instantaneous change, loosely accompanied by a punk music soundtrack—well, hell. *Fuck* democracy, right? You know what's right, so fuck second thoughts, fuck dialogue, fuck everyone else. Just do it, *maaan.*

Punk was, and is, about defiance, and resistance, and self-reliance; it was, and is, anti-authoritarian, youthful, loud, creative, independent, unique. Punk was wonderful, except on those occasions—more than rare, less than frequent—when it wasn't. When it became the apotheosis of extremism and hate. When it actually became worse than the worst of the society it was seeking to change.

Most young people, and certainly most punks, don't set out to become extremists and haters. But most punks, to put a fine point on it, aren't George Burdi and Gerry Hannah.

Meet George and Gerry—for whom "If the Kids Are United" is just some stupid fucking song.

—

It's Saturday night, May 29, 1993, around 8:25 P.M., at the Boys and Girls Club on Nepean Street in Ottawa. Outside the old brick building, in a residential area on the west side of Ottawa's downtown, some six hundred protestors—many of them punks— are screaming epithets or chanting slogans: "Racism is the refuge of the weak and the afraid" and "Save our land! Smash the Klan!" Holding the protestors back, or trying to, is a vastly outnumbered group of police officers. Inside the hall are six dozen or so neo-Nazi skinheads, present to witness a rare performance by the punkish- sounding band RaHoWa, short for Racial Holy War. Outside on the club steps, chatting with a few of his pals in the Church of the Creator's self-described Security Legion, is George Burdi, RaHoWa's lead singer. Surveying the melee mere feet from where he stands, Burdi looks immensely pleased with himself.

On this night, Burdi is a few weeks away from celebrating his twenty-third birthday. He's a large man, about six feet tall and more than two hundred pounds. His muscular arms are littered with tattoos, one of which reads TO THINE OWN SELF BE TRUE; his latest, of which he is very proud, is the three-point symbol of South Africa's pro-Nazi Afrikaner Resistance Movement. His hair is cropped short, but not so short that he could be mistaken for a skinhead. His hairstyle is one of the things that help distinguish Burdi from his many followers—found in Ottawa's Boys and Girls Club tonight, but also across Canada and the United States. Front man for a punk neo-Nazi band, leader of the Canadian branch of the virulently, violently racist Church of the Creator, Burdi stands out from the crowd. He always has.

Burdi and his skinhead followers laugh as the protestors throw eggs at them, none of which hits its mark. At 8:45 P.M., two sizable explosions are heard, not far from where I am standing with my notebook and tape recorder; someone is throwing cherry bombs. Burdi strolls inside the club, shaking his head. At 9:15, another cherry bomb detonates as fifteen members of the riot squad arrive.

At that moment, as the protestors start to chant "Cops and Klan, hand in hand," RaHoWa launch their set of noisy, ham-fisted pro-Nazi anthems. Inside the old club, as police surveillance videotapes show, the assembled skinheads swill more beer and give more fascist salutes. The music throbs through the walls, flush with menace. Outside, the crowd of protestors is starting to thin out; a rock slams against the front door. Inside, Burdi and his band are all swagger and machismo, as usual. Leaning forward, his features pinched, Burdi launches into one of RaHoWa's most popular numbers, a cover of Nancy Sinatra's sixties hit "These Boots Are Made for Walkin'." Burdi has changed the lyrics:

> *These boots are made for stompin'*
> *And that's just what they'll do*
> *One of these days these boots*
> *Are gonna stomp all over Jews . . .*

The police watch as skinheads go wild, the space in front of the club's tiny stage a hurricane of slam-dancing. RaHoWa's rock 'n' roll, if it can be called that, isn't the intense, high-speed punk played by Minor Threat or Bad Religion; most often, it has a thudding, sluggish tempo, like those punk outfits midway on the road linking hardcore and metal. RaHoWa isn't very good, but that seems to be beside the point. "Boots" has roused the skinheads, so Burdi leads RaHoWa into another favourite, "Third Reich." The former straight-A high school student bellows the lyrics, which are more an incitement to genocide than an actual song:

> *Kill all the niggers, and you gas all the Jews*
> *Kill a Gypsy and a coloured too*
> *You just killed a kike, don't it feel right?*
> *Goodness gracious, darn right!*

It is more than a profoundly disturbing scene; it is *fucking sick*. How is it that someone is permitted to advocate genocide, with a smirk on his moonish face, and suffer no consequences whatsoever? How is it that Burdi and his pals were able to rent the Boys and Girls Club under false pretences—one of their female acolytes told the club she needed it for a "private dance"—and then be permitted to provoke a riot? The police officers, some of whom have been observing the proceedings inside the club, look genuinely shaken.

About thirty minutes after they began, the members of RaHoWa stop playing. George Burdi and his followers start consulting with the police about the best way to get themselves and their equipment out of the club. The discussions continue for a long time. It is evident that the Ottawa Police assume the evening's excitement is at an end and the burly young racists are planning to crawl back under the rock from whence they came.

This assumption, the police and others would later agree, was a big mistake.

Years later, interviewed in Toronto, George Burdi attempts to downplay that fateful night in May 1993. And, to save time and because he has my attention already, he seeks to minimize the significance of his decision to fuse punk rock sounds to neo-Nazism and white supremacy, and market it with Wall Street savvy— something that no one, in North America at least, had done before. "Much has been made about my apparent genius for recognizing the seductive attraction of rock, and using it as a vehicle for my opinions," he says. "But there was no such premeditation. I was also seduced. I listened to music non-stop since I was a boy." Uh-huh.

Born in June 1970—with, he once said with a straight face, "some kind of destiny"—George Burdi was raised in the affluent north Toronto suburb of Woodbridge. Burdi was an intelligent boy, and absurdly self-confident. His father owned an insurance company; his mother encouraged George and his younger brother,

Andrew, to read as much as possible. During one family vacation
in the United States, when he was twelve, Burdi claims to have read
twenty books, apparently of the view that the mere reading of
books equates with gaining actual knowledge. As he later told *The
New York Times,* in a lengthy profile the newspaper published about
the brainy young Canadian racist, "I read 14 books in two weeks.
In grade five, I was tested and given a college-level reading level
and a genius-level I.Q. I read everything from Thucydides to Plato
to Nietzsche." It is unclear what impact Nietzsche's musings about
the "vulgar" Jews and the "affirmative Aryan religion" had on a
grade five student. But in the same school year, one of Burdi's
teachers at St. Gerard's Elementary School in Mississauga told his
parents that the thoughtful altar boy "was going to be someone very
important in the future."

"Before RaHoWa," Burdi says, "I had been in a couple of other
bands; just kids' stuff, but loads of fun nonetheless. When I was
twelve years old, I won a talent show [at St. Gerard's] singing 'Cum
On Feel the Noize.' The guitarist was my age, the drummer was ten,
and the bassist was our forty-year-old music teacher, full beard and
all. It was quite the sight! We did two shows in our packed
auditorium, five hundred kids going completely nuts. We did two
encores, each time playing the same song. I signed dozens of
autographs. Everyone was sure I was going to make it big someday."

Listening to him, even when he is recalling a grade-school
talent show, it is evident that George Burdi's favourite subject is
George Burdi. His ego, even by rock 'n' roll standards, is immense.

In 1985, Burdi enrolled at De La Salle College, a Catholic boys'
school in Toronto, where students wore uniforms and were usually
the children of the well-to-do, like George. One of his favourite
teachers, Lee Hardy, recalls that Burdi quickly revealed an
unwillingness to accept other points of view. In those days, as Hardy
recalls—and as Burdi never fails to point out to whomever is
interviewing him—his closest friend was a promising Filipino youth.
But there were early portents of the troubles ahead, says Hardy:

"Any type of philosophy that tied in to the Nazis, George was always front and centre." On one memorable occasion, when De La Salle students were permitted to abandon their school uniforms for something "special," George Burdi chose to show up in a homemade Nazi uniform. When De La Salle celebrated a Black Pride Month, Burdi lobbied (unsuccessfully) for a White Pride Month. And so on.

In his second year at De La Salle, Burdi says that "fell in love" with a girl from a neighbouring private girls' school; her father, he says, was an active participant in the Canadian far-right movement. In a bid to gain the girl's favour, and her father's approval, Burdi expressed an interest in learning more about neo-Nazism and white supremacy. In very little time, he was chummy with long-time racist right leaders such as the Western Guard's John Ross Taylor, Citizens for Foreign Aid Reform's Paul Fromm, Holocaust-denying author David Irving and, most significantly, Nazi publicist Ernst Zundel. A portly, German-born Hitler enthusiast who funded neo-Nazi groups around the globe, Zundel took a great interest in George Burdi, drawing the young man deeper into the pig swill of organized hatred. Zundel even permitted the ambitious De La Salle student to use the computers at his fortified downtown Toronto home, and to help put together Zundel's Holocaust-denying newsletters. "The time I spent with [Zundel] I would ask questions and just listen," Burdi says. "And soon, the only way I understood National Socialism was as a creative, positive force and ideology."

Inevitably, Burdi's extracurricular activities were noted at De La Salle College, says Lee Hardy. So, too, the changes in his appearance: in grade ten, Burdi had had an average physique; by the twelfth grade, says Hardy, he had become strikingly muscular—there were hallway rumours that he was consuming steroids. Burdi's brother Andrew told Hardy that his brother was "weird" and that "he's gone off the deep end." Evidence of this wasn't difficult to find, says Hardy. One day, following a student presentation about Hitler and Nazism, Burdi rose in Hardy's history class and declared that the Holocaust had been "a good policy," while the Jews "are a bunch of crybabies." When Hardy attempted to point out that the fact of the Holocaust was beyond historical dispute—and that millions of Jews, gays, liberals, clerics, dissidents and disabled persons had been systematically exterminated by Adolf Hitler's fascist regime—Burdi merely shrugged. "That's insignificant," he said. Later, Burdi told an appalled Hardy that he no longer believed in conventional history—he believed in "revisionist" history, the type manufactured by the likes of his new friends Ernst Zundel and David Irving.

Burdi's racist involvements "put a tremendous strain" on his relationship with his family, he says, and caused endless, bitter arguments. His parents were devastated by the seismic change in their son. Following his graduation from De La Salle, in 1989, Burdi enrolled for a few listless months at the University of Guelph. While there, lurking in the shadows at coffee houses and campus bars, he discovered a racist theology that made Zundel and Irving's intellectualized hatred seem decidedly meek: the Church of the Creator. Thereafter, George Burdi's slide into the abyss was steady and swift.

Of the many neo-Nazi and white supremacist variants in existence, the Church of the Creator (COTC) was among the most violent and extreme. At first, Burdi says that

SKINHEADS OF THE

RACIAL HOLY WAR

even *he* found the COTC's propaganda too much: "I read it, and actually it scared me, it was so radical. It just turned me off. I said, 'Wow, this is psycho.' And then, as time went on, those ideas I had read didn't leave my mind. They had planted a seed of doubt, and I wanted to find out more." The COTC's "idea," Burdi found out, was called Creativity—and Creativity took the position that it was "a racial religion" whose goal is the "survival, expansion, and advancement of [the] White Race exclusively." A Creator, as Burdi came to call himself, does not believe in God. Race, to the COTC, was ne plus ultra: the white race is "nature's highest creation." Jews and non-whites—called the "mud races" by the COTC and a few other equally psycho neo-Nazi affiliations—were subhuman and the enemy, deserving of death.

Skipping classes at Guelph, Burdi read *The White Man's Bible* for the first time. In it, the COTC's founder and self-anointed "Pontifex Maximus," Ben Klassen, defames Christians, blacks and other minorities, although it is Jews who come in for the strongest disapprobation. In Klassen's 452-page "bible," published for the first time in 1981, Jews are described as the "mortal enemy" who are plotting to take over the world by "mongrelizing," and thus destroying, the white race. "Working towards the niggerization of America is the Jewish race," Klassen wrote. "Pushing, clawing, propagandizing with a fury unparalleled in history, the Jews are working towards their ultimate historic goal—total enslavement of all the races of the world."

Unlike many other far-right pseudo-religions, who fear police investigations and prosecutions and temper their rhetoric accordingly, the COTC was unabashed about its willingness to use violence to achieve its goals. Wrote Klassen, "We of the CHURCH OF THE CREATOR are not hypocrites. We openly state that some people need killing, that killing has always been with us and will always be with us . . . Killing our enemies, too, is under certain circumstances a necessary measure for the survival of our own race. Therefore we condone it, and it, too, is no sin in our religion." The COTC has achieved notoriety on a global scale for the violence of its members: across North America and Europe—and in places like South Africa and Russia—"Creators" have been convicted of scores of hate-motivated murders, robberies and vicious assaults.

Undeterred by all of that—and perhaps aware of the avalanche of publicity that would attend the establishment of the first chapter in Canada—George Burdi phoned Ben Klassen at the COTC's headquarters in rural North Carolina. They spoke at length. As impressed as Ernst Zundel had been, Klassen arranged for the inquisitive young Canadian to travel to the fortified COTC compound in the Blue Ridge Mountains in January 1990. Following what Burdi calls "a mental and emotional cleansing period," and individual tutoring sessions with Klassen, whom he claimed to idolize, Burdi returned to Canada.

He dropped out of Guelph and severed all contacts with his family; his parents "weren't thinkers," Burdi later told me, contemptuously. The young Creator started crashing at flophouses in downtown Toronto, most often in the company of racist skinheads. By the fall of 1990, Burdi had formed RaHoWa. "One of the early bassists in the band had a punk rock background, and he always said that true punk rock wasn't trying to sound like punk rock—it just did," says Burdi. "Most of the time, what got dubbed punk rock, especially the sub-genre known as Oi!, was just badly played metal. What made it so attractive [to me] was that it was *real*."

Oi! music—the "real" punk derivative that RaHoWa played, and that was (and remains) favoured by skinheads around the globe— ultimately had its origins in the British subcultures of 1950s. The skinheads' forerunners were the Teddy boys, the virile faction that became immensely popular in the U.K. in the early 1950s and, some twenty years later, would achieve a brief resurrection at Let It Rock, Malcolm McLaren and Vivienne Westwood's clothing shop in the King's Road.

Teds, as they called themselves, were drawn mostly from the British lumpenproletariat. They were a bizarre, foppish underclass trapped in menial labour and dead-end, Hobbesian lives. The Teddy boys favoured long Edwardian coats, tight trousers, bootlace ties, greased-back hair (à la Elvis Presley) and suede shoes referred to as "brothel creepers." The Teds loved Presley's music, and that of Sweet Gene Vincent and Jerry Lee Lewis. They also loved to fight— at dances, on street corners—with whomever met with their disfavour. Most often, the Teddy boys targeted non-whites in

Britain's growing West Indian community. The fabled Notting Hill race riots of August and September 1958 were mostly the handiwork of the Teddy boys, apparently enraged that a black man had spoken to a white woman in a pub; hundreds of them thereafter went "nigger hunting," armed with iron bars, butcher's knives and weighted leather belts. But it was their final act of insurrection, for the Teddy boys were on their way out—the early 1960s was dominated by another subculture, the Mods.

The Mods were fond of stylish Italian suits, oversized army parkas and short haircuts. Like the Teddy boys, they toiled in lowly jobs; but, unlike the Teds (whom they despised and with whom they often battled), the Mods were not racist. At night they could be seen jetting around city streets on shiny Vespa and Lambretta scooters, or loitering in clubs and record shops that played the music they revered: black soul sounds from Little Stevie Wonder, Marvin Gaye and the classic Tamla Motown artists. In amphetamine frenzies, the Mods danced through the night to their beloved soul sounds, stopping only at dawn to slouch back to the drudgery of their clerical jobs.

By 1966 or so, the Mods—like the Teddy boys before them—were in decline. One group of Mods had gravitated to the arty, fashion-conscious Carnaby Street scene. The other group—the one out of which George Burdi and his ilk would eventually sprout, weed-like—became the Gang Mods, or Hard Mods. The Hard Mods wore clothing that would not get in the way of a fight: snug work pants, army jackets, industrial boots and suspenders. They had a tough look, and a tougher lifestyle. By 1972, the Hard Mods had become known by one name, the one that stuck: skinheads.

Tight, rolled-up jeans, Ben Sherman shirts, collarless flight jackets: these formed the skinhead uniform. Most of all, however, the skins became instantly recognizable for their cherished, meticulously shined Doc Marten boots. "Docs," as they were called, were designed by a German podiatrist for working people forced to stand on their feet all day; they were immensely popular in the United Kingdom for the comfort and style they offered. The skinheads loved the boots because they were good for stomping adversaries in street fights. After all, the skinheads, according to University of London professor Dick Hebdige, one of the leading authorities on British youth subcultures, were "designed to make anyone who has even the smallest stake in the present scheme of things cross over to the other side of the street."

Sadly, these days, most of the skinheads one sees strutting down city streets have had some involvement with neo-Nazism and white supremacy. But at the beginnings of their "movement," the skinheads were not racist. In fact—ironically, amazingly, truly—the skins were anything but. In inner city areas such as Lambeth or Brixton, in South East London and North West Kent, skins mixed easily with non-whites at clubs and halls, dancing to the choppy, echo-laden tunes of roots reggae, popularized in Britain by the self-described "rude boys," who had brought it with them from Jamaica. The skinheads borrowed some of the rude boys' fashions (such as the crombie jacket), and—as some sociologists observed—even some of the Jamaican mannerisms and argot. The skinheads' music, that which they loved more than any other, was the black man's music. It had various names—ska, bluebeat, rocksteady—but it was all Jamaican, and it was all black. There were no white bands that could, or did, play reggae and ska, but the skinheads did not mind.

The skinheads adored the Jamaican stars as much as the black kids did: acts such as Prince Buster, Desmond Dekker, the Maytals, the Melodians, the Skatalites and the Ethiopians. While most of the artists who played ska and bluebeat were routinely ignored by the major record labels, some half-hearted attempts were made to take commercial advantage of the burgeoning rude boy–skinhead subculture. In 1969, for example, a sloppy little record called "Skinhead Moonstomp" was released by the seminal reggae label Trojan. The song was performed by a group calling itself Symarip, made up of black skinheads: "I want all you skinheads to get up on your feet/ Put your braces together and your boots on your feet/ And give me some of that old mooooonstompin'!"

Ska was music for the poor, by the poor, and it was popular among the skinheads and the rude boys because most of them were poor, too. It is extraordinary, given the reputation that skinheads would acquire in a decade or so, but it *did* happen, nonetheless: in dance halls across Britain, skinheads and Jamaican kids could be seen dancing together, defending each other.

But the alliance of skinheads and blacks was not to last. The Jamaican kids started to gravitate towards a more politicized reggae, promoting Rastafarianism and, if you listened closely enough, no small amount of antipathy for whites. The skinheads, as a result, started to look for their own music—just about the time that punk was rearing its spiky, technicoloured head.

The skinheads liked punk. It was aggressive and unafraid of a good scrap, just like them. It pissed people off, and the skins liked that, too. So, in the early days of punk, in both London and New York, skinheads attended gigs, and even formed a few bands of their own. But the punk-skinhead alliance was an uneasy one. At the start, in 1977 or so, punk attracted a mélange of counterculturalists—gays, lesbians, Rastafarians, metalheads and art students—with whom the skinheads did not mix easily. In those days, punk claimed an affinity for those who were nonconformists and those who had been victimized by mainstream society. But, however much they aspired to be regarded as leftist, anti-establishment and therefore tolerant, punks were not without their blemishes.

In the late seventies and early eighties, in both Britain and North America, organized racism grew bolder. Spurred on by high rates of youth unemployment and a widespread distrust of prevailing immigration policies, groups on the neo-Nazi, white supremacist fringe started to enjoy a renewal of popularity. In his important sociological text titled *Punk Rock: So What?*, London cultural studies professor Roger Sabin recounts a series of terrible firebombings and murders targeting British Asians. "What was punk's response?" writes Sabin. "The most striking impression is one of silence." Many punks, who often like to style themselves as progressive vanguards against any and all expressions of intolerance, were conspicuously absent from the fight against hate.

The National Front was reaching its political zenith and revitalizing itself with new skinhead recruits, but not all punks were silent. Bands such as the Clash, for example, were at the very forefront of the anti-racism effort. But in his book, Sabin provides ample evidence that many punks had precious few lessons to offer skinheads about peace, love and understanding. Siouxsie and the Banshees, one of the earliest U.K. punk bands, appeared to have a chronic inability to understand that there was a clear distinction between punk-style shock and Nazi-style stupidity. On one of the band's songs, "Love in a Void," Siouxsie Sioux screeches that there are "too many Jews for my liking." Sioux's claim that the lyric was unrepresentative of the band's point of view (she later stated that it was actually about "too many fat businessmen," thereby demonstrating that she did not get the point at all) was not assisted by her penchant for wearing swastika armbands, goose-stepping onstage and making fascist salutes in the direction of her fans.

But Siouxsie was not alone in her imbecility. The Damned's Rat Scabies told the music press in July 1977 that Handsome Dick Manitoba, of the seminal New York punk combo the Dictators, was "a fat Jewish slob." The Stranglers recorded a song called "I Feel Like a Wog." The Models had one titled "Nazi Party" (as in, "I wanna form a . . ."). The Clash's long-time manager, Bernie Rhodes, remarked in a 1978 *Record Mirror* interview that "a lot of Pakis deserve" to be the targets of hate-motivated violence. Adam and the Ants' song "Puerto Rican," meanwhile, asked why a girl would "go waste it on a Puerto Rican . . . Gonna strike a matchstick on his hair . . . Girl, you're gonna make me cry/ I won't let that dago by!"

Some American punks weren't much better. In 1977, Johnny Ramone described his band's sound as "pure white rock 'n' roll, with no blues influence." The designer of the Ramones' famous presidential-seal-style logo, Arturo Vega, contemptuously dismissed concerns about the band's apparent use of crypto-fascist imagery—

and his own well-documented penchant for painting swastikas—by saying, "The people that are gonna be offended are the ones that have something to hide. The people that act so defensively are always the ones that are closet fascists." Punk was shocking, in effect, so it was alright for punks to use racist imagery to shock.

That, of course, is bullshit. As University of Wisconsin cultural studies professor and punk theorist Stacy Thompson has written, "Nazi accoutrements produce more than shock." Swastika imagery was everywhere in punk in the early days, like some sort of foul, unkillable virus: on Johnny Rotten's T-shirt, which also featured an inverted crucifix, and the word DESTROY; on the swastika armband frequently worn by Captain Sensible of the Damned; on Sid Vicious's infamous red shirt—the one he actually wore in Malcolm McLaren's witless film, *The Great Rock 'n' Roll Swindle,* as he strolled through the Jewish quarter of Paris, assaulting women (mere weeks, it should be noted, before he plunged a knife into his girlfriend's abdomen). While few people would suggest that an addled junkie like Vicious was capable of a memorable political judgment about *anything,* it shouldn't be forgotten that Sid Vicious persuaded his friend Johnny Rotten to embrace plainly anti-Semitic lyrics in "Belsen Was a Gas":

> Belsen was a gas I heard the other day
> In the open graves where the Jews all lay
> Life is fun and I wish you were here
> They wrote on postcards to those held dear
> Sergeant majors on the march
> Wash their bodies in the starch
> See them all die one by one
> Guess it's dead, guess it's done
> Oh dear, I don't care

He left the band many months before "Belsen Was a Gas" made its noxious debut on the Sex Pistols' set list, but Glen Matlock grimaces when the song (which could easily have been covered by George Burdi at a RaHoWa show) is brought to his attention. Asked if there is a line, even for punks, that you don't cross—and if race and ethnic hatred, and "jokes" about the Holocaust, are far beyond the line—the Sex Pistols' bassist does not quibble. "At that stage [in punk], it became anything goes," he says, shaking his head. "I actually challenged Sid about 'Belsen,' and he said that people had gotten it wrong, and he said that it was supposed to be ironic. Ironic, that's what he said."

Matlock laughs derisively. "Yeah, they sure won over a lot of people with *that,* didn't they?"

In punk's early days, skinheads were more observer than participant. They hung out at punk gigs mainly because they did not yet have a music to call their own. Around 1977, that changed with the christening of the British punk sub-genre called Oi!, the one that George Burdi would later find so exciting.

Championed mainly by the British music paper *Sounds,* and no one else, Oi! was punk rock stripped down to its base elements: loud, simple and aggressive, without any of the musical or lyrical artiness that punk, even in 1978, was starting to embrace (cf. Wire's first album, *Pink Flag,* which was made up entirely of three-chord rants, some only seconds long; their second effort, *Chairs Missing,* made frequent use of—God forbid—synthesizers in extended Pink Floydish dirges). The groups associated with Oi—at the start, anyway—were Cockney Rejects, Angelic Upstarts, Bad Manners, Cock Sparrer and, most of all, Sham 69. Sham, as they were called by the many who loved them, were (too easily) dismissed as a derivative second- or third-generation punk band. But the kind of punk music Sham played wasn't devised to invite the affections of the skinheads; in fact, Sham's songs were most often an attempt to bring punk back to its roots and promote unity among young people, from skins to rude boys.

Unfortunately for everyone concerned, and for Sham 69 in particular, the quartet's noisy, sing-along punk anthems attracted violent skinheads in droves. "Skinheads are back!" Pursey hollered at one infamous London performance—a statement he would later come to regret. Pro-fascist skins, many of them associated with the neo-Nazi National Front, regularly disrupted gigs by Sham 69 and the other Oi! bands. Many years after Sham 69 first burst on the scene, Pursey told me, "Even though I'll give anybody their rights, we're a democracy and all that, but rights have to be intelligent in some way. And we didn't see fascism as democratic or intelligent. It's going backwards." Unable to prevent their skinhead followers from embracing fascist philosophies, Sham 69 simply stopped playing in public and, in time, broke up.

The skinheads, meanwhile, only grew fonder of white supremacy and neo-Nazism. The British neo-Nazi and white supremacist groups—which had been attempting to reverse declining membership for years—grew exceedingly fond of the skinheads, whom they regarded as the new order.

Oi! became a music for racists, if not—as one British historian wrote—the actual music of racism. The two racist organizations that first recognized Oi!'s tremendous potential were the National Front and the British National Party (BNP). Formed in February 1967, following the merger of three xenophobic U.K. groups, the National Front was anti-immigrant, anti-Semitic and ambitious. In the general election of 1970, the fledgling party of racists fielded candidates in select ridings, capturing as much as six percent of the vote. By the time of the 1979 general election, the Front was fielding candidates in more than three hundred Parliamentary districts and was winning up to twenty percent of the popular vote. The BNP, meanwhile, was created in 1982 by John Tyndall, a founder of the National Front. With more than a hundred branches across Britain, the BNP was more successful than the National Front, actually winning several council seats in and around London. Its principal policy was the "resettlement" of non-whites to "their lands of ethnic origin."

For the skinheads, all of this represented a victory at two levels. First—following the rupture between skin and rude boy subculture some years earlier—they finally had a musical style that was wholly and indisputably their own. Second, thanks to the likes of the National Front, Oi! was well on its way to acquiring a political philosophy whose simplicity (because all racist, anti-Semitic doctrines are, in their foul essence, profoundly simple) was completely aligned, and uncannily so, with the nascent skinhead world view. Out of this collision of music and fascism was born the prototypical neo-Nazi and skinhead prophet: Ian Stuart Donaldson.

Born in August 1958 near Blackpool in Lancashire, Donaldson and his grammar school chums formed Skrewdriver in May 1977. The Sex Pistols, he later admitted, were a "vital" influence. Beefy, acned and shrewd, Donaldson attended the Pistols' fabled gig at the Lesser Free Trade Hall in Manchester, where they shared the bill with the Buzzcocks. To Donaldson, punk was "full of energy;" he, like so many others, wanted to be part of it. Later that year, Skrewdriver released the single "You're So Dumb," an anti-drug song, on the otherwise respectable independent Chiswick Records. Around the time of their second Chiswick release, *Anti-Social,* Skrewdriver dropped its punkish look and adopted, wholesale, the skinhead sartorial style. Donaldson—like George Burdi and a few others a decade and a half later—started to muse out loud that "punk music . . . was becoming too left wing."

The appearance of pro-Nazi skins at Sham 69 gigs eventually drove the band out of existence and Jimmy Pursey into retirement from music for many years, but for Ian Stuart Donaldson and Skrewdriver, the marriage of skinheads, neo-Nazism and Oi! offered plenty of opportunity. Donaldson says, "Sham cut their own throats by slagging off [skinheads], and that's what destroyed them in the end." For his part, Donaldson started attending National Front meetings in Blackpool, and became a card-carrying member of the Front in April 1979. Skrewdriver threw itself into the racist rock business with a vengeance.

By early 1982, Skrewdriver was attracting disturbingly large crowds at both the fabled 100 Club in Oxford Street and the Skunx in Islington. At one of those live dates, Donaldson erased any remaining doubts about where he and his band stood on the issue of race, declaring that they were "racial nationalists"—in effect, that the British nation should be the homeland to only one race (theirs). When the U.K. press grew increasingly (and understandably) critical of both the band and the whole Oi! sub-genre,

Donaldson was undeterred. To express his contempt for the popular Rock Against Racism fundraising concerts—organized to draw attention to the growing threat posed by the National Front, the British National Party and others like them—Donaldson re-activated Rock Against Communism, a pro-Nazi front, in 1982. Simultaneously, he established the White Noise label for future records by Skrewdriver and assorted other neo-Nazi bands that were flourishing in both the British and North American skinhead scenes.

Skrewdriver's first release on White Noise was the notorious *White Power* extended play single—with "Smash the I.R.A." and "Shove the Dove" on the flip side. The title track's lyrics effectively represented the first time that anyone, anywhere, had explicitly married neo-Nazi and white supremacist sloganeering with rock 'n' roll. The results were sickening:

> *I stand and watch my country, going down the drain*
> *We are all at fault, we are all to blame*
> *We're letting them take over, we just let 'em come*
> *Once we had an Empire, and now we've got a slum*
> *White Power! Forever*
> *White Power! Today*
> *White Power! Forever*

Before it gets too late
Well, we've seen a lot of riots, we just sit and scoff
We've seen a lot of muggings, and the judges let 'em off
Well, we've gotta do something, to try and stop the rot
And the traitors that have used us, they should all be shot

The song went on to become a solid underground hit, reissued many times; years after the fact, "White Power" continues to be covered by neo-Nazi skinhead bands around the globe. But the good times, for Skrewdriver at least, didn't last. With his beloved National Front fractured by infighting and in decline by the mid-1980s, Donaldson led Skrewdriver and some other groups to form another label, Blood and Honour, in 1987 ("Blood and Honour," naturally, is a rendering of an SS slogan found on the daggers of the Hitler youth corps). Blood and Honour would subsequently go on to become a highly successful operation, peddling pro-Nazi and white supremacist records, magazines and merchandise around the world, while simultaneously enlarging the membership rolls of dozens of fascist organizations. Its website is an international, virtual neo-Nazi gathering place.

After Donaldson's death in September 1993—in a car accident, on the way to a far-right meeting—Blood and Honour was taken over by Combat 18, a brutally violent neo-Nazi group that had originated in the BNP (the "18" in the group's name refers to Adolf Hitler's initials, the first and eighth letters of the alphabet). In 1994, Combat 18 formed the pro-Nazi label ISD (Ian Stuart Donaldson) records; among the British Oi! bands that would achieve notoriety on the label were No Remorse, Razors Edge and Celtic Warrior. (Ironically, Combat 18's preference for money over ideology angered many within the neo-Nazi movement on both sides of the Atlantic—among them one "Eric Hawthorne," who wrote on a skinhead Internet listserv in June 1996 that Combat 18 "has opportunistically risen to fill the void created with the untimely passing of Ian Stuart, and have proceeded to defile his memory by using his good name to promote their self-serving interests." Eric Hawthorne was the pseudonym used by George Burdi before his decision to go public with his involvement with the COTC.)

With White Noise, Blood and Honour, ISD and other racist record labels that subsequently appeared in other countries, neo-Nazi and white supremacist organizations, once moribund, started to flourish again. For them, the young skinhead resurgence represented new members, new influence and astonishingly large revenues. An alphabetical list compiled by the Anti-Defamation League of the countries that have produced hatecore bands, while already out of date, gives one a sense of the magnitude of the problem: Argentina (groups like Nuremberg); Australia (Kommando, White Noise and two dozen other bands); Austria; Belgium; Brazil; Canada (Aryan and Odins Law); Czech Republic (Apartheid and a dozen others); Denmark; Estonia; Finland (Hate Crime and others); France (Kristallnacht and scores more); Greece (Der Sturmer); Hungary; Ireland; Italy (SS-20 and a couple dozen other groups); the Netherlands; Norway; Poland (Zyklon-B and many, many other hate bands); Portugal; Russia (Terror National Front and dozens of others); Scotland; Slovakia; Serbia; Spain; Switzerland; Ukraine; Uruguay— and in Germany, Britain and the United States, literally hundreds of racist rock bands, many of them disturbingly popular, with names like the Klansmen, White Law, Gestapo, White Aryan Rebels, Aggravated Assault, Berserkr, Definite Hate and Jew Slaughter.

Interpol estimated in 1999 that the groups, and their labels, generate US$3.4 million in sales every year. In Poland, for example, some racist rock 'n' roll bands can sell more than thirty thousand albums, as many as mainstream pop acts. In that country alone— with a population of thirty-nine million—Interpol says that more than fifteen thousand people are "intimately involved" with the skinhead hate rock scene.

All of the hatecore bands—*all of them*—partly owe their existence to Ian Stuart Donaldson. And a goodly number of them owe a great deal to George Burdi, too: after all, it was Burdi, more than anyone else, who helped turn the global hate rock business into a well-oiled, multi-million dollar machine in the lucrative North American market.

Quite a few observers (including neo-Nazis in the bands noted above) regard Ian Stuart Donaldson as George Burdi's inspiration, if not the person he actually aspired to be. When it is pointed out to him that his hateful music had a profound emotional impact on many skinheads, as Donaldson's had, the Canadian demurs. "I always sought to get out from under the polemics of what I was doing, to branch out and evolve as an artist, which is always important for any creative person," Burdi told me in a recent interview. "During my time making white power music, I always felt self-limited by what I could write about. All of the ideas were so derivative."

That's unadulterated horseshit, of course. George Burdi did not seek to get out—nor did he attempt, as he puts it, to "branch out and evolve"—even when he was being sought by law enforcement agencies in two countries for assault and tax evasion. Even when he was facing lengthy jail terms and huge fines. Even when his name had become synonymous with some of the vilest expressions of hatred many people had ever seen. Even then he didn't try to get out, or "evolve." Even *then*.

No, George Burdi did not get out. Instead, like his forebear, Ian Stuart Donaldson, George Burdi got in *deeper*.

As near as anyone can figure, George Burdi's steel-toed boot slammed into Alicia Reckzin's face at around 11:45 P.M., within the shadow of the War Memorial, not far from Parliament Hill. At the time, Reckzin—a five-foot-nothing single mother and punk fan, active with anti-racist groups in the Ottawa area—was on the ground because she had tripped while running away from George Burdi and the dozens of skinheads who were beating up anyone who got in their way.

According to the Ontario Court of Appeal, whose version of the evening's events has not been disputed by anyone (save George Burdi), what happened was this: "[Burdi] led his followers in an angry charge across the street to attack the anti-racist demonstrators. One of the victims of that charge was [Alicia Reckzin], who was struck on the head while running from Burdi's supporters. When she fell, she was kicked several times on her right side. She saw Burdi kick her in the face and utter: 'This is the cunt that started the whole thing.' As a result of the assault, [Reckzin] suffered a broken nose, temporarily lost consciousness, and had memory problems for weeks."

It was, said the court's three judges, in a unanimous February 1997 decision that finally sent George Burdi to prison, "a brutal assault committed in the name of racist ideology."

The attack on Reckzin also happened, in part, because the police made a mistake. Following the RaHoWa gig at the Boys and Girls Club, the skinheads did not go home—contrary to what the police were expecting. Instead, they went straight to Parliament Hill, the seat of Canada's national government. As they made their way towards the Hill, at around 11:00 P.M., Burdi and the sixty-odd skinheads following him urinated on residents' lawns, bellowed at passersby and threatened non-whites who crossed their path. Wearing a COTC Security Legion sweatshirt and smoking a cigarette, Burdi gave impromptu interviews to the few reporters willing to get close enough to the parade of neo-Nazis; he answered their questions with the aplomb of a seasoned politician, and smiled a lot.

They marched right onto Parliament Hill. No one stopped them. A few RCMP officers observed the scene, clearly incredulous, but they did not intervene. On the manicured lawn near East Block, Wolfgang Droege—Burdi's comrade-in-arms and the leader of the white supremacist Heritage Front—gave a blessedly short speech. The assembled skinheads chanted "*Sieg heil*" a few times, and then "White power!" After that, Burdi started to speak, his voice still hoarse from RaHoWa's performance: "They thought it would be difficult for us to take Parliament Hill! For a second, I want you to imagine something: I want you to look around the field here. This is the square where we will hold our victory rally . . ."

One of the skinheads yelled, "Field of dreams!"

Without missing a beat, Burdi nodded, punching the air with his fist. "Yes! This is the field of our dreams. This country was built by our forefathers, who came here and, out of the vast wilderness, forged a destiny for our people. And, through great hammer blows, we will win that destiny back. For this land was once ours! And we are now a dispossessed people! But no longer shall we hide, and no longer shall we cower in the shadows! Now we are ready! We are at the forefront. We are standing on Parliament Hill, declaring that this battle has just begun!"

The skinheads erupted in screams: "White power! White power! White power!" Their voices echoed off the dark Parliament Buildings as the Mounties continued to stand by. Burdi, his voice almost completely gone, kept hollering: "We are here tonight declaring that, yes, the white man is standing up! They think they will make us go the way of the dinosaur, that it is all over for the white people. That it's all over for the white race . . . but we are here tonight declaring that there will be a future for our people. We will have a land, a sacred soil, that we will call our own! And we will never yield!"

Whatever his other faults, George Burdi is a formidable public speaker. His speech, impromptu and entirely without notes, would have been much more impressive were it not for the fact that it was promoting Nazism—and taking place, unmolested by law enforcement, at the very symbol of Canadian democracy. Burdi led the skinheads in a chant. "What do we want?" he yelled.

The skins screamed their reply: "White power!"

"And when do we want it?"

"Right now!"

"And what is the only solution?" Burdi bellowed.

"The final solution! The final solution! White power!"

A small group of protestors gathered near the entrance to the Prime Minister's Office, in the Langevin Block, across Wellington Street and directly opposite Burdi and the neo-Nazis. One of them threw a bottle that shattered on the asphalt. Burdi sneered. "These people can't stand the sight of us standing here," he said. Rocks started to sail back and forth, as more RCMP cruisers sped to Parliament Hill, their sirens wailing.

At exactly 11:40 P.M., an animal roar filled the air, and the skinheads charged across Wellington Street at the protestors, who immediately scattered and started running for their lives. "Holy shit!" one police officer exclaimed, sprinting to his cruiser.

For the next thirty minutes or so, anarchy—real, actual, get-pissed-and-destroy anarchy—reigned along the streets on and near Parliament Hill. A boy, no more than fourteen or so, was pushed down by one skinhead and kicked in the face. Blood streamed out of his mouth and nose. Some of the skinheads extracted small billy clubs they had hidden in the folds of their bomber jackets and started to beat tourists and bystanders. People could be heard screaming throughout Ottawa's downtown core; tires screeched as non-white cab drivers attempted to get out of the area. Near the Lord Elgin Hotel, Burdi and a few others caught up to a terrified Alicia Reckzin. When Burdi was finished with her, her face was a mass of blood and gore; the resulting fracture to her nose came within a hair's breadth of her eye sockets.

Burdi was charged with assault causing bodily harm. Almost immediately, neo-Nazis in the United States—prompted by a group of COTC members in Los Angeles—started up legal defence funds for him. Burdi was convicted by an Ottawa jury (all white), and sentenced to a year's imprisonment for the assault on Alicia Reckzin. He spent a month behind bars, and was released when his lawyers filed an appeal. By his own admission, he emerged from prison consumed by bitterness and hate, and more committed than ever to the neo-Nazi movement. Knowing well the power of racist rock, he threw himself wholly behind RaHoWa and a new venture, something called Resistance.

"In 1995," he says, recalling those heady days, "we played a show in Montreal to over five hundred skinheads. It was at that point that I realized we had reached a turning point. The whole crowd, francophones and all, were singing every word to every song we played.

"I remember the feeling looking out over this sea of bodies. It felt like time had slowed down . . . the energy flowing to us from the audience was electrifying. I could hold the microphone out over the crowd, and they would just scream the lyrics for me. The mosh pit was so insane I actually felt like we should play a slow song, just to prevent someone from getting killed . . . We had no idea so many people listened to our music! No idea."

But with Resistance Records, he and everyone else would find out, and soon enough.

It might sound like an exaggeration—that George Burdi's Resistance Records was conceived in hate—but it isn't. Resistance was in the hate business, and business was very good, right from the start.

For Burdi, it all made perfect sense. As with RaHoWa's memorable 1995 gig before five hundred skinheads in Montreal, hate rock—hatecore, as some call it—was the ideal propagandizing tool. "Music alone cannot save our Race, granted," Burdi wrote in a secret email letter to other skinheads in June 1996. "But our music is precious to us, and highly effective as a recruiting tool . . . compact discs cannot alone accrue to political victory [*sic*] for the White Race, but the actions of the international agents of ZOG [the Zionist Occupational Government, a term used by the racist right to describe governments and agencies that oppose them], in trying to stop the spread of White Power albums, demonstrates with perfect clarity that Big Brother knows compact discs are more effective than anything we've ever employed to destroy the system."

Hyperbole, but this was George Burdi, after all. In 1993, when he was twenty-three, RaHoWa recorded an album that had been financed by a European racist rock label called Rebelles Européens. Shortly after *Declaration of War* was completed, Rebelles Européens folded, but Burdi and his band kept Rebelles' advance so that they could (in a neo-Nazi twist on the punk Do It Yourself ethic) issue the record themselves. As Burdi later admitted to the Southern Poverty Law Center, a U.S.-based group that monitors hatecore activity: "The intention was only to release RaHoWa stuff, but I started getting demo tapes like crazy from other bands. I thought, hey, maybe I can release some of these as well. It cost only $2,000 to record a skinhead band, and it was easy to flip the profits from one into the next one. Soon we had a magazine, five or six people working for us, and twelve or fifteen bands signed. There have been all kinds of rumours about different people giving seed money to start Resistance, but in fact there was no one."

Along with the record label, the centre of Resistance's operations, the company also maintained an impressive-looking website and published a glossy neo-Nazi magazine, *Resistance*, which contained hatecore news updates, interviews, record reviews and features about National Socialism, COTC, the National Alliance and the Aryan Nations. "We established a viable model that other skinheads could follow, and the whole music scene grew from that," Burdi says. "We explained it to anyone who would listen. Suddenly, it went from a couple of white power labels to a couple of hundred. I'm sure many were just a P.O. box and a guy living at his mom's house, but it worked."

Incorporated in January 1994 with RaHoWa associates Jason Snow and Joseph Talic, Resistance Records operated out of Michigan's Highland Township, outside Detroit—in part to keep the company beyond the reach of Canadian hate laws. (The fact that another Resistance co-founder and COTC member, Mark Wilson, lived in Michigan apparently played a role in Burdi's decision.) Among the skinhead bands Burdi signed were Nordic Thunder,

Aggravated Assault and Aryan; later, Berserkr, Centurion, Max Resist and the Hooligans joined the Resistance stable. In very little time, Burdi and his business partners were shipping CDs to about forty European hatecore labels—who, in turn, sold CDs by the bands Burdi had signed. The money started to flow in; soon, Burdi was able to live entirely on Resistance income.

It was a very profitable operation. "If we sold CDs in bulk wholesale, profit would range from $3 to $6 [U.S.] on each disc," Burdi says. "A CD cost $2.20 to produce, including a dollar for the band. They would retail for $15, and you wholesale them at $6 or $8 or $10. Small distributors could get a second income by buying fifty discs from us wholesale and turning a $10 profit on each one.

"From 1994 to early 1997, we sold more than sixty thousand CDs and tapes, maybe as many as a hundred thousand. The vast majority of sales were wholesale, and every quarter was twice the sales volume of the previous quarter. Our website went up in 1994, and each month we would profit a couple thousand dollars from that."

The Resistance website carried an enticing caution: "WARNING—The music promoted by this Web Page has been deemed unacceptable by Big Brother . . . If you are easily offended, TURN BACK NOW . . . If you are bold and independent-minded enough to think for yourself, PROCEED." Purchasers of CDs could use credit cards over a secure server. Through the website, Resistance eventually sold T-shirts, books, calendars, flags, jewellery, postcards, posters, videos and even watches with "88" on the face ("8" representing the letter "H" in the alphabet; "88" representing "HH," or "Heil Hitler"). With the additional business generated by the website, Burdi and Resistance were earning US$1 million in annual revenue.

Like a lot of criminals, Burdi and his Resistance colleagues were not paying taxes on all of that revenue. So, in 1997, Burdi's world fell apart. On April 10, officers with the Michigan State Police Treasury Division, wearing bulletproof vests and carrying assault rifles, raided Resistance's headquarters. Also co-operating in the police action were the Ontario Provincial Police and the Michigan Department of the Treasury. On the same day, the OPP arrested Burdi in Windsor: the Ontario Court of Appeal had reaffirmed his 1995 conviction for the assault on Alicia Reckzin. George Burdi went back to prison.

Burdi claims that he realized the futility of all of it while inside—the futility of RaHoWa, the COTC, Resistance, Oi!, skinheads, neo-Nazism and white supremacy, all of what his life had become—and he resolved to get out. In 1998, he sold his interest in Resistance to Willis Carto (the leader of the anti-Semitic Liberty Lobby) and Todd Blodgett (a former White House press aide to Ronald Reagan). In the following year, Carto and Blodgett flipped Resistance's catalogue to William Pierce (the leader of the viciously racist National Alliance, and the author of *The Turner Diaries,* the far-right novel that served as the blueprint for the April 1995 Oklahoma City bombing that claimed the lives of 168 men, women and children). Pierce's National Alliance controls Resistance to this day; Burdi has never revealed how much he made out of the deal.

When he was finally paroled, Burdi returned to Toronto and let it be known that he had become a vegan, that he meditated and that he had embraced Hinduism. He also became engaged to an Indo-Canadian woman and formed a new band called Novacosm, which featured two non-white members. Plenty of people suspect that he has not fully renounced his former life; at the same time, police agencies agree there is no evidence he has returned to it—and, on occasion, he has provided some information to anti-bias groups seeking a better understanding of the hatecore movement. Burdi deserves credit for that much, at least.

Reaching him in the modest one-bedroom apartment where he now lives, in a rundown part of Toronto, I ask George Burdi a final question: Is punk *still* capable of being captured by the extremes, on the left or the right?

Of course, he says. "No one political perspective has a monopoly on punk. Yes, sure, there were more leftist punk bands.

But the rightist bands were there from outset as well. They were fewer in number, but they were still just as passionate, weren't they?"

"FUCK YOU! FUCK YOU! FUUUUUUCK YOOOOOOU!"

Calgary, Alberta, Canada: it is Friday, April 18, 1980, just around midnight, and Gerry Useless—his real name is Gerry Hannah, but everyone in the West Coast Canadian and U.S. punk scenes knows him as Gerry Useless—is onstage with the Subhumans. It's dark in the hall, and the air is thick with the stench of spilled beer and sweat.

Up on the ancient stage, Brian Roy Goble, the hapless vocalist known as Wimpy Roy, is trying to be the singer. Over on the side, Mike Graham is slashing away at his guitar; behind him and Goble, Jimmy Imagawa is flailing away at his drum kit. Gerry Useless, meanwhile, is more or less centre stage, legs splayed. He is wearing a threadbare white T-shirt emblazoned with the words TRUE LOVE in red. Below that is a large and detailed diagram of an erect penis sliding into a disembodied vagina. Gerry Useless plays bass guitar, but at the moment he is apoplectic, wild-eyed with rage, in fact.

"FUCK YOU! FUCK YOU! WE DON'T CARE WHAT YOU SAY, FUUUUUUCK YOOOOOOU!"

The target of Gerry's rage is the Calgary Police Service, some of whose members are in the process of shutting down the punk concert at the Victoria Community Hall, located just north of the Calgary Stampede Grounds. Hundreds of punks have come to see the Subhumans—one of Vancouver's best-known punk outfits— play in a place they rarely visit. The next day, the newspapers would estimate that more than five hundred people were there when the police knocked open the doors to the place; the punk fans had paid $4 to get in, and most had learned about the gig through word of mouth. In April 1980, in places like Calgary, punks did not advertise—they played wherever there was a stage, and reluctantly shut things down when the police showed up. Which they often did.

"WE DON'T CARE WHAT YOU SAY, FUUUUCK YOOOOU!"

The Subhumans are playing one of their signature anthems, composed by Gerry Useless. It's called "Fuck You," naturally, and it's usually a lot of fun, and everyone usually gets to sing along in a weird punk campfire kind of thing. But not tonight; tonight, Gerry isn't giving anyone else a chance to sing along, including the Subhuman's lead singer. Gerry is bellowing the song's lyrics—screaming them, actually—at the two dozen police officers flooding into the Victoria Community Hall. His face is so red, it seems possible that his head will explode at any moment.

"FUCK YOU! FUCK YOU! FUCK YOU!"

The police would later tell the media they received numerous noise complaints from residents in the vicinity. Punks have been relieving themselves outside, too, because the hall's washrooms have been trashed. In the men's bathroom, one of the toilets has been

cracked open, spilling water everywhere; someone has kicked a hole in the wall big enough to walk through. The promoters of the gig are a few members of the other punk bands on the bill, lesser-known local bands with names like the Mild Chaps, the Sturgeons and (you guessed it) the Hot Nasties. A few of the teenage Calgary punks have pooled their own money to rent the hall, and then waived getting paid so that the Subhumans could. Eyeing the extent of the damage, and knowing they will have to pay for repairs out of their own pockets, the Calgary punks aren't entirely opposed to the notion that the gig is being shut down. None of them is surprised to see the police, certainly, because the police close down their gigs all the time. Gerry Useless, however—who shouted at some of the locals earlier on because he wanted more money—is one pissed-off punk rocker.

"WE DON'T CARE WHAT YOU SAY, FUCK YOU, YOU FUCKERS!"

For Gerry Useless, the presence of the police is a big, big deal; the Subhuman's bassist is suddenly a live wire, leaping all over the stage, more animated and energetic than he has appeared all night. It almost seems as if Gerry is, well, more interested in the presence of the police than he is in the presence of his fellow punks.

Which, as the whole country will shortly learn, he actually is.

"FUCK YOU! FUUUUCK YOOOOOOU!"

Gerry Hannah was, he stresses, "an upper-working-class kid." Not, he also stresses, "a lower-working-class kid." It's unclear why the distinction is important to him, but in a January 2002 radio interview, he says the words "working class" quite a few times just the same. He also throws around a lot of stuff about "rebellions," and "revolutions," and "alternative culture," and "political action," and whatnot. Gerry is preoccupied by those sorts of things, still, so many years after he stopped being a punk and became what he describes as an "urban guerrilla." He's nearly fifty now, but he still talks like an aspiring revolutionary.

Of Scottish, Irish and Spanish heritage, Gerry Hannah was born in North Burnaby, a Vancouver suburb, and named after a missionary. His father died when he was very young; thereafter, Hannah was raised by his churchgoing mother, with whom he is very close. He lived on the main road leading up to Simon Fraser University, and his early years, Hannah recalls, were spent running around in the woods on Burnaby Mountain. In grade two, he met his friend Joey Keithley—the DOA front man Joey Shithead. Another elementary school chum was Brian Goble, the future Wimpy Roy and lead singer of the Subhumans. Ken Montgomery, who adopted the name Dimwit when he drummed for DOA, the Subhumans and the Pointed Sticks, hooked up with Hannah, Keithley and Goble in grade five or so, when his family moved to

Canada from the United States. The four were more or less inseparable after that. They lived within a three-block radius of each other, and they did everything together. "The four of us grew up together on Burnaby Mountain," recalls Shithead. "Gerry was the fourth amigo."

With his rugged good looks, and his well-documented intensity, Hannah was also "the hip outcast," Shithead says. He was the first to sprout bushy sideburns and long hair—and he was the one most often kicked out of school. Shithead continues: "Gerry was usually given to a streak of fanaticism, shall we say. Like, that was definitely clear when we were teenagers, and he wanted us to become a band, out in the woods. Without electricity." That fact provides a revealing glimpse into Gerry Hannah's perspective on what was going to become his life.

The Burnaby North High School foursome, along with a couple of others, loved Black Sabbath, and played the British heavy metal group's *Paranoid* album endlessly. They resolved to start their own group and started practising covers of songs by Jimi Hendrix, the Doors, Bob Dylan and the Moody Blues in Hannah's basement when his mother was at church. In 1975, after spotting an advertisement in *The Georgia Straight* weekly newspaper about a commune near Lumby, in British Columbia's interior, Hannah started trying to persuade his friends to move there.

"How the fuck are we going to be a rock band out in the country?" Shithead asked.

Impressed by the unrestricted use of acoustic instruments at a John Denver concert, Hannah recalls that he had an answer. "I had very strong feelings about technology, and feelings about hydro-electric dams and the manufacturing industries that produce musical equipment," he says. "I felt that perhaps we should be getting away from that kind of thing, and become more dependent on acoustic instruments that didn't require that kind of huge infrastructure behind them." (That notwithstanding, Hannah does admit that he made regular use of electrical hair dryers before Subhumans shows, to fluff his wavy locks. "I took a long time in the bathroom," he says, without the faintest hint of irony or humour or self-awareness.)

So Hannah, Keithley, Goble and Montgomery hitchhiked to Lumby, a remote town located in the North Okanagan, midway between Vancouver and Calgary. "We packed our bags and left," says Hannah. "When we got up there, we found it wasn't exactly what we were looking for."

Why did they go? "We didn't like what was going on in mainstream society, and we wanted to get back to the land. We wanted to live an alternative lifestyle," Hannah claims. But Shithead disagrees. "We told Gerry to screw the acoustic thing and [we] rented some electric amps," he says. The group, at that point calling themselves the Resurrection, abandoned the squatter's lifestyle and moved to nearby Cherryville, where there was electricity. Gerry and Joey rented a big house on the highway using their Unemployment Insurance benefits. After several months, when their money ran out and the locals had taken to threatening the longhaired Vancouverites on a regular basis, the band headed home. Gerry Hannah's back-to-the-land experiment had come to an inglorious end.

Back in Vancouver, the high school dropouts—all of them had abandoned their studies just prior to graduation, to Shithead's regret later on—played occasional gigs at high school dances, under the name of Stone Crazy. During the day, the Stone Crazy gang worked at a food processing company. Their first paying gig was in June 1977, in Merritt, B.C., at a motor inn. They were joined for the performance by Simon Werner, a Brit who'd been recruited to play guitar along with Shithead. Before being roundly booed offstage, the group played a cover version of a song by a band they had been listening to a great deal: "Beat on the Brat" by the Ramones. They also played the first song Shithead ever wrote (a later staple of DOA shows), "Disco Sucks." On the way back home that night, Werner suggested the group abandon the cover songs and start a punk band that played originals. All agreed, save Gerry Hannah. He said he didn't like punk rock.

In the summer of 1977, Hannah worked the railroads between Vancouver and Swift Current, Saskatchewan, saving his money for an electric piano. On July 30, the Furies, Vancouver's first punk band, headlined a fabled show at the Japanese Hall; soon enough, bands with names like the Dishrags and the Lewd were putting on shows too, and attracting a surprising number of kids. When Hannah returned to Vancouver, things were very different: Shithead had shaved his head and purchased a black leather biker jacket, just like the ones the Ramones wore. Hannah and his keyboards, it seemed, were no longer wanted; the group was taking a new direction. Hannah wasn't happy, to say the least. "Then I started listening to the music that they were listening to," he says. "The Sex Pistols, the Clash, the Damned and the Ramones and stuff. It didn't take me long to see what they were seeing—that this was the rebirth of rebellious music."

The new group, sans Hannah, needed a name. One North Burnaby alumnus suggested "Joey Shithead and the Marching Morons." The Shithead part was kept, but the Marching Morons appellation was discarded in favour of the Skulls—because "it was mean," Shithead says. In no time at all, the Skulls started gigging before enthusiastic crowds in and around Vancouver. Gerry Hannah watched from the sidelines.

While the Vancouver punk scene was growing, it was not growing fast enough for the Skulls. Supported by Gerry Hannah— "who had fuck all to do in Vancouver" anyway, notes Shithead—the Skulls decided to move to Toronto. There, they believed, they would be better appreciated, and possibly even offered a record deal. They rented a van and headed east in November 1977. Most of them had never been as far as Ontario before.

In snowbound Toronto, bored (and with the Skulls playing far fewer gigs than anyone had expected), Gerry Hannah decided to form his own band. It was, in the parlance of the Vancouver punk scene, a "fuck band"—just for fun. Hannah, who played bass, called it Wimpy and the Bloated Cows. Werner played guitar and Shithead kept the beat; Brian Goble became Wimpy, and the nickname stuck. Gerry Hannah, somewhere around December 1977, became Gerry Useless.

In a rented house on the western fringe of downtown Toronto, Gerry Useless started writing his own punk songs—stuff like "Slave to My Dick," and "Fuck You." Says Shithead, admiringly, "Gerry was working on some cool songs . . . he penned [those] two classics while playing bass in our basement."

You call us weirdos, call us crazy
Say we're evil, say we're lazy
Say we're just the violent type
Kind of dumb, not too bright
We don't care what you say—fuck you
You tell your friends we're really sick
Short-haired fags on a commie trip
And you should know 'cause you're so cool
Number one, nobody's fool
We don't care what you say—fuck you

After five disastrous months in Toronto, and a briefer but equally ill-fated sojourn to Britain, the Skulls and Gerry Useless decided it was time to return to Vancouver. Shortly thereafter, Wimpy and Useless formed the Subhumans.

Despite an unfortunate tendency to periodically veer into heavy metal—a tendency they shared with their pals in DOA and Black Flag—the Subhumans were a pretty good punk band. Very good, actually. But the fact is this: whatever the Subhumans achieved, in their three years of existence, will always be overshadowed (and devalued) by what Gerry Useless did after he left the band. Some people may dispute that, but it's a fact, nonetheless: Direct Action, or the Squamish Five, became a lot better known than the punk quartet calling itself the Subhumans. And that *sucks*.

It can't be disputed, however, that Gerry Useless himself came to consider the Subhumans to be a lot less important than Direct Action. It's why he quit the band and went underground, after all. "I didn't really feel there was a lot of hard-core commitment [in the punk scene], on a political level, for that kind of work," he says, adding that he didn't like punk rockers "who just shouted political lyrics from the stage, or the crowd." He liked people "who put their money where their mouth was." Or, in Gerry's case, put *bombs* where other people's *bodies* were.

For anyone who ever saw one of their chaotic shows, it certainly seemed like the Subhumans were doing more than simply shouting "political lyrics from the stage." The Subhumans were intensely political, in a way that other punk bands (particularly North American ones) were disinclined to be in the 1970s. After all, in places like the United States or Canada, it was difficult to advocate the anarchy and class warfare the Sex Pistols and the Clash sang about. The sort of economic breakdown that had beset Britain—characterized by massive unemployment, collapsing public services and actual race riots—was not happening to the same degree in North America. But the Subhumans and a few others (notably DOA, along with the Dead Kennedys, Black Flag and Minor Threat) were unsatisfied with the way things were, and they regularly challenged their audience to press for radical change. For instance, in September 1979, Hannah helped initiate Rock Against Radiation, an outdoor concert in Vancouver's Vanier Park that featured DOA, the Subhumans, the Pointed Sticks and the K-Tels protesting both nuclear weapons and nuclear power. More than three thousand people showed up. The event was a fantastic example of the positive, proselytizing power of punk. Everyone was impressed, except Gerry Hannah. He wanted more.

Interviewed at length on a Vancouver radio station in 2002, Gerry Hannah admits that, "the Subhumans were a real powerhouse," adding, "DOA and us were like two heads on the same animal. We were both quite political. We didn't shy away from doing benefit concerts [or support] causes that challenged the status quo." But back in 1980 or so, Hannah had grown very impatient with punk, punk rockers and democratic change. Fatefully, one of the Rock Against Radiation co-organizers was Brent Taylor, a peace activist whom Hannah knew from Vancouver-area punk shows. Taylor introduced Hannah to another peace activist, a woman named Ann Hansen. For Gerry Hannah, the encounter with Hansen would have life-altering consequences.

The Subhumans toured non-stop between 1979 and 1981, playing wherever someone was willing to take a chance on them. Across Canada and the United States, the band would headline or, often, support some other act. Among the bands they enjoyed playing with, Hannah says, were the Dils, X, the Dead Kennedys and pre–Henry Rollins Black Flag, a particular favourite of Hannah's. In the summer of 1980, Hannah assisted the shambolic Hermosa Beach, California, punk band in obtaining gigs at community halls across western Canada—and even acted as a de facto manager, bullying local punks for more money for Black Flag. (Hannah's leftist credentials, apparently, frequently took a backseat to terrestrial preoccupations such as money.)

But all the while, Hannah's patience for democratic societal change was wearing thin. He recalls that he was alarmed at the time about the military interventions by the Reagan administration in Central America, and enraged that no one was doing anything about it. "I was becoming more and more politicized all the time," he says, "because I was more and more aware of what was happening in Central America . . . I mean, [the Reagan administration was] brutalizing, raping and murdering tens of thousands of people! I was feeling . . . I was pretty choked with this stuff that was going on. I felt pretty frustrated that nothing seemed to be working [and no one] was trying to stop this stuff."

At around the same time, Hannah met Julie Belmas. Just nineteen years old, with short, jet black hair and pale blue eyes— and by all accounts as beautiful as Hannah was handsome—Belmas was associated with a group of Vancouver punk rock women who called themselves the Bowery Girls. For the most part, the group did little more than hang out and party together, but Belmas was, like Hannah, interested in more action and a lot less talk.

The pair attended earnest sessions of things like People Struggling for Society to Be Free, which was a support group for imprisoned members of the radical American Indian Movement. Hannah also ran into Belmas at meetings of a number of different groups agitating against U.S. involvement in El Salvador. "Julie and I were both hardcore punk rockers . . . I was really impressed by [her]," he says. The feeling was reciprocated; very soon, the two were intimate, and talking about a life together living in the woods, away from the venalities of modern society.

Hannah and Belmas started spending more and more time with Ann Hansen, Brent Taylor and Taylor's roommate, Doug Stewart. The Subhumans bassist seemed to be in awe of the far-left militants; his friends say he was becoming increasingly radicalized. Joey Shithead watched the transformation with growing concern: "He, they, chose the wrong methods . . . there's a lot of things in this world that need changing. But the better way to go at it is the path of peaceful resistance. Be the epitome of that. They didn't."

Wimpy Roy, too, was suspicious about what was happening to his long-time friend. Before Hannah went "underground," Wimpy challenged him one night at a party. "You're up to something," he said, but Hannah laughed it off.

"For one thing, [Wimpy] knew that I had a gun," Hannah says now. "And it wasn't a hunting gun, either." It was, he says, a semi-automatic M22 assault rifle, with a twenty-round clip. The rifle closely resembled the revolutionary's traditional weapon of choice, the AK-47. (Later on, Hannah also acquired a 9-mm Luger that, he remembers, "was incredibly easy to aim.")

Hannah's fellow gun-toting guerillas were a diverse group. Brent Taylor was the son of a pair of professors, and a former high school track and field star. Described as a genial, easygoing fellow, Taylor had somehow become an advocate of violent leftist revolution. Throughout the late 1970s, he travelled North America, orbiting ever closer to extreme anarcho-leftist outfits like the Prairie Fire, the George Jackson Brigade, the Symbionese Liberation Army and the related New World Liberation Front (a terrorist cell responsible for a series of bombings in the San Francisco area at around that time). Taylor himself later achieved some notoriety in 1979 when, as part of a group calling itself the "Groucho Marxists," he tossed a pie in the face of Conservative leader Joe Clark during a visit to Vancouver. (Ironically, the stunt earned him a spot on a police computer—which would turn out to be a key factor in his capture.)

Later, Taylor joined the Seaforth Highlander regiment of the Canadian Armed Forces and earned a dishonourable discharge— but not before getting free lessons in the handling of weapons and explosives, which made him a more effective revolutionary. "I knew Brent Taylor from way back," says Hannah. "He'd been around the punk scene for a long time and he was very political . . . [and he was doing] all kinds of naughty things." He laughs without elaborating.

Taylor's roommate in 1980 was Doug Stewart, a University of British Columbia dropout with an interest in math and physics. Stewart had been an early convert to disarmament, and was initially associated with Pacific Life Community, a moderate group opposed to the installation of Trident missiles at a submarine base in nearby Washington State. Like Taylor and Hannah and the rest, Stewart grew impatient with gradual, peaceful change, and in time applied his formidable knowledge of science to the construction of bombs and fuses.

Ann Hansen—whom Taylor had met in 1979 or so, while spray-painting anti-government and anti-corporate slogans on the sides of buildings and construction sites in Ontario—was even more committed to the urban guerilla cause than Taylor. A product of the wealthy suburbs around Toronto, Hansen attended the University of Waterloo and, in 1979, spent six months in France and Germany, ostensibly to research a paper on "radical activism." In reality, Hansen's preoccupation was assisting the Red Army Faction, otherwise known as the Baader-Meinhof group—a terrorist organization that killed or kidnapped a dozen West Germans in the mid- to late 1970s. As she recounts in her book *Direct Action: Memoirs of an Urban Guerilla*, in Europe she embraced the notion that violence was an appropriate response to the violence that was being done to the environment and poor people; no one asked her, it seems, whether that calculation could end up making her as morally deficient as the governments and corporations she despised. By 1980, her Baader-Meinhof education complete, Hansen moved to Vancouver to work for prison abolition and a half-dozen other causes.

"Julie really started hanging around with Brent and Ann Hansen and Doug Stewart," recalls Hannah. "They were doing a lot of little, um, low . . . you know, minor-scale actions. And then I was asked if I wanted to come along and help them do some things. And I did."

At the start, the unnamed group didn't do much that was significant—or, to put it another way, they didn't do anything for which they were later charged by the police. (Hannah admits that the group broke many laws in this period, but he refuses to say which ones.) After much deliberation, the group of five decided on their first hard-core political "action"—an attack on the Amax Molybdenum Mine near Alice Arm, British Columbia, to protest toxic discharge into local waterways. In May 1981, Taylor, Hansen and Belmas broke into the offices of the Ministry of the Environment in Victoria, set off flares, spray-painted graffiti, smashed windows and poured red paint over the carpets. Around the same time, they undertook a similar break-in at the Amax corporate offices. They would later tell friends the break-ins had been a "buzz."

Gerry Hannah, who was still Gerry Useless at night, made a choice. "It was suggested to me that I get a rifle while it was still legal to get a rifle," he says, without indicating who urged him to do so. "So that, if I needed to go underground, or whatever, I would be able to. So I ended up selling my synthesizers.

"At the time, I had a bunch of synthesizers, and I was intending to write scores for documentaries. Kind of a Brian Eno thing. But I ended up selling them and buying an assault rifle and getting heavily involved with what Brent, Ann, Julie and Doug were up to at the time." He laughs. He seems to find it terrifically funny, this buying-guns-to-shoot-people stuff. Fucking hilarious.

Hannah moved into a rented house in Burnaby with Belmas, Taylor and Hansen (Stewart lived elsewhere). Gerry Useless, fun-loving punk from Burnaby Mountain, had become Gerry Hannah, urban guerilla. Around this time, Hansen and some other activists—unnamed—broke into the home of a gun collector and stole Magnum handguns, pump-action shotguns and assorted rifles. At any given time, the five maintained a cache of nearly two dozen weapons. In late 1981 and early 1982, the group devoted itself to target practice in remote rural areas near Squamish, a logging town north of Vancouver. They collected books about how to break into cars, clean assault rifles and even build land mines; they stole other people's identification. Robberies, office-trashings and vandalism became regular activities. When the group was in need, they shoplifted; Hansen proved particularly adept at stealing cars. They kept busy.

Says Hannah, "I ended up kind of being in a situation where I was one of their support people. I was a petty thief. I helped them procure the resources they needed."

Reading about the Action Directe guerilla group based in France—a group that claimed responsibility for a series of late-1970s bombings and brutal murders targeting politicians, officials and businesspeople—the five B.C."guerillas" were mightily impressed. They decided to call themselves Direct Action.

In the early days of Direct Action, in 1981 or so, Gerry Hannah was different from the others not merely because he was a minor celebrity, and a punk rocker of note, but because he was wildly hypocritical. On the one hand, Hannah declined to get personally involved in many of the group's bombing missions because they were what he called "too high level." On the other hand, he claims, "I supported [the bombings] totally." Asked to explain the contradiction, Hannah says, "It's kind of a technicality or something like that." Something like that.

Hannah finally abandoned his punk rock life. "I didn't go to gigs once I was underground. Not at all. I didn't have any contact with the punk community at all. We had to completely stay away from all of that stuff." Hansen would later recall that Hannah told her he was "sick and tired of all the bullshit in the music scene."

According to Hansen, it was a stressful time for Direct Action. She later wrote, "The tension [in] our lives had been relentless. We never took a break, never went to the beach for a day of doing nothing, never took a casual walk in Stanley Park, never slept in or hung about the house lazily reading a book on a rainy day. Our group was on a mission, and we lived each day with the zeal and the fervour of people who believed that their every action was so important that the survival of the planet depended on them . . . Urban guerillas do not take vacations."

Earlier in 1982, the hard-working group of terrorists stole a half-ton of Toval dynamite from a construction site; later, they located nearly 2,000 pounds of explosives at another remote site owned by the provincial highways department. Direct Action's next "action" was, therefore, to be a big one: blowing up the remote Cheekeye-Dunsmuir hydroelectric transmission line, near Squamish, in May 1982. Direct Action (and many others) were strenuously opposed to the adverse impact the hydro project had

had on the environment. So, early in the morning of May 31, Hansen and Stewart—aided and abetted by Belmas, Taylor and Hannah—blew up four shunt reactors with 400 pounds of the stolen dynamite. The explosion was powerful enough to wake up residents 10 kilometres away. No one was hurt, as expected, but Direct Action was giddy with their victory: the Cheekeye-Dunsmuir project was grounded for two months, and the publicly owned power utility lost nearly $5 million. Moreover, they weren't caught.

Their next move was to be even bolder. Sometime in the summer and early fall of 1982, Direct Action selected their target: Litton Systems, in Toronto. Litton manufactured the guidance system for U.S. cruise missiles. Hannah explains why Direct Action selected the company: "[The cruise] was a missile that was being designed by the United States that could be launched from air, sea or land . . . it was designed to carry a nuclear payload. It was considered by the Soviet Union and many other people in the world to be a first-strike nuclear weapon. Canada was playing a very active role, as it always does, in helping the American military achieve their goals.

"Every day, practically, before the action that we did came down, there had been groups outside the Litton plant in Toronto trying to shut the plant down, trying to stop it. [Bombing Litton] was the only logical and sane position to take in the whole thing."

In October, following weeks of meticulous preparations with Hannah and Stewart, Hansen, Taylor and Belmas drove across Canada in a van packed with 550 pounds of stolen dynamite, listening to the Dead Kennedys and DOA. Hannah remained in Vancouver, and while he fully supported the bomb plot, he knew that the Litton attack was dangerous: "We had upped the ante on ourselves. It was no longer nickel and dime political action. This was serious stuff. It just changed the whole landscape for us."

The Litton plant was located in an industrial zone not far from Toronto's airport, and the facility bordered on a major highway that was used by hundreds of thousands of people daily; when Hansen and the others cased the place, they would have seen that. Most of the plant was surrounded by a tall chain-link fence, and a guard tower was located near the main entrance. When the group saw the proximity of the guard tower to the building they intended to blow up, Direct Action debated whether all 550 pounds of dynamite would be necessary. Taylor decided the issue: "Anything less than 550 pounds would just be a symbolic bombing," he said, as quoted in Hansen's book about the group. "We want to get the idea across that sabotage should be used to cause real financial damage, to deter investors from going ahead with their deadly projects. We can learn from the Red Army Faction bombing[s]."

Most people don't actually talk like that, or behave like that, of course. But the five members of Direct Action weren't like most other people. They were fucking idiots.

They were *subhuman,* you might say.

On October 15, 1982, at about 11:15 P.M., Hansen drove her van onto the neatly trimmed lawn at Litton and parked it beside building 402. She flicked the toggle switch on the bomb's timing device and stepped outside. Beside the van, she deposited a fluorescent orange box on the ground. A stick of dynamite had been taped to the box. On the other side, Direct Action had written: "DANGER EXPLOSIVES— Inside this van are 550 lbs. of commercial dynamite which will explode anytime from within 15 minutes to 25 minutes after the van was parked here. The dynamite will be set off by two completely separate detonating systems. Do not enter or move the van—it will explode. Phone the police immediately and have them block off Highway 27, City View Drive, Dixon Road and other roads surrounding the Litton Plants and have the workers inside the plants moved to protected areas. Nearby hotels and factories should also be notified so that no one will be hurt by the blast. On top of this box is an authentic sample stick of the dynamite contained inside the van. This is to confirm that this is a real bomb!"

Hansen jogged to the getaway car, where Brent Taylor was waiting. They drove away. A few minutes later, they picked up Julie Belmas at a bus stop. Her job had been to call Litton's two security guards on duty that night and warn them about the bomb. She told Hansen and Taylor it was clear that the security guard, Maxwell Spencer, "just didn't understand" what she was saying about the bomb. Despite that, the three made no other warning calls. They did not decide to call off the bombing.

Security guard Terry Chikowski was thirty-three years old, married and a volunteer peewee hockey league referee; Maxwell Spencer, meanwhile, was older, a former church minister. The two men conferred nervously about the call from the anonymous young woman, which they had taped. Chikowski urged Spencer to immediately call the police, which he did. Within minutes, three squad cars arrived from 23 Division in Etobicoke, sirens wailing. After the officers ascertained that the van appeared to contain a bomb, Chikowski ran into building 402 to warn workers to get out. He started to yell a warning to one worker, James Tayles, and was in mid-sentence when the bomb went off, slightly after 11:30 P.M.

The explosion was massive. Building 402 was levelled; when the dust settled, thick steel cables could be seen in the concrete slabs that had once supported the structure. There was a massive crater where Hansen had parked the van; parts of it flew more than a hundred feet out onto Highway 427. At the plant, ten people—ten regular, normal working people, not malevolent politicians or unscrupulous corporate executives—were badly, badly hurt. One worker, Barry Blunden, had his skull fractured by the bomb, along with a broken collarbone, legs and fingers. A police officer, Mervyn Dennis, had severe facial lacerations, a fractured leg and permanent hearing loss. Another constable, Guy Courvoisier, was knocked unconscious. Meanwhile, out on Highway 427—onto which parts of Ann Hansen's stolen van had rocketed, resulting in two major accidents—another score of people were seriously injured.

But it was Terry Chikowski's injuries that were the worst. His body was ripped open by the blast; his internal organs were literally hanging out of gaping wounds when ambulance crews found him. Reached for an interview at his home in the Toronto area, Chikowski politely, and dispassionately, recalls what happened to him on that terrible night. "Well, I've still got afflictions as a result of the injuries." He pauses. "Well, look, let me tell you what they were. My back was split open approximately fourteen inches, and I had four pounds of muscle that were blown out of my back. I had a portion of one rib blown out of my back. My spleen was disintegrated. I had four ribs snapped off the spine and four others cracked. A hole was blown in the lower left side of my stomach. [My] left lung and left kidney collapsed—but they brought them back up during surgery."

He pauses again, then gives a dark laugh. "My diaphragm was split, and the surgeon said that was kind of a saving grace, because when they opened me up in the front, they would have had to cut my diaphragm anyway—to remove the fragments of glass from my heart."

The most horrible injury of all, however, came from a brick— a brick that had once been part of a wall at building 402. Says Chikowski, "Where the muscle left my back, they had to surgically remove half a brick that was embedded there, along with a piece of sheet metal. It was apparently sticking out of me, similar to a shark's fin." The doctors later told Terry Chikowski that, had he not been in good physical shape, the brick would have passed straight through his body, in the spot where his heart is located. He was in intensive care for a week—with more three hundred stitches outside his body and more than six hundred on the inside. The surgeons also left "three or four" clamps inside him, he says, to hold together strips of shredded muscle and tissue. He was moved out of intensive care on his tenth wedding anniversary.

And what does Gerry Hannah have to say now about all of this carnage? Not very fucking much. That he supported the bombing, for starters. And, when describing Terry Chikowski's injuries to a Vancouver radio audience, Hannah blandly observes how the young man's back contained, in the vapid jargon of the military planners he professed to loathe so much, "embedded material." He declines to say much more.

Hearing Gerry Hannah's assessment of his injuries for the very first time, Terry Chikowski gets a little mad. "They can call it political all they want," he says. "It was definitely a criminal act. Max and I had nothing to do with manufacturing any cruise missile guidance systems at Litton! *We* didn't do that! [Hannah and Direct Action] had a total disregard for human life. A total disregard.

"They just went and did what they wanted to do, and the rest of the world be damned."

In the wake of the bombing, Direct Action experienced the first faint stirrings of self-doubt. The group issued a lengthy communiqué that essentially blamed the injured for their wounds: "Accidents happen," they wrote. "We were mistaken in believing that the Litton guards and police would be on top of things . . . all injury to the workers could have been avoided if the guards had promptly evacuated the Litton plant, as they obviously should have."

Says Hannah: "[The Litton attack] was too much for us to handle, and we went too far."

But the doubts did not last for long. Back in their revolutionary nest in Vancouver, the group recovered their sense of high moral purpose, and started plotting more bombings—and even an armed robbery. In November 1982, Hansen, Belmas and another still-unidentified woman (it was important that women alone carry out the "actions," Hannah says, without the assistance of men, because men produced and acquired pornography) bombed three Red Hot Video stores in North Vancouver, Surrey and Coquitlam. All but one of the video outlets was levelled. The Red Hot chain was targeted, Hannah recalls, because it offered patrons access to what Direct Action considered to be violent pornography. "Revolutionary change needed to be made in society," Hannah says. "I was hoping that more and more people would do that sort of thing, I guess."

On January 20, 1983, a cloudy day that threatened rain, Direct Action was in another stolen van on Highway 99, heading to Squamish for yet more target practice. Hannah says the five had been readying themselves for the robbery of a Brink's truck at a Vancouver-area department store. Unlike in the Cheekeye-Dunsmuir bombing or the attack at Litton, Hannah had decided to play a very active role in the robbery. Of the Brinks guard, Hannah says, "We were going to take him down." He wouldn't hesitate to kill the man, Hannah would later suggest, because the man was "an agent of the State."

He, they, didn't get the chance. On an isolated stretch of highway, at a phony road closure (done up to resemble a hydro-related job, ironically enough) dozens of heavily armed police officers surrounded the van. They had had the group under surveillance for some time. The urban guerrillas of Direct Action—or, as the media quickly dubbed them, the Squamish Five—were no more. "I don't know if we would have wanted to shoot our way out of that situation," says Hannah. "We would have all been killed, for sure. They had way more guns than we did."

Things did not go well for Direct Action after that. Doug Stewart was sentenced to ten years' imprisonment for the Cheekeye-Dunsmuir bombing and a weapons charge. Brent Taylor received twenty-two years for a string of crimes, including possession of weapons and explosives, conspiracy to commit robbery, possession of stolen property, auto theft and the Litton bombing. Ann Hansen was sentenced to life for an equally impressive list, along with the Red Hot Video bombings; she reacted to the sentence by throwing a tomato at the judge. Julie Belmas was sentenced to twenty years, but this was later reduced to fifteen on appeal. And Gerry Hannah—the former punk rocker named Gerry Useless—was handed a term of ten years, mainly for the planned Brink's robbery. "I was sentenced in 1984 and released in 1988," he says.

By 1992, the last member of the group to be released, Brent Taylor, had been paroled. According to *Saturday Night* magazine, he drifted into drug addiction. Stewart changed his name, renounced his radical past and became an electrician, and now lives in obscurity somewhere in Vancouver. Taylor and Hansen both reside in the Kingston area, where Hansen makes cabinets and has started organizing again for prison abolition. Belmas—now calling herself "Juliet"—publicly renounced her fellow revolutionaries and became a born-again Christian.

And Gerry Hannah? Gerry Hannah, once Useless, lives in the interior of British Columbia, in a place without a phone and (finally) without electricity. He drives a snowplow for a living. And he doesn't give interviews, one of his friends says, unless he agrees with your politics.

"FUCK YOU! FUCK YOU! FUUUUCK YOU!"

The five hundred or so punks are starting to leave Calgary's Victoria Community Hall. Some punks are pissing on peoples' lawns or knocking over trashcans and such. A few arrests are threatened, but with one exception—a really drunk old guy outside the hall who took a swing at one of the cops—nobody is actually detained. Satisfied that they have finally seen Vancouver's fabled Subhumans, the Cowtown punks are heading home. Few are upset that the gig has been shut down, with the obvious exception of Gerry Useless.

"FUCK YOU, PIGS! FUCK YOU!"

A few of us—because, yes, I was there that night, being the guy principally responsible for bringing the Subhumans to Calgary— stand at the back, observing Gerry. The rest of the Subhumans are watching him, too. Gerry is screaming himself hoarse, but none of the cops seem to care, or notice. Gerry keeps at it, even after the rest of the band stops playing.

"FUCK YOOOOOU! FUCK YOU!"

Here's the thing: to Gerry Useless, the police were malevolent agents of the enemy state, there that night to oppress him, and to crush dissent, and to spread fascism and stuff like that. But the rest of us knew the police had finally arrived because, basically, we *had* been playing too loud.

"FUCK YOU!"

FUCK ART, LET'S DANCE
(or, fuck dancing, let's get artsy)

On December 10, 1977, Lester Bangs wrote the best 177-word definition of punk rock—and rock 'n' roll itself, maybe—ever. It is a definition that is testament to Bangs's writing genius, and also to the musical genius of the Clash (about whom Bangs was writing a massive three-part feature for *New Musical Express*). It is also a definition that persuasively disposes of this book's central thesis—that punk is inherently angry and political, and that it encourages self-actualization as a means to change the world—and just about every other po-faced cultural theory about punk gathering dust in forgotten corners of libraries everywhere.

In his definition, Lester Bangs is describing a Clash gig one night in Bristol, and what Joe Strummer—"an angry live wire, a fury unleashed on the stage," Bangs calls him—is doing:

It was one of those performances for which all of the serv-
iceable critical terms like "electrifying" are so pathetically
inadequate, and after it was over I realized the futility of
hitting Strummer for that interview I kept putting off on
the "politics" of the situation. The politics of rock 'n' roll,
in England or America or anywhere else, is that a whole
lot of kids want to be fried out of their skins by the most
scalding propulsion they can find, for a night they can pretend is the rest of their lives, and whether the next day
they go back to work in shops or boredom on the dole or
American TV doldrums in Mom 'n' Daddy's living room,
nothing can cancel the reality of that night in the revivify-
ing flames when for once if only then in your life you were
blasted outside of yourself and the monotony which
defines most life anywhere at any time, when you supped
on lightning and nothing else in the realms of the living or
dead mattered at all.

Not all of punk rock was about politics, or artistic expression,
or self-actualization, or always being pissed off. Sometimes, it really
was about what Lester says it was: having a good time. Sometimes,
punk was just as important when it declared (as punk label Stiff
Records did in 1977 on a T-shirt reading FUCK ART, LET'S DANCE) that
it was okay to simply have *fun*. That's what this chapter is about:
punk bands who were more about *fun*, and less about *fury*.

Got it? *Fuck* that political, artsy shit—let's dance!

The Ramones were perfect.

For all of the eighties, and the parts of the seventies and nineties
that they were together, the Ramones were ubiquitous and constant.
Whenever and wherever you saw them—and, in all, there were 2,263
shows to see—the punk rock quartet from Forest Hills, New York,

generally looked the same, and generally sounded the same, too. This is not to say that the Ramones did not eventually learn to master their instruments (they did), or that they did not periodically dabble in some aural experimentation (they did that, too, usually with unsatisfactory results). But, for a generation, the Ramones were a constant in the punk rock universe. Some would say that the Ramones *were* the entire punk rock universe—because, like God, they created it.

For most of the twenty-two years in which they were together, the Ramones were counterculture icons, which is an oxymoron, a contradiction in rock 'n' roll terms. Sid died, the Clash slipped into self-parody, and countless other punk outfits came and went. But, for those of us who were getting inexorably older, there would always be Da Brudders Ramone—Tommy, Joey, Johnny and Dee Dee— writing and playing three-minute (sometimes two-minute) bursts of rock 'n' roll brilliance. No politics, no cant, no artistic pretensions: the Ramones were sort of like the early Beach Boys, but loaded up with chains, biker jackets and songs about chainsaws (there were some undeniable ABBA and Bay City Rollers influences in there too). And *fun*—the Ramones, more than any band before or since, championed the cause of fun.

At the centre of the ceaseless pop music genius that produced "Blitzkrieg Bop," "Rock 'n' Roll High School" and "Sheena Is a Punk Rocker," were the four original Ramones, the ones principally responsible for their first four truly perfect albums: *Ramones, Leave Home, Rocket to Russia* and *Road to Ruin,* released in rapid succession between 1976 and 1978 (although, truth be told, Marky Ramone played drums on *Road to Ruin,* while Tommy Ramone produced it). If you ever plan to get stranded on a desert island somewhere, those are the four punk albums to bring along.

Joey, the singer, arrived in the world in May 1951 as Jeffrey Hyman—which, as he came to recognize in 1971 or so, wasn't a very cool moniker for a rock 'n' roller. For a blessedly short while, he wore pink boots, adopted a glam persona and dubbed himself

"Jeff Starship," playing in something called Sniper. By 1974, when the Ramones got together, he had become Joey Ramone—and he would remain Joey Ramone until he died.

Tall and gangly, skinny enough to make an NBA centre look squat, Joey Ramone resembled an enormous leather-jacketed praying mantis. Onstage, he was always the same: face hidden behind an unsightly bush of long black hair, eyes lost behind a pair of dark, ever-present sunglasses. He would stand there, feet splayed, one hand gripping the microphone stand and the other punching the air, usually out of time to Tommy Ramone's efficient drumbeat.

His voice was no finely tuned instrument, which was precisely why the planet's suburban adolescent misfits—punks, in short—loved him so deeply. He was a punk; he was everyone's first punk. His band's music was not merely different from the self-indulgent, technically perfect, coma-inducing arena rock that so many others (viz. Supertramp, Fleetwood Mac, the Strolling Bones) offered up with about as much emotional attachment as an annual report. It was, in fact, against all of that. The Ramones' sound was loud and fast and snotty, and it was about things that a lot of us could relate to: hanging out at 7-Eleven, drinking Slurpees, getting hassled by knuckle-dragging, mouth-breathing Led Zep goons in high school corridors just about anywhere in the industrialized democracies.

With just a few chords and a rock-steady beat, the Ramones sound wasn't merely different; it was a *revolution*. Evidence of their punk parentage isn't difficult to locate: they started playing punk rock in 1974, when Johnny Rotten was still a long-haired Alice Cooper fan, and Joe Strummer was an R & B singer in a pub rock band, and everyone else was still in nappies. The Ramones' first live set happened on March 3, 1974, at Performance Studio, and their first gig took place on August 16, 1974, at New York's soon-to-be-legendary CBGB's. The Sex Pistols didn't play their first show until November 6, 1975, at St. Martin's School of Art in London—more than a year later. But that won't deter the naysayers and the know-it-alls, of course.

They'll tell you the Stooges, or the MC5, or the New York Dolls invented punk rock, but that's bullshit. Many of those bands were in the thrall of fucked-up hippies and/or junkies with anger issues, their earliest albums filled with wads of fatuous psychedelic nonsense. The Ramones, meanwhile, were The First Punks. Believe it.

Always to Joey's right (and always to the Right), for two decades or so, was Johnny Ramone, the band's guitarist. Born John Cummings on Long Island in October 1951, he was the only son of a builder. A baseball fanatic, a Republican and a natural athlete, Johnny gave up on sports around the time he met Tommy Erdelyi in the cafeteria at Forest Hills High School. For a time, the pair joined a local garage rock band, the Tangerine Puppets. Johnny's guitar was a blue Mosrite, purchased at Manny's Guitar Center on 48th Street in January 1974—at $50, it was the cheapest guitar in the place. He dropped out of college to work construction jobs; at nights, he learned rock 'n' roll. Early on, Johnny acquired the distinctive playing style that would distinguish his work with the Ramones—a tricky downstroke, with his Mosrite dangling somewhere in the vicinity of his knees. With Johnny, there were no frills, no stupid guitar solos. Just a wall of deafening, fast, catchy punk rock. (He also was the band's de facto leader, and berated the others to practise, save money and show up on time.)

On the other side of Joey was Dee Dee Ramone, the band's bassist and one of the most influential figures in punk rock; his preoccupation with comic books, household cleaning products and junk culture are seen in many of the group's songs. Born Douglas Colvin in September 1951, Dee Dee (a name he selected, he wrote in his autobiography, because it was "pretty outrageous") was a so-called Army brat. His father, an officer who fought at the Battle of the Bulge, led the Colvin family to postings in Tokyo, Massachusetts and Munich. Like Joey's, Dee Dee's home life was turbulent and difficult; his father, he later said, subjected him and his mother to beatings. And, like Joey, Dee Dee chose rock 'n' roll as a means of escape (as things turned out, he chose drugs, as well).

After leaving the senior Colvin to the military back in Germany, Dee Dee, his mother and his sister settled in Forest Hills in 1968, just in time for high school. Bored, restless, Dee Dee discovered Greenwich Village, glue-sniffing and hustling near the intersection of 53rd Street and Third Avenue—an experience that was to serve as inspiration for one the Ramones' best songs (titled, naturally, "53rd and 3rd"). In and around 1972, following exposure to the Stooges, the Dolls and the Dictators, Dee Dee decided to try his hand at rock 'n' roll, perhaps reasoning that he had already tried pretty much everything else. An attempt to form his own band failed, as did an audition with a group called the Neon Boys (later to be rechristened Television by its founders, Richard Hell and Tom Verlaine). Dee Dee then started talking about putting together a group with his drinking buddy Joey, who lived in a Forest Hills apartment complex nearby. Johnny, happily, also lived in the neighbourhood and was interested in some kind of a musical venture. The Forest Hills trio would sometimes venture out to see the Dolls or the Stooges. (The fact that all four Ramones were from Forest Hills was not irrelevant; unlike the Manhattan bands of the era—the ones across the East River, such as Television or Blondie—the Ramones disdained artsy New York artificiality.)

At first, Dee Dee was the vocalist and Joey played drums; Johnny was always the guitarist. When they got near a stage, they figured, they would wear the same uniform that they favoured during the day: jeans, T-shirts, tennis shoes and black leather jackets. They hated the stuff that was on the radio that year—John Denver and Barbra Streisand had the bestselling album and single, respectively. The Ramones would play rock 'n' roll like they thought it should always be played—simply, with no frills. Like their lives depended on it.

But something was missing. Tommy Erdelyi was born in January 1949 in Budapest. At the age of seven, he emigrated with his family to the United States—specifically, to Forest Hills. Tommy had known Johnny since their high school and Tangerine Puppets days, but they had lost touch when Tommy relocated to Manhattan. In 1974, after purchasing his Mosrite, Johnny phoned Tommy to say that he and Dee Dee were hoping to form a band. Since high school graduation, Tommy had busied himself learning how to be a sound engineer, as well as how to play a range of instruments. He was interested in Johnny's new musical venture, so he invited the trio to play at an East 20th Street rehearsal space, Performance Studio, which he ran with another Forest Hills High alumnus, Monte Melnick. Tommy and Monte (who would go on to become the Ramones' tour manager, soundman, babysitter and driver for their entire existence) were impressed; Tommy, in fact, was impressed enough to briefly manage the group and, eventually, join up. He became the drummer, freeing Joey for vocal duties. Dee Dee came up with their name, inspired by Beatle Paul McCartney's early stage pseudonym, Paul Ramone. Sire Records signed the group in the fall of 1975. The Heavens parted: the Lord God had given mankind the Ramones.

Many years before he lost his life to lymphatic cancer in April 2001 (too young, too soon, at the age of forty-nine), I spent part of an afternoon with Joey Ramone, interviewing him as he sat in his apartment on East Ninth Street, south of Union Square. He was unfailingly polite and patient, even when dealing with someone who was more of a fan than an actual journalist. I asked him what the Ramones meant. What they stood for. Joey Ramone didn't even hesitate. "*Excitement*," he said. "That's what we want. We want to show kids that the real spirit of rock 'n' roll is to pick up a guitar and form a band, do it yourself. And, you know, up until recently, it seemed like you had to have been playing for, like, twenty years to have any chance at all. But that's bullshit, y'know what I mean?

"Everything just got so far away from what it was supposed to be. When rock 'n' roll started, it was supposed to be *fun and exciting*. And the fun and excitement got taken away and thrown out. It got dull and boring, y'know? But now things are picking up again. There's sparks in there. There's sparks in it again. Things will keep getting better."

Thanks in no small measure to the Ramones, things actually *did* get better.

The Ramones first album (called, appropriately, *Ramones*) was recorded, legend goes, for about $6,000 (U.S.) in February 1976. Taped up in the rafters at Radio City Music Hall, produced by Craig Leon and Tommy Ramone, the session lasted seventeen days. Mixing took ten hours. The album clocked in at just under thirty minutes and contained fourteen songs. It was released in April 1976 on the Sire label, which later became home to Richard Hell and the Voidoids, Dead Boys and the Talking Heads. *Ramones* contained songs (sometimes very, very short songs) with titles like "Beat on the Brat," "I Wanna Be Your Boyfriend" and the band's frenetic cover of Chris Montez's "Let's Dance." On the black-and-white jacket, Tommy, Johnny, Joey and Dee Dee slouched against a brick wall, near a schoolyard down the street from CBGB's. Along with the biker jackets that became their most enduring symbol, they wore T-shirts and jeans with the knees worn through. They looked like thugs; they looked like they would not hesitate to mug an old lady for a few bucks. My friends and I stared at that picture more than once, wordless: there could hardly be a more conscious rejection of corporate rock 'n' roll, and what it had become, than that astounding photograph. It was almost as if the Ramones had changed pop music by simply standing there and getting their picture taken.

The first time I dropped that Ramones LP onto my tinny turntable in the basement of our southeast Calgary home, I could not believe my ears: I could make out, barely, Joey's voice, yelping lyrics that were alternately funny and stunning. Along with that, a crescendo of guitars and drums, ripping through three-chord riffs like a chainsaw. As if to drive home the point, one of the songs was titled "Chainsaw." A lot of people feel it's one of the most wonderful rock albums ever made. (I think it's the best.)

The first Ramones record was what rock 'n' roll had been meant to be in the first place: simple, fast, loud, and calculated to irritate your parents. It was, along the way, a kick in the slats of the bloated corpse of the rock "business," which—circa 1976—had become utterly disconnected from the lives of real kids. After the album came out, a lot of things started to happen. For instance, when Malcolm McLaren spotted the Ramones (while he was in the States, unsuccessfully attempting to transform the New York Dolls into some sort of a political statement), he was, like everyone else, awestruck. McLaren dashed back to the U.K. to create another rock band, one that would rely heavily upon the sound of the Ramones, which he would call the Sex Pistols. When Sid Vicious received an invitation to join, he stayed up all night, practising bass to the Ramones' first LP.

But the Ramones weren't like the Pistols, at all. Where the Pistols became proponents of anarchy and class-based nihilism, the Ramones were rarely political. They figured the fans did not come to hear a group of musicians lecture them about politics, and they were right. (The most notable exception to this came much later: Joey's angry take on Ronald Reagan's decision to visit a German cemetery containing S.S. soldiers, which he called "Bonzo Goes to Bitburg"; Johnny disapproved, because he thought Reagan was a great president.) The Pistols and their ilk were also preoccupied with fashion, and their fans favoured safety-pinned earlobes and technicolour tresses. The Ramones, and their fans, stuck with the biker jackets, T-shirts, jeans and tennis shoes.

Like me, a million other kids saw the Ramones more times than you can count, in towns and cities right across the United States, Canada and Europe. Their shows were typically attended by people who were anything but typical: Brit-style punks, metalheads, art school types, skateboarders, university students and even honest-to-goodness bikers. They would always play the same way: heads-down, straight-out rock 'n' roll. No chitchat between songs: just Joey occasionally mumbling "thank you," and then Dee Dee hollering "one-two-three-four" before every tune (if the spirit moved him, he'd do the count-ins in German, too). And then another sonic barrage, washing over you like a wave of heat.

Many years after the fact, Hilly Kristal sits on a dilapidated old couch near the grimy front windows at CBGB's and gives a little smile when he is asked about those days. Kristal looks to be in his seventies now, and he admits that he doesn't stick around much anymore to see bands at his club. But he is still Hilly Kristal, the guy who gave the Ramones their first opportunity to play in public. Ipso facto, he is one of the very few people who can legitimately claim to have created punk, and thereby rewritten rock 'n' roll's script.

Behind his wispy beard and his big shaded eyeglasses, Kristal is gazing out onto the noisy intersection of Bowery and Bleeker, just up from SoHo, where CBGB's is located. Back in the summer of 1974, just a few months after it opened, the bar wasn't much to look at; back then, in fact, it wasn't even considered safe to be close enough to clap eyes on the place. Patrons were charged a buck to get in. Nowadays, CBGB's (an acronym for Country, Bluegrass and Blues) is considered an extremely significant piece of pop culture real estate—it is "legendary," says *New Musical Express*. In recognition of that fact, an adjoining bit of East Second Street has been renamed Joey Ramone Place; out front, the pedestrian crossing light features a punk rocker instead of the standard WALK symbol, and the DON'T WALK icon, instead of a warning hand, is the traditional rock 'n' roll pinkie-and-index-finger salute.

As Hilly Kristal remembers the Ramones at the start, dozens of tourists stream in to buy CBGB's T-shirts, pullovers and belt buckles. Hilly Kristal sells a lot of CBGB's T-shirts, his staff says. "Well," Kristal says, "they were probably the worst band I had ever heard, when I first heard them. They were even worse than Television. I mean, they just weren't together. Their amps were breaking down, and they were yelling at each other onstage. It wasn't a very good beginning." He laughs at the memory.

He continues, "But, well, they really wanted to play. They *really* wanted to play. They had great energy. And there seemed to be a lot of interesting things going on, you know? I had heard about the new bands. People were talking, and there were these bands [with] no place to play. And I put Television and the Ramones, both of them together, on Sundays. I hadn't been open on Sundays, and I figured I had nothing to lose. They really wanted to play, so I kept putting them in, and they got better."

Kristal suspects the turning point came when he spoke with Joey Ramone about the band's musical competence. The Ramones were never going to make it, Kristal told Joey, if they did not learn to play their instruments better. Joey, he says, took the advice to heart. Within a short time, says Kristal, the band was capable of playing more than a dozen songs in about twenty minutes. He adds, "All of a sudden, it came alive."

There is a commotion at the door, and an impressively bald, bespectacled man in a biker jacket ambles in, looking for Hilly Kristal. Says Kristal, "Let him in, it's John! He's from *Punk Magazine!* Hey, wanna do an interview? Maybe you'll get in the book!"

The unexpected newcomer is John Holmstrom. If Hilly Kristal is the man who gave the Ramones (and therefore the punk movement) their start, then John Holmstrom is the man who gave the movement a *name*. He drew the cartoon on the Ramones' *Road to Ruin* LP cover, as well as the one on the back of *Rocket to Russia,* and, most importantly, is the long-time editor of *Punk Magazine*—the magazine that predated *Sniffin' Glue* and all of the other punk zines. He's the guy who (along with the magazine's "publisher," Legs McNeil) appropriated the unflattering word "punk" from the pages of *Creem* magazine to describe the newest New York bands, particularly the Ramones.

A long-delayed, long-planned interview with the CBGB's guru turns into a chatty Ramones primer led by Hilly Kristal and John

Holmstrom. (Which, when you think about it, is a lot better than an interview, anyway.) Says Kristal, "What *made* them? I'd say, them doing twenty songs in seventeen minutes without stopping. Whose idea was that? It may all have been their idea. It happened in August [1974], I think. Boy, when they did *that*—ZOOM!"

Says Holmstrom, "When they took Joey out of the drums and made him the singer, and Tommy started drumming for them . . . once they got that chemistry going, they had a really unique sound. I mean, Tommy had worked in the music business. He had real musical ability."

Kristal nods. They seem completely unaware of my presence. "Tommy was one of the best. A good drummer, and he was on the ball. He kept it all together, as long as he was there," Kristal says to Holmstrom. "They needed him, because they were so sloppy at the start. Sloppy, sloppy, sloppy. You could hardly hear anything. And somehow, at some point—it happened. I mean, it was like, boom. All of a sudden they were different." He pauses. "They *really, really* wanted to do it. They were sincere, and they were great guys."

Kristal is advised by one of his staff members that he is wanted on the phone. He excuses himself and encourages Holmstrom to continue the interview. The editor of *Punk Magazine* shrugs and agrees. Asked why Hilly Kristal took a chance on the Ramones, Holmstrom says, "Hilly's a businessman. I think he had his regular crowd in here [in the summer of 1974] to keep him in business. Remember, he was in the Bowery, and he was probably paying next to nothing [in rent] in those days. I mean, you were considered to be taking your life in your hands if you walked into this neighbourhood at night. People were *frightened* to come to CBGB's. It had this reputation, you know? There were no other clubs here, and there weren't all these expensive apartments and stores here back then. So you had a lot of refugee rock bands who had no rock clubs to play in, in New York. And Hilly provided the only place in New York that offered a place to play for bands that wanted to play original music."

Hilly Kristal returns and points at Holmstrom. "Did you tell him about the end of the summer of '74? Because, all of a sudden, you know, I mean everybody came here. The Ramones turned everybody on, you know? Just high-energy, non-stop, song after song . . ." He trails off; Holmstrom is grinning, looking like he has heard these stories many times in the past quarter-century. "It was like . . . a thing."

It was, indeed, A Thing. Everybody seemed to love the Ramones. After that summer, the music press, in particular, was in love with the leather-jacketed moptops. Lots of ink was spilled, and few adjectives spared, to promote the notion that Da Brudders Ramone represented the salvation of rock 'n' roll. "The Ramones are a band that the London rock scene could really use," wrote Charles Shaar Murray in *New Musical Express* in November 1975. "They're simultaneously so funny, such a cartoon vision of rock and roll, and so genuinely tight and powerful that they're just bound to enchant anyone who fell in love with rock and roll for the right reasons." *NME*'s Julie Burchill reviewed a May 1977 performance by the Ramones at Eric's in Liverpool—at which Burchill actually fought her way through the mosh pit to stand at Johnny's feet: "Everyone had warned me how much this forced assimilation into the Ramones world of decibels would hurt, but I was oblivious. It sounded great to me . . . The words are totally indecipherable, but so what? This ain't a Wittgenstein tutorial, this is rock 'n' roll." In *NME*'s September 1976 review of the single "Blitzkrieg Bop," Roy Carr declared, "Truthfully, I've never heard so much positive rock energy being generated . . ." In its May 1977 review of "Sheena Is a Punk Rocker," Charles Shaar Murray rhapsodized, "Look, all the Ramones songs sound like hit singles and then don't sell, but this song is so flat-out delightful that not even the nasty, boring, dull-as-bleedin'-ditchwater Britpublic will be able to resist it."

On the Ramones' home continent, the reaction was much the same. "For me, it blows everything else off the radio," declared Robert Christgau in *The Village Voice*. Much later, *Rolling Stone* would conclude, "By melding such hook-laden tunes with an aggressive stance, high volume, and no-frills songwriting, the Ramones became one of the most important rock bands of all time." *The New York Times,* meanwhile, would come to regard the Ramones' first LP as one of the twenty most influential records of the twentieth century— ranked right up there with albums by the likes of Frank Sinatra, Billie Holiday, Miles Davis, John Coltrane and others. Notwithstanding the enthusiasm the Ramones engendered, notwithstanding the actual *love* a lot of people had for them, they paradoxically never achieved the sort of commercial success they so richly deserved. In the United States, for example, their brilliant first LP was purchased about seven thousand times. That's it

On the one hand, that shouldn't matter: punk wasn't supposed to be about rock 'n' roll sales, it was about getting back rock 'n' roll's soul. But, on the other hand, is it acceptable that, just days before he, too, succumbed to cancer, Johnny Ramone was obliged to frantically sell off his beloved baseball and rock 'n' roll memorabilia on a website so that his widow would have some way in which to live?

In conversation with Joey Ramone, in the front half of the eighties, it was evident that record sales preoccupied the band more than they liked to admit. When discussing the Ramone's commercial appeal, Joey seemed torn. He wanted to get rock 'n' roll back to its roots—back to fun, back to simplicity, back to reality. Punk was the way to achieve that. But, simultaneously, it clearly frustrated him that so much dreck occupied so much space on the Top Ten charts.

Here's part of that conversation, never before published. I started by asking Joey how, generally, things were going for the Ramones.

Joey: It's pretty much the same everywhere—it's crazy. It's very well-received. It's very receptive. The kids really just want to let loose and have a good time, you know? That's the way it is. We just finished a tour of Europe, and it was great. It was crazy all over the place, you know?

Me: Are the critics still onside?

Joey: The media and the press are so stiff—they're just so serious. But the kids, they know what they've come to see. They really want to have a good time, you know? That's what it's really all about.

Me: So what are the Ramones all about?

Joey: We're not phony. We're not into hype and bullshit. We're not into all that star bullshit stuff, you know? We're just guys. We just want the best for us and our audience, you know? That's it.

Me: But why do so many kids listen to bullshit, then? Why is bullshit found on the charts, and not the Ramones?

Joey: Well, kids today, they're either brainwashed or . . . a lot of people, I can't believe it myself, a lot of people don't even know who the Beatles were or the Kinks, when they hear one of their songs. They think it was written by someone else. It's sick, you know? Coming from our point [of view], it makes you really pissed off, you know? But, finally, the radio is turning around, and now the groups dominating the charts are the newer groups . . . you see fewer and fewer of the older groups. Whereas before it was heavily dominated by other stuff. So that's great.

Me: Does it bother you that a lot of people are now hailing the Ramones, and before they would never give you the time of day?

Joey: There's always those latecomers who catch onto things last, you know what I mean? But the fact that they catch on at all is vital. It's healthy. In that way, it's probably the best time for rock 'n' roll in years . . . Whether they come [to our shows] because it's trendy or the hype or, you know, they're just coming to see something that they don't understand . . . just the fact that they're coming, you can change them around, you can change their way of thinking. That's important, you know?

Me: Some people try to lump you in with metal groups, and the metal sound. What do you think about that? Are the Ramones into the metal crowd?

Joey: It's just like this fucked-up crowd of people that just want to take Quaaludes and get drunk all the time. I don't understand it. It's just bullshit. It's so negative. It's terrible.

Me: What are the Ramones fans like?

Joey: Our fans are totally dedicated to us.

Me: Why can't they get the charts to reflect that, then?

Joey: The radio, up until recently, has been dictating to everybody what to listen to . . . so that they stay happy, I guess. They don't want anybody making waves, like we do. They try to deter anybody from listening to anything but that kind of music, you know?

Me: There's no more sense of rebellion in music. A lot of groups seem to be trying to sell to kids, as well as their parents . . .

Joey: There are so many groups like that now. There's no . . . it's just junk. It's alright for your parents . . . the radio, they try to force it on you, this is what you're supposed to like, so that way they can sell it to everybody. I'm glad people are saying "Fuck that. I'm sick of this shit, I'm going to listen to what I'm going to listen to." But it's hard, when the only stuff on the radio is shit. So we say take a stand, and say enough is enough.

Me: But nothing ever seems to change. Why aren't the Ramones on the radio? Why aren't any of the good punk groups on the radio?

Joey: The thing you gotta remember is to keep plugging and keep pushing . . . people are going to try and stop you . . .

Me: But the major labels won't give any of the punks a chance . . .

Joey: Put it out yourself. Or find a smaller label. They're more concerned about you than the big labels. The [big ones] don't care. It makes no difference to them . . . But there are new labels all the time. It's better to go with somebody like that. They're concerned about you, whereas the other labels, all they're concerned about is sales. And if you don't sell, they drop you, you know?

Me: But doesn't all of that frustrate you? I mean, the Ramones write great songs! You should be selling millions of records . . . doesn't it frustrate you?

Joey: It's been a constant uphill climb for us. It's been like smashing our heads against a wall. And, you know, it will probably always be that way. But you just can't let it get you down, you know? If you stop, no one is going to give a shit about you. It's just you who can make it happen.

Me: Why do the British punks have an easier time getting on the charts over there? How are they different from North American punks?

Joey: There were a few good groups to come out of it, you know? There were a few genuine groups to come out of it. But a lot of it was crap, as far as I am concerned. Especially with the whole punk fashion part . . . it was all bullshit, you know? It probably did more harm than good, in fact. Because it just kind of set things back. There was just so much that was in bad taste that it made it harder for everybody, you know? A lot of the groups were just about shock and shock . . . the groups that really cared about the music and wanted to change things, like we do, found it ridiculous. That whole thing with the Sex Pistols and the swastikas and all that bullshit. It just fucked things up. It was stupid.

Me: What do you think about the Pistols?

Joey: I can see some pros and cons. But, with the Pistols, it was about Malcolm [McLaren] trying to make a quick buck off of everybody, which he did. And the fucking band didn't see anything. Even the band! What they got, it was a joke.

Me: Did they mean what they said about anarchy, do you think?

Joey: It was all a big hoax. All the English media, they take it so seriously. It was all bullshit, and I knew it when it happened. What's the point of getting into politics, anyway? It's like the Clash, you know? They were always politically oriented, and they talked about how they hate the rich and they don't want to know about this or that. Then they come to New York and go to Studio 54, where all the fucking rich assholes are, and they hang around with Andy Warhol and drive around in limousines. They're just a bunch of hypocrites, you know? And I like the Clash, but you know . . . they're full of shit! [He laughs.]

Me: Will you guys ever get political?

Joey: You can't get involved in politics. It just backfires.

Me: Don't the Clash make some good points, even when they're being political?

Joey: It gets to me when I have a discussion with somebody about it . . . I don't want to badmouth the Clash. It's not a big deal, but it's just so hokey. It's just so ridiculous. They're a good, exciting group, even if [*London Calling*] is just pitiful. They really went out of their way to be middle of the road with that one, and make it, you know? Their first album was just great, though.

Me: Did you guys invent punk rock?

Joey: When we went to Europe the first time, there was nothing over there. The music they listened to was pub rock. Dr. Feelgood and stuff like that. We played a couple shows there, and the whole thing really kicked off, you know? I mean, a lot of people are really misinformed about where it all started, you know what I mean?

Me: But you guys get hits in Britain, don't you?

Joey: In Britain, [the groups] want to be number one and on top of the trends . . . they know it's fixed, though. [He laughs.] It's really exciting to be in a place where the punk groups, the new groups, they dominate, and they lay down the rules. Everybody gets [their records] played and everybody gets a chance. But back in the States, there's a million stations, and it's really hard to break through.

Me: Blondie made it . . .

Joey: Yeah, well, we stuck to our guns. We didn't sell out like Blondie did, or nobody else like that, and do disco, you know?

Me: Has it changed them?

Joey: They think they're big stars now. Too big to talk to you.

Me: Well, thank you for talking to me!

Joey: It's not about being big, anyway, it's about being an asshole. Doing interviews and doing radio, it's the only way to get to the people. They're the ones keeping you alive. That's what it's all about.

Me: The Ramones, to me, created punk and made rock 'n' roll fun again. Am I wrong? Did you guys change anything?

Joey: I think we've changed a lot. We've created a whole new sound in music. What we wanted to do, we've done it. Things are going to get better. It's healthy. It's really got me excited. Things are going to get better, you'll see.

For the Ramones themselves—and despite the hopeful tone with which Joey concluded our conversation—things didn't "get better" by much. Those first four albums probably represent their zenith. For Joey, Johnny, Tommy and Dee Dee, however much they tried, however many amazing shows they played, however many wonderful songs they wrote, the big time never quite arrived. Too soon after Joey's death from cancer, Dee Dee—who had quit the band to pursue an ill-advised and ill-fated career as a rap artist—died of a heroin overdose in July 2002 at his Los Angeles home. Then, slightly more than two years later, Johnny lost his life to prostate cancer, also in L.A., after half a decade's struggle with the disease. Of the original foursome, only Tommy is alive; the guys who came later, like Marky, C.J. and Richie, are still around, too.

Even though he seemed to be conceding that the Ramones would never hit the big time—as he said, almost ruefully, " . . . it will probably always be that way"—Joey Ramone's desire to sell a few more records was never far from the surface throughout the interview, and throughout his musical career. Without him actually coming right out and saying it, you could hear it in Joey's voice: if shitty, stupid bands such as Van Halen or Fleetwood Mac could sell records crammed with shitty, stupid songs, why couldn't folks give the Ramones a break, just for once? Would it have been so very difficult to put "Sheena Is a Punk Rocker" on the radio? Would anyone have gotten hurt? Would it have placed Mick Jagger's bank balance in jeopardy?

By missing out on the Ramones when they were still around, millions of kids lost out—hell, *Western civilization* lost out. But it would be a mistake, a *big* mistake, to conclude that the Ramones' inability to sell a kabillion albums in any way minimized their many achievements. They created the punk rock sound, and arguably punk rock itself. They launched the careers of scores of bands, from the Sex Pistols to Pearl Jam to Green Day. They embodied the DIY ethic before anyone knew what it meant, let alone tried it. They returned rock 'n' roll to its rebellious, raw roots. And, mostly, they made a lucky few feel good. They were *fun*.

While Joey Ramone admitted that things "have been a constant uphill climb," and that "it's been like smashing our heads against a wall," he also said it's important not to let it get you down—whether you're a Ramone or not. In words that should be scrawled on the grimy, sweaty walls of every dark and dingy garage, in every messy basement and rehearsal space, wherever acned young bands are tuning up, starting out, he said, "If you stop, no one is going to give a shit about you. It's just you who can make it happen."

And *that,* perhaps, was what the Ramones were sent by God to do—not to sell as many records as Fleetwood Mac or Van Halen, or to overthrow governments, or to persuade anyone to dye their hair pink. The Ramones were sent here to make a few of us feel good. To make us misfits feel that we belonged (to something, anything), and that we could start a band if we wanted to.

We did, we did. And, *Christ,* did we ever love the Ramones. And we still do.

In performance, as they make fart jokes and urge young girls to remove their tops—which young girls do, without hesitation, and in great numbers—it's hard to picture Blink-182 backstage, sipping mineral water and quietly discussing Noam Chomsky. And political change. And the nature of art.

"I think it's the responsibility of art, in general, to get people to think," says bassist Mark Hoppus. "Whether it's political or not. And sometimes, it works. I think art is a vehicle for thought, and it's how you use it, I guess. We use Blink primarily to provoke emotions in people—just like any other band does. Whether it's about breaking up with a girl, or whether it's the destruction of your family life, or whatever. I mean, Bad Religion use it as a vehicle to express [their politics], song by song. I think it is art's responsibility to do that, but not just about politics. About anything."

He pauses. "Yeah. Responsibility is a really weird word, you know?"

I ask him whether art has any responsibility at all—to change things, or to persuade.

"I think its only responsibility is to provoke thought," he says.

Guitarist and vocalist Tom Delonge, who has been listening to his long-time bandmate, starts to interview Hoppus himself: "When you write songs, do you write them thinking they will evoke reaction, or do you write them for yourself?" he asks.

The band's handler looks apprehensive. The interview—one of only two Blink-182 will grant on this tour stop—is already running overtime. But Hoppus and Delonge ignore him, and continue discussing art.

"When people come and say to us that a certain song does something for them, you know what is interesting?" Hoppus says to Delonge. "I remember in literature class in high school, I would sit there almost in disgust about how much detail we would use to talk about someone's work. And I would think, 'There is no way the author thought of this, or that, when they wrote the next paragraph. They were probably just trying to get to the next paragraph.' And whether they did or they did not is not my point. My point is that art is what someone gets from it. It is not complete until someone takes something from it and forms their own conclusion." He smiles. "It's a cool way to think about everything."

Delonge, apparently, agrees. The two of them—multi-millionaire punk rockers—stare off in the middle distance, saying nothing. No jokes about titties, or references to penises, or even wisecracks about boinking the next-door neighbour's hot mom. Their handler, seeing his moment, declares that the interview is over, so sorry, must move along, thank you so much. Hoppus is unfazed. He turns to me and stares intently. "Do you have any other questions, Warren? This is interesting."

Interesting? You want *interesting?* As horrified as some people will be to hear it, the fact is this: Blink-182 are, arguably, the spiritual heirs of the Ramones. They write songs about girls, and cars, and the flotsam and jetsam of popular culture—just like the Ramones did. And they write poppy punk songs—just like the Ramones did. But unlike the Ramones, whom they plainly adore with an intensity that is almost frightening, Blink-182 sell an extraordinary number of records. They therefore have a lot more money than the Ramones did; Blink-182 probably have more money than God. So why *them,* and not the Ramones? Why did they make it, and not Tommy, Johnny, Joey and Dee Dee? The boys in Blink-182 wonder about that themselves, sometimes, but they ain't complaining. Which raises another Blink-182–related dilemma, and one which we will get to shortly: *Can* you play wacky, nutty, empty-headed punk-pop forever and a day? *Should* you, even if you can?

Formed in 1991 or so in the global surf-punk capital of San Diego, the band's original lineup was guitarist and vocalist Tom Delonge, bassist Mark Hoppus and drummer Scott Raynor. At the start, they called themselves Blink.

Hoppus—tall, thoughtful and the band's philosopher on this night—was born in March 1972 in California. When he was fourteen, his parents divorced, and he relocated for a time to the U.S. national punk capital, Washington, D.C., to live with his father. He received his first bass guitar and amp at age fifteen, in exchange for a paint job. Until bitten by the punk bug, he wanted to teach high school English.

Delonge, meanwhile, made his debut in December 1975 in San Diego. He decided to form a band with Hoppus when he was in his mid-teens. The pair were big fans of the Ramones, Bad Religion and the germinal California punk-pop heroes the Descendents—a collection of geeks who were the first, on the West Coast, anyway, to write a lot of songs about fast food and girls, and none at all about class warfare.

Blink produced a Did-It-Themselves EP, *Fly Swatter*, in 1993. In 1994, they came out with another self-released record—this time a full-length album called *Buddha.* They started to attract attention. In 1995, the threesome signed to indie label Grilled Cheese/Cargo and released *Cheshire Cat.* It was a huge hit in Australia, of all places.

Around this time, Blink learned that a forgettable Irish techno band was also called Blink. Concerned about getting sued, the band added 182 to their name, and no one—including the band—knows precisely what it signifies. (If you want them to, they'll speculate for you, which offers them yet another opportunity to relate masturbation jokes.) The big time beckoned: Blink-182 was invited to join the 1996–1997 Warped Tour, earning in the process a higher profile and proximity to other bands on the tour that year, among them Pennywise and NOFX. Following the tour, and following appearances in countless skate, surf and snowboarding videos (the band members remain hard-core skateboarding aficionados), their third LP, *Dude Ranch*, was released. Debuting in 1997, *Dude Ranch* sold impressively, going platinum in Australia and gold in the United States. Suddenly, Hoppus and Delonge were drawing the affections of a slew of major labels.

Shortly thereafter, Raynor—abruptly, mysteriously—was out. (According to Raynor, the reason was that he wanted to go back to school; according to those around Hoppus and Delonge, the reason was that hoary old rock 'n' roll chestnut, artistic differences.) Travis Barker—short, much-tattooed, formerly with the Aquabats—was in. Much to the chagrin of SoCal punk purists, Blink-182 signed with MCA, who in the summer of 1999 released the band's fourth—and multi-million-copy-selling—album, *Enema of the State.* On the cover: porn queen Janine Lindemulder, a band favourite. Lindenmulder also played a "nurse" in the band's "What's My Name" video, which was shown on MTV and elsewhere approximately five billion times.

After *Enema of the State,* things got a little crazy for Blink-182. The rulebook has always been clear: punk bands aren't supposed to enjoy much in the way of commercial success. That's how it had been for the Ramones and plenty of others, and that's how it would be for everyone else. But by 1999, Blink-182 had thrown away the rulebook, and were making money like they were printing it themselves. People, *lots* of people (in places as far-flung as Europe, Australia, Asia and the Americas), apparently liked the idea that punk should be fun. In no particular order, the Blink boys won a Teen Choice Award and a Blockbuster Music Award, and they appeared on the MTV Video Music Awards 2000, where they performed "All the Small Things" for an audience of millions and picked up Best Group Video. Later, in Europe, they won an MTV Europe Award for Best New Act. Along the way, they played once on *Saturday Night Live* and twice on *The Tonight Show.* They also opened the Billboard Music Awards. In between, Blink could be found on the covers of *Rolling Stone, Teen People, Teen* and *CosmoGirl.* Even if they hadn't sold any records whatsoever, the trio could have comfortably retired from the sales of Blink-182 merchandise.

Nobody could ever accuse them of being as earnest as Ian MacKaye, or as anti-corporate as many of the Epitaph punk bands. Hoppus and Delonge have always been clear about who they are, and what they hope to achieve—and socialist world revolution does not rank near the top of their priorities list. But it is equally clear that the boys in Blink-182 are not the infantile, hormone-charged post-adolescents many assume them to be. Nor are they in any way unintelligent—five minutes of conversation with them makes that clear. Instead, it is obvious that Blink-182 *act* dumb. They *act* silly. So, um, why?

It's not like Blink is incapable of being political. Delonge, for example, is proudly anti-Republican, and the band uses its popular website to urge fans to register for the vote, and then to mobilize against the likes of George W. Bush. They've participated in benefits designed to raise funds for anti-Bush causes. And they donate money to a variety of causes, among them groups that help children afflicted with HIV, Habitat for Humanity and Stand Up for Skateparks, which builds skateparks for kids in low-income neighbourhoods.

For a band that reaches so many millions of pairs of ears; for a band that is plainly more intelligent than they let on; for a band that could have a tremendous worldwide impact in a sober, serious way—why, er, songs about boobs and dinks and farting? Why the shows that resemble frat house parties on a massive scale? Why so poppy and, therefore, less punky?

Hoppus has agreed to be interviewed first, and he has batted this one over the back fence many times before. And, besides, he doesn't think following in the Ramones' footsteps is necessarily a bad thing. At all. "I've always been drawn to melody, to something I can sing along with, you know?" says Hoppus, who has an intense, direct gaze. "The first time I heard the Descendents, the very first time I heard punk at all, was when I heard the Descendents song, 'Silly Girl.' I had heard of punk rock before, but had never really been exposed to it. That was fast music. It had a lot of energy, and they were singing about things I cared about."

Such as?

"Girls. Not fitting in at school. Problems with your parents," says Hoppus. "And I could sing along with it. It was real." "Real" was what the guys in Blink-182 had experienced in their lives; race riots, military occupation and grinding poverty were not things they had experienced, so they didn't sing about that stuff, Hoppus says.

Just as I ask Hoppus whether punk, by definition, should be about weightier matters, Delonge lopes into the room. Like Hoppus, he's wearing track pants and a T-shirt. He has a genial, easygoing way about him. Hoppus says to Delonge, "We were discussing if it is possible for us to have rebellion in our music."

"Yeah," says Delonge, stretching out on the couch where he has taken a seat. "I think it's possible. But rebellion in what sense? I think most people assume punk rock is a music of rebellion, and that it should be against society or governments or have some kind of a political reasoning behind it. But I think that the essence of punk was really just to avoid conforming to the society around you. I think you are being sincere, actually, when you record a record that is just absolutely abstract, and different, and [the] 180-degree opposite of what everyone expects of you. That way, they don't know what to expect of you. That's what we try and do. We're not scared to try and do anything."

That isn't the view of some Blink-182 critics, of course. The band's detractors—and, in the punk movement, there are many of those—assert that Blink sold out long ago, and that Hoppus and Delonge are terrified to try anything that may ultimately jeopardize the sales of their CDs. Hoppus and Delonge have heard the criticism before. Delonge shrugs. "If you think about the Sex Pistols, they wouldn't have hesitated a second," he says, sounding a tad defensive. "They would have tried to take their music to the largest possible audience, you know? Being on a major label, TV shows and stuff, doing everything you possibly can to get as many people as you can to hear [your music] . . . I mean, the Clash did that, too. The Ramones would have done that, if they had been given the chance.

"But I do remember when I was a kid, and having these meatheads in school [starting to] play the songs that I loved, and I was so pissed off. I was actually sad. But, when I really thought about it, I shouldn't have been sad that people are finally catching on to good music. That's being a snob."

True enough, true enough, and Hoppus is nodding, too. "For me, punk rock has always been about doing whatever you want to do. What you feel is right for you. It's less about a specific style of music. It's more about a spirit than a musical style."

Their handler looks like he is about to have a coronary; he wants the interview over *now*. Blink-182 have to play very soon, before a sold-out crowd of thousands, but the band's founders want to leave their guest with the clearest possible distillation of their views. Punk cred, Hoppus and Delonge say, is attitudinal. The way in which you give expression to that attitude—and the things you choose to rant about—can, and should, be up to you. At the end of the show, it doesn't matter if your music is wholly apolitical, they say. What matters is that you are playing loud, fast tunes on your own terms. And if someone dismisses you as "fun," then so be it. Blink-182 can live with that criticism, if it is one. The Ramones got it, too, way back when.

"Punk has become part of the mainstream, just as rock 'n' roll became part of the mainstream," says Hoppus, standing up. "Just as much as hip-hop is becoming part of the mainstream. Just as much as other styles of music—styles of music that rebel against society and conformity—sometimes acquire popularity and become part of the mainstream. It's all cyclical. It happens.

"And we think it's healthy, too. It means walls are being broken down between the genres—and that people are more open to different kinds of bands. And that's good, right?"

Well . . . sure. Probably. *Yes.* Delonge and Hoppus move out the door. In the distance, the shrieks of untold thousands of teenage girls (and boys) is heard. Soon enough, I regret to say, quite a few of them are going to be topless.

There'll be fart and penis jokes aplenty, too.

It's the first thing you notice, and there can be no denying it: Billy Idol looks *old.*

Decked out in lots of black—black jeans, black shirt, with a black T-shirt underneath, two revolvers emblazoned across his chest—Idol still sports his trademark bleached-blond punk hairdo and favours a lot of jangly silver jewelry on or near his wrists, neck, fingers and ears. But the founding front man of punk-popsters Generation X turns *fifty* this year; he's got a couple of teenage children; and the bags under his eyes bear no small resemblance to the treads on a pair of high-end Michelin snow tires.

It's not a criticism, per se; I mean, all of us are getting older, whether we like it or not, and are thereby experiencing new and unwanted hairlines, waistlines and facial lines. Unlike the rest of us, however, the rebel yeller's formerly youthful features have been preserved in MTV video amber—and, when his videos are occasionally rebroadcast by a veejay in a nostalgic mood, we get reminded, jarringly, that Billy Idol is no punk spring chicken. By his own admission, he's partied a lot, and it shows.

Billy Idol is, however, a genuinely funny and friendly sort of bloke, with a firm handshake and a desire to be helpful. He's almost impossible to dislike, however much he, and his famous videos, have been lampooned by satirists as diverse as Van Halen's David Lee Roth and Eminem. He doesn't take himself particularly seriously, which is not something that can be said about quite a few of his contemporaries.

Born William Michael Albert Broad in Stanmore, Middlesex, in 1955, Billy—as he delights in telling you—was kicked out of Boy Scouts for "snogging" with a girl. He was an inattentive student, and was therefore called "idle" by one of his teachers—the very name he later gleefully adopted. When he was nineteen or so, Billy quit his studies at Sussex University and relocated to London, where he hooked up with fellow Sex Pistols fans Siouxsie Sioux, Steve Severin, Sue Catwoman and Clash guitarist-to-be Mick Jones. The gang, which favoured shocking clothes and behaviour, called themselves the Bromley Contingent, named after a South London suburb where a few of them had lived.

In 1976, the year that Britain was set ablaze by the Ramones' first album, Billy put together the punk group Chelsea. Idol played guitar, while Gene October supplied vocals and Tony James played bass. When October left in that same year, Idol and James stuck together and formed Generation X. Right away, the band—with their unabashed pop sensibility and their unapologetically image-conscious stance—were noticed. *Record Mirror* called them "one of the most entertaining and vibrant bands to spring from the initial British new wave explosion." In *New Musical Express,* tongue in cheek, Tony Parsons called them "clean punks" who were therefore "[a] menace to our kids." Idol, Parsons wrote in January 1977, "while coming out with the standard lines putting down age, stagnation and the establishment, looks pretty enough for girls whose big sisters used to swoon over Marc Bolan."

And that, pretty much, was Billy Idol's punk rock dilemma. He and James were capable of writing terrific punk tunes, as they did on Generation X's eponymous first LP—songs like "Your Generation" or "Kleenex." They knew the punk scene well, and they had been involved with it from the outset (in James's case, with Mick Jones in London SS). But they were, unarguably, too *pretty.* Unlike Joe Strummer or Johnny Rotten, Billy Idol and his band members all had excellent dental work. Unlike Sid Vicious or any member of the Damned you care to name, Idol and Co. had unblemished skin.

Hell, in one interview, they unwisely (and untruthfully) declared that they did not drink or take drugs.

In the early eighties, after Generation X had broken up, and after he had moved to New York City to pursue a solo career, Billy Idol set about consuming drink and drugs with the zealousness of a convert making up for lost time. While racking up numerous hits with the execrable "Mony Mony," "White Wedding," "Hot in the City," "Eyes Without a Face," "Flesh for Fantasy," "Cradle of Love," and so on, Idol bought a motorcycle, moved to Los Angeles and energetically devoted himself to drug addiction. In 1994, he nearly killed himself with an overdose.

Apart from his bit roles in films such as Adam Sandler's *The Wedding Singer,* no one heard much from Billy Idol for most of the decade that followed. It was time to sit back and do a bit of evaluation, Idol says, particularly in light of the fact that he had become a parent. He laid low.

In the new millennium, Idol put out a greatest hits collection and starting gigging again with his post–Generation X songwriting partner, Steve Stevens. In 2005, the pair put out another record, their first in more than a decade. It doesn't sound very punk, but Idol doesn't give shit about satisfying the purists, and never did. He gives one of his trademark sneers. "In punk, you had artists who were maybe painters who'd make music," he says. "There would be people who were artists, who were journalists. You had people turning things on their heads. I mean, someone like me, who wasn't the greatest guitar player in rock, or the greatest singer, could end up writing songs and singing. Punk meant you weren't non-musical just because someone *said* you were non-musical . . . There was a need to give people a chance to do different types of things."

In Idol's view, that willingness to be different applies to *punk,* too. Unlike many punks, or former punks, Idol is not offended by punk-popsters like Blink-182 or Good Charlotte in the slightest. Punk could hardly challenge rock 'n' roll's orthodoxies, he suggests, and then turn around and promote its own orthodoxies. That's hypocrisy. "[Some punks] lost sight of what it was all about," he says. "It's not just about music, it's not just about fashion. It's not just about three-minute songs, not about two-minute songs and seven-minute songs. It's about *passion.* It's about being *alive,* about what you really think is right, what you want to do, and not being fucked over by some little sod with the right shoes, you know?"

Fair enough (and he's wearing big black boots, in case you are wondering). But did Billy Idol have to, well, become such a fucking pop star? I mean, was it absolutely necessary that he go and do something awful like that?

"Look," he says, "if you have a hard time growing up or whatever, you know, you can sing about that. It's your choice. But I think it was Johnny Rotten who said that 'We don't want all the punk bands to be the same.' Fine. So, why should every punk band have to be political? That's my point.

"That's what Rotten asked for, really, isn't it? John asked for all of us to be ourselves and to do the music that matters to ourselves. So I did that. I did music that was much more true to me."

Billy Idol's music may be hard to *listen to* now, but it's certainly hard to *argue* with him. Looking older than he used to, but sounding wiser than he perhaps once was, Idol shakes my hand and walks out to the next interview.

Okay. But, the thing is this: punk rock lost its way. It got off track. It became what it was trying to change. As a consequence, a lot of it sucked.

Which brings me here, to this moment, backstage at a cavernous outdoor theatre beside Lake Ontario on a humid summer night, watching dissolute musicians and aging groupies circle one another, each unsure who is the hunter and who is the hunted. I am bored. Waiting. Despairing. Wondering how the fuck I ever agreed to interview something like Good Charlotte. Even worse: *waiting* to interview Good Charlotte.

Good Charlotte, the painfully earnest, fun-loving, spiky-headed popsters from Waldorf, Maryland, are not really punk rockers. Sure, they form part of the lineup at the Vans Warped Tour. Sure, they sport technicolour tresses, and a couple of them periodically wear black leather biker jackets to photo shoots. Sure, they know (and sometimes talk about) the life-altering significance of the Ramones, or Minor Threat, or the Clash, and they regularly get called "punk" by mainstream media folks. But they ain't punks.

Ask Joel Madden, one of the twins who founded and front Good Charlotte. He'll tell you. Are Good Charlotte punk? "We're definitely not a punk band," he says. "We love a lot of punk bands, and we're influenced by a lot of different punk bands. But Good Charlotte's never been a straight-ahead punk band." So there.

When Joel—along with guitarist Billy Martin and bassist Paul Thomas—arrives backstage, accompanied by assorted handlers and hangers-on, he and the others certainly resemble punks. Pale and tattooed, they look like they haven't had three squares in their entire twenty-something lives. But instead of launching a barrage of cuss words in the direction of the old fart doing the interview (as the Sex Pistols did, famously, to Bill Grundy on the *Today* show circa December 1976), and instead of firing off a phlegm rocket at whomever happens to be nearby (like the Damned's Rat Scabies used to, with gusto, also back in 1976)—they offer gentle handshakes as they slide into plastic patio chairs. And friendly smiles. Smiles!

Joel, twenty-five, is about 5'9" and could easily pass for sixteen. Billy, the youngest at twenty-two, stands closer to six feet, and tonight favours a dark skinhead kind of look. Paul, meanwhile, is all of twenty-three and sports a ball cap. And says precious little.

They are exceedingly (and depressingly) polite and thoughtful. They don't throw the patio chairs around or get their security guys to punch me out—even when they hear the "Are you punk?" question for the zillionth time. They don't even roll their eyes. They've been on the receiving end of that particular query more times than they'd like—they told *Rolling Stone,* in a cover story a while back, that everyone asks them that—but they answer the question patiently. Nicely. Even when I try to provoke them a little bit, because it would make for a better story.

Nope—looking at them, listening to them, it is exceedingly difficult to picture Good Charlotte shooting out TV screens (as Elvis did), or rolling in glass and smearing themselves with peanut butter (as Iggy Pop did), or doing bad things with pieces of fish and compliant groupies (as Led Zeppelin did—allegedly). You just can't. They're too fucking nice to be punks. The entirety of their repertoire, in fact, seems to be directed at making their many fans feel good.

So, ipso facto, can Good Charlotte be blamed for killing off punk rock—for turning it into what it has largely become: homogenized, sterilized, white suburban frat boy pop? A bunch of bands who wouldn't know political commitment if it bit them on the arse? A bunch of bands who think it's funny, in Joe Strummer's immortal phrase, turning rebellion into money? Like, say, the cynical old men in Offspring? Like the cynical old dowagers fronting the Jurassic Park iteration of Blondie, who claimed to be punks but never were?

Well, actually, no. Because Good Charlotte have always been clear about what they are, and what they aren't. Joel says, "We have a lot of freedom being in this band. 'Cause we can do whatever we want. People are going to hear a lot of different things on our records. You either love us or you hate us."

At the start, there wasn't much of either—there was mainly profound indifference. Formed by Joel and his slightly beefier twin brother, Benji, in 1996, while they still attended La Plata High School (Class of '97), on the outskirts of their hometown, the band-to-be was characterized by a lot of ambition and—dare we say it—a lot of heart.

They came by it honestly, it should be said, and not without a lot of actual pain. On Christmas Eve, 1995, their father (who they freely describe as a drunk and a bully) abandoned Joel, Benji, their mother and two other siblings. He left, slamming the door, never to come back. His wife and children were evicted from their home and forced to accept charity from relatives and others. Their mother, meanwhile, was repeatedly hospitalized with debilitating lupus.

Joel and Benji—who thereafter assumed their mother's surname, wanting no further acknowledgement of their father's existence—took a succession of dead-end, minimum-wage jobs at their local mall, the St. Charles Towne Center. After seeing the Beastie Boys perform in early 1996, the Madden twins were determined to form a rock 'n' roll band, one that would eventually bear the name of Good Charlotte, taken from a distantly remembered children's book.

The band's founding lineup (the Maddens, guitarist Martin and bassist Thomas) attended La Plata High. Following graduation in June 1997, and a pilgrimage to the fabled Gilman Street punk club in San Francisco, the band started gigging relentlessly in and around Waldorf. In December 1999, the group was invited to play a showcase in New York City. A deal was signed with Epic five months later; their eponymous first album debuted in September of that same year.

Their approach to their music was established early on. Encouraged by their high school music teacher in their junior and senior years, Benji and Joel had started writing songs with lots of punk-style rhythms and major chords. And lots of punk-style honesty about the troubles that beset their family—most often with what Joel admits is an "embarrassing" degree of candour and detail. Here's a sampling from "Little Things," one of the band's biggest hits to date:

> *Like the time Mom went to that institute, 'cause she was*
> *breaking down . . .*
> *Like the car we had that wouldn't start, we had to walk to get*
> *around . . .*
> *And that same year on Christmas Eve, Dad went to the*
> *store . . .*
> *We checked his room, his things were gone, we didn't see him*
> *no more . . .*

Asked about his willingness to write lyrics about so many intimate details of their lives, Joel shrugs. "With me, when I write, it's almost like a page out of a journal. Sometimes I hear the songs and get a little red-faced because it's personal shit . . . A lot of the lyrics and the ideas for the songs are mine. A lot of it is me. The shit we're been through and all that. I think that, on some of the songs, all of us as a band can relate to the words." The others nod.

Martin adds, "A lot of our stuff comes from similar experiences. We live together all the time. We try to be there for each other. We're friends."

The most extraordinary example of Good Charlotte's willingness to plumb the depths of Middle America's dysfunctionality—and their own, perhaps—is "Head On." If Good Charlotte requires redemption by the rock 'n' roll gods (although, if even half of their life story is true, they don't), then "Hold On" provides it. From their gazillion-copy-selling album *The Young and the Hopeless,* the song—and the video that promotes it—is a brutally frank examination of teen suicide (which, the Centers for Disease Control tells us, kills more people than homicide, by a long shot):

This world, this world is cold
But you don't, you don't have to go
You're feeling sad, you're feeling lonely
And no one seems to care
Your mother's gone and your father hits you
The pain you cannot bear . . .
Hold on, if you feel like letting go
Hold on, it gets better than you know . . .

Joel says, "It's controversial, because people don't want to hear about that stuff." "Happy," says Thomas, sneering like the punk he says he isn't. "Yeah, exactly," adds Joel. "And that's not how the world is, I think. In America, sometimes people totally ignore that stuff. So they need to have it put right in front of their faces."

The video certainly does that. In it, Bob Burt, a retired school athletics coach, cries as he recalls his nineteen-year-old daughter, who killed herself with a deliberate drug overdose. Says Burt, "It's not the right order of things. You're not supposed to bury your children. They're supposed to bury you." He pleads with young people thinking seriously about suicide—and the Centers for Disease Control says one out of four do—to get help.

In another jarring scene from the video, twenty-four-year-old Daphne Dachstbani describes what is left of her life after her boyfriend, with whom she lived, killed himself. "I knew he was depressed, but he was scared to get help," she says. "Well, now it's too late."

Good Charlotte made the video with the direct involvement of the American Foundation for Suicide Prevention. The organization carefully reviewed the Maddens' lyrics before agreeing to offer their expertise. And they were impressed, apparently. Unlike many rock acts, it was clear that Good Charlotte had no interest in making suicide seem in any way cool.

The rest of us should be impressed too, quite frankly. They may be cute, and cuddly, and anything but punk. They may be polite to a fault. They may be, God forbid, a nice bunch of youngsters who want to make their fans happy. But it's apparent that Good Charlotte's willingness to confront their demons in public—as they do in "Hold On"—is a good thing. Following its release, the band received dozens of letters from kids who had reconsidered suicide, and sought help, after seeing the video. What other band can say such that?

"As a band, we sat down, and we said that if the song saves one life, the whole record is worth it," Madden says. "It's worth it for one kid's life, isn't it? Our purpose, the reason why we think we're here on earth, is to make some kid's life better. You know what I mean?"

I do. It ain't necessarily punk, but that's okay.

—

The apostate punks who embraced fun—the ones who thought it was okay to dance—were not the only ones who fell away from the Punk Rock Catechism and thereby earned the disdain of the punk purists. There were also the punks who turned Stiff Records' famous phrase on its head, and in effect declared: "Fuck dancing, let's do art!" They weren't always angry or political, and they weren't typically having fun and dancing a lot, either: they were the artsy ones, the punks who saw punk as synonymous with experimentation. To them, punk was a formless form, or expression without limits. It was art.

There are tons of bands and artists in this category, which is why the Subway Sect, Public Image Ltd. and Wire deserve a bit of scrutiny. Because, amongst the arty punks, the Subway Sect, Public Image Ltd. and Wire were simply the best.

Public Image Ltd., despite the corporate affectation, was really the property of only one person: Johnny Rotten, who in 1978 quit the Sex Pistols and returned to calling himself John Lydon. Following the anarchic collapse of the Pistols' disastrous January 1978 tour of America, Lydon was livid. He sulked for a while in New York, and Jamaica, and then London. He wanted to condemn the Pistols and everything they had become, but Lydon was also determined to condemn rock 'n' roll itself. Disappearing from public view was not an option: he had become too famous, and he still had too much to say. Simply carrying on and forming another punk band was also impossible: too many other artists tried to do that, post-breakup, and they inevitably ended up looking like pathetic shadows of their former selves. Lydon embraced a third option— forming a "band" that really wasn't.

So Public Image Ltd.—or PIL, as they were often known—set about irritating as many people as it could. Joined by his old schoolmate Jah Wobble (né John Wardle) and former Clash guitarist Keith Levene, John Lydon and PIL became infamous for playing entire concerts behind screens, or with their backs turned to the audience, or both. For refusing to play for more than thirty minutes. For playing the same songs more than once in the same set. And

Lydon, naturally, did his level best to anger even his most devoted fans—most often through insults flung from the stage.

As maddening as they were, as pretentious as they could be, PIL were also impressive. Their first single, "Public Image," contained a riff so catchy that U2 stole it for their own first single ("I Will Follow"). PIL's first album, also called *Public Image*, contained a number of dub-heavy "songs" that stomped all over the traditional verse-chorus-verse-chorus-verse structure of every other rock 'n' roll (and punk) composition in the universe. A good example of this was found in "Religion," which featured Lydon's voice, and no instrumentation whatsoever: "Do you pray to the Holy Ghost when you suck your host/ Do you read who's dead in the Irish Post/ Do you give away the cash you can't afford/ On bended knees and pray to Lord/ Fat pig priest, sanctimonious smiles/ He takes the money, you take the lies."

Their second album, *Metal Box,* was fucking revolutionary: inside a stamped film canister, three twelve-inch discs contained some of the most original and creative music any punk had ever produced. One hit single from the album, "Death Disco," chronicled the death of Lydon's mother due to cancer (following her death, Lydon was crippled with grief and disappeared into Toronto's suburbs for many days, mourning his loss while living with his mother's sister). Following *Metal Box,* PIL went through a seemingly endless number of lineup changes. Its music was changing all the time, too: sometimes atonal chanting, sometimes catchy pop tunes. The only constant, it seemed, was Lydon's presence.

Lydon, typically, refuses to allow Public Image Ltd. to be categorized: the venture, he says, was deliberately designed to resist the sort of pigeon-holing that rock critics and fans do too often. "There's been many guises of PIL," he says during his Toronto visit. "It would be too difficult to pick one particular period [that was my favourite].

"I don't really write music, really. I'm into everything. There are certain songs I wrote while in PIL that the Pistols would have never touched. 'Religion' and things like that. And so I keep moving on."

Wire had the same attitude. Formed in the original punk wave in 1976, Wire were—at the start—bona fide punks. The band comprised Colin Newman on vocals and guitar; Bruce Gilbert, also on guitar; Graham Lewis, on bass and occasional vocals; and drummer Robert Gotobed. They made their London debut in December 1976, and then started capturing attention with shows at the Roxy. Signed by Harvest Records, Wire set about recording what remains one of the best punk albums ever, *Pink Flag*. The album features twenty-one songs in just thirty-five minutes, some of them just a few seconds long. More than half of the album's songs, in fact, whip past in less than ninety seconds. *Pink Flag*—stripped down, raw and immensely tuneful—became one of the most influential albums to come out of the punk era. Its songs have been covered by everyone from Ian MacKaye's Minor Threat to REM, and flat-out copied by Elastica. Wire seemed destined for great success.

And then, abruptly, dramatically, Wire changed course. The band became idiosyncratic, complicated and, incredibly, *arty*. One year after the 1977 release of *Pink Flag*, the band produced *Chairs Missing*—and, the year after that, *154*. Not only were *Chairs Missing* and *154* different, the albums sounded like they had been recorded by completely different *bands*. On *154*, Wire offered up songs such as "A Touching Display" (seven minutes of echo-laden droning that challenged even the most die-hard fan) and "A Mutual Friend" (which, among other things, didn't even accommodate a 4/4 drumbeat). The two LPs, while brilliant, seemed determined to reject every punk convention.

But Newman, like Lydon, cheerfully dismisses the notion that Wire is even a band. "We were all friends when we started," he says. "At the moment, it's just an umbrella, really. If you have been doing this for years, like we have, it's normal for various people to go off on various tangents."

Pressed about the astonishing change of sound found on *154*, and how it seemed to be a conscious rejection of punk, Newman muses. Most of the album's subversive sounds, he says, are due to him. "There's quite a lot of me on *154*," says Newman. "It's a much more baroque album; there are many more layers to it . . . we have moved so far away from [the art school categorization], now. We don't ever really seriously gravitate in one way or another. We don't like labels."

No kidding. During an interview, I point out to Newman (as it has been pointed out to him and his colleagues before) that if Wire stuck with the sort of simple, catchy punk tunes found on *Pink Flag*, they would have become extraordinarily rich. After all, REM made the band a small fortune with its cover of "Strange," from the first Wire LP. Hasn't Newman been tempted to dispense with the artiness and make a bundle of loot, as so many others have done? Newman laughs. "I don't really care about it, one way or another," he says. "I've got no axe to grind. I'm not going to tell [other bands] what they should be doing—it's really up to them, isn't it? But I know what you're saying. My dad is always saying the same thing!"

Vic Godard's Subway Sect ended up charting a similarly arty course, but less deliberately than John Lydon or Colin Newman. Formed with the encouragement of Sex Pistols manager Malcolm McLaren in London in 1976, the Subway Sect were unlike their contemporaries from the outset. Not only could they not play their instruments, they didn't actually *possess* any instruments. Where the Clash and the Sex Pistols dressed in the most colourful, outrageous clothing they could find (or create), Godard and his pals favoured hues of grey—even showing up for gigs wearing bland V-neck sweaters. And, while most punks were writing tunes that could be as melodic as those by ABBA (whom many of them, from the Pistols to the Ramones, secretly adored), the Subway Sect distinguished itself with a sound that was a cacophonous crescendo of clutter.

The band's personnel included Godard on vocals, Rob Simmons on guitar, Paul Myers on bass and Paul Packham on drums. They made their live debut in September 1976, backing the Pistols at the 100 Club Punk Festival. The gig was to be the Subway Sect's first; they were invited to play because, band leader Vic Godard says in an interview, Malcolm McLaren had met them at his clothing shop, and he liked them. They dyed their clothing grey.

The unique way in which the Subway Sect were granted an opportunity to play at the 100 Club festival demonstrates how fully Malcolm McLaren was in control of the scene in those days, quaint theories about anarchy notwithstanding. Godard says, "We went to McLaren's office, and then we all went on this two-mile walk. McLaren sort of questioned us about everything—you know, music, what do we listen to and all that. He was into the same sort of stuff as us, except he was really into the Doors, and we didn't like them at all. But that was the only thing we disagreed on." McLaren paid for a rental space for the Subway Sect, around the corner from his shop, and told the band he would come by after a week and decide if they would be invited to join the bill at the festival. The Sect practised from eight in the morning until seven at night, every day, for a week.

"So I remember on the Friday, we were really nervous 'cause we thought, you know, this is it. And, I mean, we were awful. Absolutely awful. Really awful. But he must have liked the lyrics. And he said, 'Yeah, you're alright. But you need more rehearsals.'" McLaren arranged for the fledgling band to practise at the Clash's space until the 100 Club gig, which they did daily until September 20. Stepping onstage, the Sect were all chewing gum. Caroline Coon, a sometimes-journalist and a charter member of the Pistols' retinue, described the Sect's first performance in this way: "Their sound is a grind of frantic, jagged dischords which, whether by chance or design, mostly resolve into acceptable patterns of unadorned simplicity." Whatever the fuck *that* means.

Godard recalls, "I just couldn't wait to get [offstage]. I wanted to, like, disband the group immediately after that. But that wasn't even our worst gig!" In the living room of his comfortable ground floor flat in Richmond, Surrey, Godard—who is self-deprecating and extremely generous with his time—says the ubiquitous Bernie Rhodes offered to manage the band after he saw their "performance" at the punk festival. That relationship provided them with a weekly wage of £15, practice time at the Clash's Rehearsal Rehearsals space and, later, a coveted spot on the White Riot tour.

Melody Maker's Coon, who knew Godard and his chums well at the start, attempts to characterize the Subway Sect's approach to music and performance: "They are unique and well-respected for the strange, avant-garde quality of the absurd in their sound—which they aptly describe as 'complete noise.' [They] are an unpenetrable [*sic*] unit, deadpan, grave and shy . . . Over the months, it has become possible to determine vestigial melodies in their music. A mine of talent."

Advised of that assessment, Godard—who now earns a living as a postal worker—has a good laugh. "When we started, we didn't want to just copy the Sex Pistols," he says. "But we thought that because they had been able to get up on stage . . . well, they could, so we could, too. Now, I'm not trying to slam it, that sort of very loud, power-chord kind of music—I mean, we *liked* them. But that wasn't really what we *liked,* you know?" The sound they wanted to emulate, Godard says, was that of the Velvet Underground and former Modern Lover Jonathan Richman—quieter, unstructured, off-the-wall kind of stuff.

It wasn't a conscious attempt to be different just for the sake of being different. Godard and the other members of the Subway Sect believed that the "punk" moniker the press had affixed to the fledgling movement was completely mistaken—not for the term, but for the notion that so many different musical approaches could be regarded as part of a single, similar sound. "The Clash were nothing like the Sex Pistols, who were nothing like the Buzzcocks, who were nothing like Siouxsie and the Banshees, who were nothing like us," he says. "So, I mean, although we were all lumped together, there was basically no order or similarity in that group of groups. There's just too many differences between them. Yet they were all lumped together into one thing."

Their minor hit, "Ambition," amply proves Godard's point. In the song, Godard insisted upon taping the ping-pong sound of tennis balls—along with a bizarre keyboard riff that was completely unlike anything else being done by his punk contemporaries. Admittedly, "Ambition" is a catchy pop song, but it is also wildly incompatible with the aggressive sounds being churned out by everyone else in the first British punk wave.

Godard, who eventually led the Subway Sect into playing jazz, swing, skiffle, Northern Soul, and a lot less rock 'n' roll, says, "We split up, we got together, we started doing all kinds of different music. I just accepted this much more broad musical thing . . . I mean, look at all of the groups that did stay together. Groups like the Ramones kept just turning out albums, and I just didn't want to be like that, sounding the same all the time. That's not growing.

"Punk was the do-it-yourself type thing, where you just don't know absolutely anything, but you get up there and have a go at it. That's my view. So, follow those punk dreams, people!"

From the age of fourteen, Jimmy Pursey used to go to discotheques. He was a regular. On one particular night, Jimmy got very drunk, crawled up onstage and started miming to a couple of Rolling Stones songs. "Well," says Jimmy, in his near-impenetrable accent, "the geezer who ran the gaff really liked it, so . . ." The gig became a regular thing; Pursey formed a band. He picked the name, he says, during a bowel movement—or, as he puts it, "after having a toilet at a football match." There on the wall of the stall, someone had celebrated the winning 1969 season of his hometown football team, Hersham. All that remained, however, was SHAM 69. Seemed like as good a name as any, so Pursey took it. Formed in 1975, the most memorable Sham 69 lineup played its first gig at the Roxy in London in 1976.

At Sham gigs, it was always Pursey that everyone watched. As *NME*'s Tony Parsons wrote, in August 1977, "Jimmy Pursey of Sham 69 is A Star. Hardly anyone has heard of him or his band, he doesn't get interviewed by *Vogue* or *Sunday Times Magazine* . . . Nevertheless, Jimmy Pursey of Sham 69 is A Star. I don't want to make this sound like I-have-seen-the-future-of-rock'n'roll-etcetera, but Jimmy Pursey of Sham 69 is one of those people who live their life in a state of constant conflict with any lifeless, soulless, joyless Established Order with which they come in contact. He's A Star because—and this may be cliché but it's totally apt—you can't ignore him, you can't forget him, and you can't help but react."

In performance, Sham 69 were powerful, incendiary, passionate like many punk bands wanted to be, but never could be. Those who saw the band onstage still say—more than two decades later—that Sham 69 were the greatest live performers in the history of rock 'n' roll. But, like the star Parsons likened him to, Pursey burned with a bright intensity and then slipped away, refusing to perform live because too many neo-Nazi skinheads were showing up, attracted by Sham's macho, working-class style (a fact that disgusted and troubled him for years after the fact). And, as Parsons also noted, Sham were indeed in a prolonged state of disagreement with the established political order. This was reflected in some of their best-known anthems, such as "If the Kids Are United," "Angels with Dirty Faces," and "Unite and Win."

But Sham 69 were about fun, too. Some of Pursey's most memorable contributions to punk were funny, colourful snapshots of working-class life that were about drinking, fighting and chasing girls—songs such as "Sunday Morning Nightmare" and "Hersham Boys." Some of his songs, such as "Hurry Up Harry," were laugh-out-loud funny. Jimmy Pursey, punk philosopher and poet, is therefore uniquely qualified to adjudicate the unanswerable, eternal question of punk rock: punk is certainly political, and it probably isn't arty. So is punk still punk if it's *fun?*

Pursey has an accent so thick and a delivery that's so fast that it's impossible to keep up without a good tape recorder and a lot of detailed notes. "Punk, really, was a coat hanger, rather than the actual clothing," he says. "In other words, if you look at it like that, you can take a coat hanger and hang whatever you want on it. It was the bare essentials, do you understand?"

Pursey has heard all about Blink-182 and Green Day and Good Charlotte and the scores of other acts that are mostly about having a good time. Asked to pass judgment on them, he doesn't even need to think about the answer. He leaps right in. "I think they're legitimate, do you understand? It's the skateboarding curriculum, or the skateboarding attitude that they've got. It's a bit like punk, but their roots are more rock 'n' roll. They're taking the sound from punk, as a musical form, rather the political form, or the stance that punk had. That's all they basically boil down to, and I've got no grudge about it."

Jimmy Pursey doesn't necessarily listen to any of the new punk-pop bands, but he refuses to dismiss them. "Those bands, at least they're playing with a bit of attitude. And, even if it's pop, it's better to play pop with an attitude. Green Day was the first of the Blink-182s, and so on and so on. They're transparent about who they are, and there's nuthin' wrong with that. Nuthin' at all, mate!"

THERE IS A FUTURE
(or, punk will never die!)

Even John Lydon—even Johnny Rotten, for Chrissakes, the punk who famously howled in "God Save the Queen" that there was "no future" for him, you or anyone else—agrees: there is, indeed, a future! There is meaning! There is opportunity! *There is a future you can create, maaaan!*

Slouched at his podium, pale, sickly, smoking in a no-smoking room, he hisses, "There are no rules, other than don't step on anyone, and don't hurt anyone." He squints. He glowers at the front row. He points at an adoring fan, who is clearly thrilled to be threatened in a room full of complete strangers. "But if you get in my way, you're going to have a serious bad time. I couldn't give *two fucks*. Makes no difference. I'll do what I want to do, anyway."

He pauses for dramatic effect, although it's totally unnecessary.

He already *is* dramatic. "That sort of spirit is what is missing . . . You have to do it yourself. You really have to. You have to get out of bed in the morning."

Pause. Drag on cigarette. Scowl. "Well, some of us do."

It's not conventional punk, admitting that there is a future. Rotten/Lydon doesn't want to come right out and admit that he is an optimist, but the fact is, he *is* one. On this day, his every word, his every pause, his every expletive, subtly suggests that he values life—his and others', too—and that he believes Anger Is Energy and Do It Yourself aren't just some minor, forgettable punk rock subculture bullshit slogans. They are ways to live your life. They are ways to make things a bit better.

His pal Sid Vicious chose to return to the heroin womb through the eye of a needle, and he killed himself (and Nancy Spungen) in the process. Too many young punks think that Sid Vicious was the Ultimate Punk, but they are mistaken. Sid Vicious—in his swastika T-shirts, with his spindly stick-arms littered with track marks, the girl he stabbed to death a jumble on the floor by the dirty toilet in the next room—was the one who really, truly believed there was no future, at least in respect to himself. He *murdered* it. He therefore missed out on a million great songs, and a million amazing new bands, and even a few pints with his mates. Forget about romantic sunsets and children playing in the park: Sid Vicious lost his shot at the future, and there's nothing fucking worse than that. Punk or no punk.

The future ain't dead, and neither is punk. Herewith, the views and insights of the ones that know—the punk pioneers, the new punks—about punk's meaning, punk's promise and punk's future. And, at the same time, some words about the Perfect Punk: the legend who most believed in fighting for the future. And, following this chapter, the Top Ten Punk Albums, Top Ten Punk Singles and Top Ten Categories of Punk Writings. In no particular order.

Give him the last word, and Johnny Rotten/John Lydon sniffs. He looks like he is about to spit, but he refrains, just this once.

"Anything I say, I *mean*," he growls, then he grins, like a fiend from the Ninth Circle of Hell.

"We mean it, maaaan!"

Glen Matlock, the Sex Pistols: "I always found Joe [Strummer] a very affable sort of guy. I got on fine with Joe. But there was always kind of a friendly band rivalry there. Just one thing I would say against him, even though he's not with us anymore . . . We just found the politics with the Clash a bit hokey, you know."

Pause. "But they were still good. Better than the Backstreet Boys!"

The Pacific National Exhibition (PNE), at one corner of Vancouver's dirty, dingy, dangerous East Side, is basically an old barn hammered together in the early part of the last century to host agricultural exhibitions. In 1957, Elvis Presley performed there; in 1964, the Beatles did. After one infamous Rolling Stones show in July 1966, a Vancouver newspaper reported, "Thirty-six teenagers were carried from an auditorium here Tuesday after a disturbance broke out during a performance by the British rock and roll musical group the Rolling Stones. Eleven youngsters were held in temporary custody in a detention room at the Pacific National Exhibition Forum during the show. Two were charged with being drunk. Police said a policeman was kicked in the groin, an usher suffered a concussion when hit by a youth, a policewoman collapsed from exhaustion and a youth suffered a broken ankle during the show. Officers said a number of hysterical girls had to be carried over a riot fence between the audience and the performers." A broken *ankle!* A spell of *exhaustion!* Goodness gracious!

While it may once have been something magnificent, by 1979 the PNE was a dank, smelly shithole. On this night, October 16, 1979—and as per the Clash B-side titled "1977"—there are no more Elvis, Beatles or Rolling Stones in evidence. And very few of the many, many police officers present look preoccupied with minor crap like broken ankles or bouts of exhaustion. As they glance here and there, plainly nervous, the cops seem much more concerned about survival—*personal* survival—and little else. The gates to the PNE are swarming with thousands of punks and aspiring punks from all over the western Canadian provinces and American states. Some of the concertgoers look completely ridiculous—punk wannabes sporting Sex Pistols T-shirts and moustaches, what Vancouver punk Buck Cherry suggests is the punk rock equivalent of an oxymoron—but most of the others are the real article, real punks. Some of them look like they are capable of killing someone with the sort of deliberation normal people reserve for flicking on a light switch. A few of them look like they *have* killed someone. It is, accordingly, a wonderful, glorious punk rock night.

Let me explain. At the mainstream rock 'n' roll gigs of the era—at, say, Rolling Stones shows—there is always the smell of dope wafting through the air, and lots of mellow, well-behaved, long-haired fans, sit in the seats to which they have been assigned. Smiling. Singing along. Sharing gourds of wine.

It's enough to make you puke.

At the best punk gigs—at *this* punk gig in particular, which is the biggest ever in Vancouver and possibly on the Northwest coast—the air is heavy with menace, but not much in the way of marijuana or hashish smoke. The drugs of choice here are cheap beer and speed—and lots of it. Accordingly, there is a thick vein of violence pulsating just below the surface, and it has everyone feeling like something *bad* is about to happen, at any moment, in an explosion of blood and sweat and spit. It feels like someone could reach out in the dark and plunge a knife in your back. Which, in a peculiarly punk way, has a tendency to make you feel more *alive*. It's a lot of fun when you get used to it, actually.

Everywhere you look, there are punks—punks in biker jackets, punks with tattoos, punks in chains, punks with safety pins gouging skin that looks abscessed. More punks, in fact, than any of the North

American punks present have seen in one place at one time. Between moments of unease, and flashes of panic, it feels like an historic night is unfolding. It feels electric. It feels like the ideal night for a show by the Clash, the biggest fucking punk rock band in the world. The Clash! *The Clash! Here!*

From their first incendiary album in 1977 (on which they raged against racism, youth unemployment and the hippies who frequented Rolling Stones shows) to their final waxing as the real Clash in 1982 (the cartoonish *Combat Rock,* which signalled the end was near, and appropriately so), the Clash were the most important punk band. The Sex Pistols were more famous; the Ramones invented the genre. But the Clash were, just as the record company sticker declared on the front of *London Calling,* THE ONLY BAND THAT MATTERS.

The Clash were political and idealistic; they were unrelentingly angry and loud; most of all, they were smarter and more hopeful than the other punk groups, the cynical, nihilistic ones like the Pistols. They believed in upsetting the status quo. They believed in peace, and anti-racism, and the power of words. They believed the future was worth fighting for. They believed in the power of *belief,* if that makes any sense at all.

The Clash were the ones who actually read books—and encouraged their fans to read them, too. They wrote songs that emphasized that politics were important (and, for me, at least, the Clash made it clear that fighting intolerance and conservatives, and maintaining a capacity for outrage, was always worthwhile). They demanded your attention. They were the first punk band to attempt to unify disparate cultures—for example, introducing choppy reggae and ska and bluebeat rhythms to their music. They were the first (and the only) band that sought to be the biggest and the most radical band at the same time—and they somehow made those two contradictory objectives work.

While political, they also knew how to put together a good, solid punk tune (or a reggae tune, or a dub tune, or even a rhythm and blues number). At the centre of the Clash were Joe Strummer and Mick Jones, who effectively became the punk world's Lennon and McCartney, churning out a lot of big hits in Britain and a few in North America, and attracting favourable critical acclaim everywhere. Some of their singles, "White Man in Hammersmith Palais" and "Complete Control," are among the best rock 'n' roll 45s ever. Their double *London Calling* LP is regularly cited as one of history's best rock albums.

They weren't perfect, naturally. Their dalliances with rebel movements such as the Sandinistas, circa 1980, smacked of showy dilettante politics. Towards the end, they seemed to lose some sense of their original mission statement (particularly when Strummer and Simonon fired Jones). But they weren't afraid to take risks and make mistakes.

They were human, which made us love them even more.

Jimmy Pursey, Sham 69: "When you start to notice your compatriots going down, it's a bit like being in the First World War. One minute, you're having a cup of tea with somebody, and the next minute they're dead. After you have been with them for God knows how long. And it's a very similar circumstance. In other words, you become quite shell-shocked for a while. Joe, he lived through that particular six months . . . And that's all punk was. It was just six months in the summer of '77."

Joe Strummer was born John Graham Mellor in August 1952, in Ankara, Turkey. His father was Ronald R. Mellor, a clerical officer for the British Foreign Office; his mother was Anne Girvan McKenzie— known as Anna—a nurse and the daughter of a Scottish farmer.

Ronald Mellor's parents, who had worked for the colonial railway in India, died in an auto accident in 1922, and Ronald was placed in an orphanage. Like his youngest son, John, would be,

Ronald was driven to succeed, and he earned himself scholarships that led to college and university degrees. After the Second World War, he joined Britain's civil service. As Second Secretary in various foreign missions, he led his wife—and sons, David and John—to postings in Cyprus, Cairo, Mexico and West Germany. Along the way, John paid attention to the local cultures and developed an intense interest in a wide range of musical styles.

In September 1961, when he was eight years old, John and his brother were placed in the City of London Freemen's School (CLFS), in Ashtead Park, Surrey. Such "public schools" are in fact independent and private, and charge for tuition. The two Mellor boys were among fifty or so who boarded at the school. In later years, John Mellor's detractors would inevitably note that he was the son of a foreign service officer, and that he had attended an elite private school. In fact, his father—of whom he was fiercely proud— was not particularly senior within the foreign service, and CLFS was made affordable for the Mellors only because the Foreign Service paid the tuition for John and his brother.

John Mellor was intensely bright. He loved movies and books and TE Lawrence, and he achieved three A levels in English, history and art. By his own recollection, he spent most of his hours reading. He also listened to music with his CLFS pal Paul Buck, who would go on to become Pablo LaBritain, drummer for the punk band 999. The pair favoured Captain Beefheart, the Kinks, the Who, the Pretty Things, Yardbirds, Dr. Feelgood, Lou Reed and Bo Diddley. John would listen to his favourites in his room at night, a tiny, tinny transistor radio pressed to his ear. In the late sixties, John Mellor became a prefect at CLFS—one of the older boys who had their own room and kept the younger ones in line. Unlike the other prefects, John Mellor was not cruel; instead, he had a reputation for a bizarre sense of humour, forcing younger students to sing Rolling Stones tunes as punishment for their various transgressions. On some days, tellingly, he would wear a T-shirt with a heart on it. IN CASE OF EMERGENCY, it read, TEAR OUT.

David Mellor, tragically, did not fare as well as his younger brother. After leaving CLFS in 1967, David grew increasingly lonely and isolated from his peers. He started to dabble in the occult and far-right politics, and even joined the National Front. In July 1970, he crawled under a bush in London's Regent's Park, swallowed more than a hundred aspirin and other medications, and died. In the succeeding years, his younger brother would rarely mention the tragedy. In one interview with *NME* in 1977, he remarked, grimly, "Suicide was the only way out for him."

For his part, John Mellor had too much that he wanted to do with his life. In 1968, when he was sixteen or so, he decided to try his hand at guitar. He acquired one from a cousin and strummed away. The first song he could play, legend goes, was Chuck Berry's "Sweet Little Sixteen." John wasn't bad, but he would later acknowledge that he was a better artist. Following his graduation from CLFS, John decided he wanted to be a cartoonist. He enrolled at the London Central School of Art, and lasted about a week. Woody Guthrie, he later recalled, helped him beat the boredom. Sharing living space with a few other art school students, John Mellor met a fiddler (Tymon Dogg, who many, many years later would join Strummer in his post-Clash band, the Mescaleros), and the pair decided to busk in the London Underground tunnels near Green Park. John—now sometimes referring to himself as Woody Mellor in trubute to his folkie hero—played ukelele. In this, his first paying gig, he scored £1.99.

Expelled from art school, evicted from a squat that had become home (his record collection was tossed out a window by the authorities), John spent the next two years doing what he later described as "absolutely nothing." When he needed money, he took on odd jobs at farms outside the city. Early in 1973, John followed a girlfriend to South East Wales, where she was studying. In Newport, he found a flat with art student Mickey Foote, a future Clash soundman, and occasionally attended lectures at Newport College of Art. To make money, he dug graves for the local municipality at Newport Cemetery. In 1970, he formed his first band, called the Vultures. Mellor was regarded as a charismatic front man, but the Vultures were not as good (*Melody Maker* later described them as "an erratic but occasionally stunning formation that played a handful of gigs before sinking without trace"), so, in May 1974, John Mellor gave up on Wales and moved back to London, and more busking with Tymon Dogg. The pair found a squat to live in.

Busking was, once again, an unsuccessful venture—Mellor was detained by the transport police too often—so he took a job moving garbage at the English National Opera. He was fired when he was discovered practising guitar in the orchestra pit. Using the £120 he received following his termination at the Opera, Mellor bought an amplifier. In the same time frame, and not long after his return to London from Wales, John Mellor recruited friends from Maida Hill's squatting community and formed his second band: the 101ers, named after the street address of the gang's squat at 101 Walterton Road. At around this time, John Mellor started to call himself Joe Strummer. He and the 101ers played their first gig at the Brixton Telegraph on September 6, 1974, and became regulars at benefits for members of the Chilean community who had fled a military coup in September 1973.

The 101ers weren't bad. They were regarded as an energetic live act, and they even cut two singles on the respected independent label Chiswick Records, one of them the catchy "Keys to Your Heart." The song was written by Strummer for his girlfriend Paloma Romano, later better known as Palmolive of the Slits.

In early 1975, Strummer got married to a South African woman named Pamela Moolman, so that Moolman could stay in Britain. The story is only relevant because—for his troubles—Strummer received £100, which he used to buy his beloved Fender Telecaster, the one he played in the Clash.

But Strummer was dissatisfied: he saw the 101ers' rhythm and blues repertoire as outdated. On April 3, 1976, he would later say, he received his rock 'n' roll lightning bolt on the road to Damascus: the 101ers were supported at the Nashville by a new group—one that called themselves the Sex Pistols. A few years later, Strummer would tell me the Pistols had been destined to break up; but on that night, the punk band's performance changed Strummer's life.

He made a decision, then and there, to quit the 101ers and join the revolution the Sex Pistols had started. "As soon as I saw them, I knew that rhythm and blues was dead, and that the future was here," said Strummer to Caroline Coon later that year. "But hearing the Pistols, I knew. I just knew. It was just something you knew without bothering to think about it. Punk rock is the music of now."

Tony James, Generation X, Chelsea, London SS: "Mick [Jones] and I started in a band together, and we used to stay in the tower block where his gran lived. We used to go to the local bar, the Windsor Castle, which was only 500 metres away, to see this band playing there, the 101ers. We didn't really truly like them, but we always thought that somehow the singer had something . . ."

London SS, the most famous punk band that never played a gig and never released a record, was variously composed of Tony James, Mick Jones, future Damned guitarist Brian James, future Clash drummer Terry Chimes, future Damned drummer Rat Scabies, future members of the Boys Matt Dangerfield and Casino Steel, and—in its latter stages—Paul Simonon, an art student who was recruited because he had been a skinhead and he looked good. (Not, apparently, for his ability to play bass guitar, which was non-existent.) Acting as de facto manager for the group, and not doing a very good job of it, was former Malcom McLaren associate Bernie Rhodes.

After London SS imploded, Mick Jones decided to teach bass to Simonon, a nineteen-year-old who also came from Brixton. Terry Chimes was recruited to supply beats, and Keith Levene was introduced to Jones and Simonon by Bernie Rhodes. A druggie, and a former teenage roadie for prog rockers Yes, Levene was immediately at odds with Jones. With Rhodes's encouragement, the group (which toyed with names like the Heartdrops, the Phones, the Mirrors, the Outsiders and the Psychotic Negatives) started practising. But they lacked a singer and a front man.

One day in May 1976, as Jones and Simonon were allegedly walking down Golbourn Road (or, depending on who you ask, Portobello Road, Westbourne Grove, Ladbroke Grove or even somewhere in Shepherd's Bush) with the Sex Pistols' Glen Matlock, they bumped into Joe Strummer. "I don't like your group," said Jones. "But we think you're great."

That was all the encouragement Joe Strummer needed. He quit what was left of the 101ers, and joined what was soon to be known as the Clash. How the band eventually got its name is a matter of some dispute: some theorize it was taken from the reggae group Culture's first album, *Two Sevens Clash,* but that record was not released until months *after* the Clash had selected their name. One apocryphal story is most likely the most accurate: Paul Simonon dryly noted that the word "clash" came up regularly in headlines in editions of the *Evening Standard.* The name seemed to fit.

Thereafter, under Rhodes's direction, the Clash threw themselves into two solid months of practising and songwriting. Their first gig happened on July 4, 1976, at the Black Swan in Sheffield. Right from the start, the Clash were compared to the Sex Pistols—who, along with the Buzzcocks and the Subway Sect, were pretty much the only punk bands gigging in Britain. Right from the start, too, the differences between the two bands were apparent: where the Pistols were almost unrelentingly negative and cynical, optimism suffused almost every song the Clash wrote. Where the Pistols were disinterested in their audiences, virtually to the point of contempt, the Clash always seemed determined to put on a good show and make their fans feel welcome. Where the post-Matlock Pistols were more about shock, and less about musical ability, the

Clash (particularly Topper Headon) were better musicians. Where the Pistols were no future, the Clash were all future. They could not have been more different: the Clash had *beliefs*.

The precise point at which the Clash stopped being just another punk band and became something special is open for debate. But something clicked for them around the time of the Notting Hill riots in August 1976. Joe Strummer and his new band had been practising for a few weeks, and had not, to that point, distinguished themselves as full-time, committed political activists; Strummer had had some involvement with causes considered important by the squatting community of which he had been part—like squatting—but that was about it. He was not, as he would later concede, a professional revolutionary. Mostly, he was a musician who aspired to be revolutionary.

The Notting Hill Carnival in West London was an annual celebration of Caribbean culture, and an innocuous affair—until a group of police officers attempted to arrest a young man on Portobello Road for picking pockets. Several passersby attempted to come to the aid of the suspect, who happened to be black. A fight broke out. By the time the resulting riots had petered out, more than two hundred carnival-goers and police officers had been hospitalized, an impressive amount of property had been damaged, and Joe Strummer, Bernie Rhodes and Paul Simonon (who had observed some of the rioting, and some of the police response) were politicized. The events at Notting Hill, they later said, were key to their political awakening; as if to emphasize the point, a photograph of dozens of white police officers chasing a small group of black protestors was placed on the back of their extraordinary first album. Their combustible first single, "White Riot," described Strummer's feelings about the Notting Hill clash.

But it's too easy, and too simplistic, to overstate the significance of a single event; after all, in the world they lived in, there was plenty to arouse the Clash's sense of political outrage—or anyone else's. In the summer of 1976, the daily life of too many young people in Great

Britain was characterized by the consequences of race riots, inflation, currency crises, police brutality and massive unemployment. The response of rock 'n' roll? "Tie a Yellow Ribbon 'Round the Ole Oak Tree," by Tony Orlando and Dawn, or "Disco Duck," by Rick Dees.

The Clash's first album contained fury and hope in equal measure. It was, and is, wondrous. It wasn't about some distant, mythical world inhabited by millionaires and models; it was about the real world, and real-world problems, occupied by real people— people who, like the members of the Clash, received £9.70 a week on the dole. It didn't lie—it was honest.

The album was recorded at the CBS studios on Whitfield Street in February 1977, with Terry Chimes as a session drummer (he had drifted away from the band, in part because he was disinterested in the increasing political focus of Strummer, Jones, Simonon and manager Bernie Rhodes)—and *without* Keith Levene (who had also been scornful of the political focus, and of the band's willingness to adhere to traditional rock 'n' roll approaches to songwriting). The signing of the Clash to CBS in January 1977 was, to many punks, a political act in itself: the anti-capitalist punk group entering into a contractual relationship with a media conglomerate, for a reported £100,000. *Sniffin' Glue*'s Mark Perry famously remarked, "Punk rock died the day the Clash signed to CBS." (Despite that, Mark Perry called the first Clash album, duly released by CBS, "the most important album ever released.")

The album was recorded over three consecutive Thursday-to-Saturday sessions commencing in mid-February 1977. When the tape was rolling, Joe Strummer had trouble supplying the vocal track for the music that had been previously recorded: he had to be holding his guitar when he sang, because it made the process more real to him. If you listen carefully to some of the tracks on *The Clash*, therefore, you can hear Strummer banging away at his much-adored Telecaster, despite the fact that it was not plugged in to an amplifier.

The album's fourteen songs are each a story in themselves. But the one that perhaps best describes the Clash—and the feel of the album—is "Garageland," which concludes the album. The song was Strummer's response to Charles Shaar Murray's caustic *NME* review of their performance at the Screen on the Green gig in August 1976. Murray remarked that the Clash were "the kind of garage band who should be speedily returned to their garage, preferably with the motor running."

> Back in the garage with my bullshit detector
> Carbon monoxide making sure it's effective
> People ringing up making offers for my life
> But I just wanna stay in the garage all night
>
> We're a garage band
> We come from garageland
>
> I don't wanna hear about what the rich are doing
> I don't wanna go to where the rich are going
> They think they're so clever, they think they're so right
> But the truth is only known by guttersnipes

When *The Clash* was released on April 8, 1977, it quickly shot to Number Twelve on the British album charts, astonishing everyone, including the Clash. Raw, angry and unlike anything anyone had ever heard before, the album elicited praise everywhere. Robert Christgau eventually called it "the greatest rock and roll album ever manufactured anywhere." Years later, Danny Kelly wrote in *NME* that it "was an opening blast so singlemindedly engaged and recklessly energized that it borders on the insane." Kris Needs, in *ZigZag,* wrote, "I can't mince words here. I've only heard it once, but I know this is the most exciting album I've heard in years. I can't think about it for more than a minute without feeling like I'm going to explode." Perry, in *Sniffin' Glue,* declared, "The Clash album is a like a mirror. It reflects all the shit. It shows us the truth." Not everyone adored it—one *Melody Maker* reviewer sniffed that it was "the tuneless repetition of chords at a breakneck pace"—but they probably just didn't get it.

What they didn't get, and likely never would, was this: the Clash, and their music, were about exposing injustice, and cruelty, and neglect. They were about stirring the righteous rage of the millions of punks who adored them. And they were about taking that rage, that fury, and pushing against the walls.

Because they were about those things, as corny as it sounds to the cynics, they gave a lot of kids hope.

Still do, in fact.

Steve Diggle, the Buzzcocks: "It was a jewel of a thing, what was happening. We all got on really well, we were well received. And then Joe and the Clash would come on, and we'd just stand in the audience with fucking shivers going up your spine. And you'd wonder, is this just happening for right now, or is this gonna be some incredible history, for years to come? It was exhilarating."

For DOA, it was a dream, a once-in-a-lifetime kind of thing: to be asked to open for the Clash, in DOA's hometown of Vancouver. They got the call from their manager when they were touring through Saskatchewan, somewhere between Regina and Saskatoon. Recalls Joey, "We'd opened for the Ramones the year before, and it was the biggest show we'd ever done in Vancouver. And the Clash, they had been there the previous year at the Commodore. The whole punk scene went there, and [the Clash] were totally cool. The day after the show they went and played soccer with a bunch of kids in one of the local parks, right? And, it was just like, these are really great, regular people. They seemed to be like their music, honest and straightforward."

Joey sips his drink and scratches his chin. "Anyway, when the [opportunity to open for the Clash] came, we immediately flew back to Vancouver."

The backing gig was going to pay DOA only $100, and their airplane tickets cost much more than that. But the band were thrilled by the prospect of playing on the same bill as the Clash. They rushed to the PNE Gardens for their sound check, a rock 'n' roll prerequisite that is vital for even the most anarchic punk band. When the Clash finished theirs—a process that, to Shithead, seemed to take far too long—DOA naturally assumed they, or at least Ray Campi's Rockabilly Rebels, would be next. They were wrong.

Mick Jones brought a young boy onstage—keyboardist Mickey Gallagher's son—and proceeded to show him how to play drums. Then how to play keyboards. Then how to talk into a microphone. Says Shithead, "We went to do the sound check, and we were sitting there, and these guys didn't really say hello. I mean, they didn't know us, right? I figured that when you become famous, you meet people all over the place, so no big deal. But when it turned out we couldn't get a fucking sound check . . . We just kept getting, you know, fucked around all over the place."

No sound check, no opportunity to meet the Clash and—the final indignity—the band's set was cut short while they were onstage. Joey Shithead decided to exact revenge, DOA style.

Minutes before the Clash were to start, Shithead made his way to a narrow tunnel that led to the PNE stage. As each member of the Clash tried to get by, Shithead stood in their way. "I was just standing there drinking a beer," he recalls, "and all four of them had to walk by. And these guys were all fucking short! They're fucking midgets! And, as they came by, I blocked each one and said, 'You guys are bullshit,' and they cowered and scurried away."

Shithead and a friend made their way to the Clash dressing room, stole all the beer they could carry, and spent the next half-hour throwing empty cans at Mick Jones as he played onstage. Until a large security guard found them and told them to immediately stop, that is.

"It was funny as hell," says Joey Shithead, laughing. "It was, like, the best concert ever. [The Clash] are great, and they're still one of my favourite bands. They have great songs. But on that night, they were acting like rock star pricks, you know?"

Tom Delonge, Blink-182: "We were in Australia, and to be honest, I wasn't a huge Clash fan at the time. It just wasn't my world . . . it was kind of before my time. Anyway, I walked up to him and said my name, and said that I played in a band called Blink-182, I was playing at this festival, and I wanted to have the honour of meeting him . . . I asked him, 'What was it like to be in the Clash in the early eighties?' And he goes, 'You know, we used to walk around saying fuck you, we're the Clash.' He said that elitist attitudes are cool when you're a kid, but not when you get older."

The show was over: hundreds of punks started to stumble out into the Vancouver night. Two of my Calgary punk rock buddies, my girlfriend and I, meanwhile, were loitering on the main floor at the PNE. We were exhilarated and exhausted. We had pooled our meagre resources to buy four train tickets to Vancouver to see Joe Strummer and the Clash in concert. From our point of view, their performance had been inflammatory, incredible, extraordinary—and had the added bonus of a mini-riot midway through.

Joe Strummer, in particular, hadn't been in any way cowed by the anger of the Vancouver crowd, even though some of it had been directed at him and his band. Instead, he seemed energized by it, as if he had absorbed the intensity of the crowd and transformed himself into a hurricane of heat and energy. Every pair of eyes in the PNE was glued to his every move. It was beyond words.

But after the show, we had no money left and nowhere to stay. Typical punks. The four of us were discussing this state of affairs when a little boy appeared out of nowhere. It was near midnight, the show long since over, and roadies were up on stage, packing up the Clash's gear. The little boy looked to be about seven or eight. He was picking up flashcubes left behind by the departed fans.

We started talking to the boy. It turned out he was the son of Mickey Gallagher, the keyboardist the Clash had signed for their Take the Fifth tour of North America. His father appeared, looking for him. And then, within a matter of minutes, Topper Headon appeared, looking for the Gallaghers.

Topper Headon was admittedly not much to look at: he was stooped, slight and pale, with spiky hair and a quiet manner. (Unbeknownst to us, he was then struggling with a serious heroin habit.) He was also The Drummer for the Clash, and had supplied beats for them going back almost to their raw eponymous first album, the one that had changed our lives forever. We were in awe.

Topper asked us where we were from and what we thought of the show. When he heard we had no place to stay, he said, "Well, you'd better come backstage with me, then."

He led us through a dark corridor to the Clash's dressing room, which revealed itself to be nothing more than a smelly old collection of lockers located somewhere deep beneath the PNE stands on the northeast corner of the building. We stepped inside, past a couple of disinterested security guys, into a room thick with the smell of dope. Off in a corner, a ghetto blaster was playing some dub reggae, and people were laughing. Along the walls there were battered grey lockers, and a few ancient-looking wooden benches were affixed to the concrete floor. And sitting on the benches—looking pink and sweaty and flushed—were the Clash. *The Clash!* I could not be certain, but it suddenly seemed entirely possible that my heart was about to explode.

Topper waved in the direction of his bandmates. "There's Mick, there's Paul, there's the gang," he said, indicating Clash roadie Johnny Green, the Rockabilly Rebels, soundman Mickey Foote, plus a group of huge Rastafarian guys. "And there's Joe. Get yourself a beer or something and make yourself at home." He ambled off.

Even now, years after the fact, it is difficult to express in words what that moment felt like—the moment when Joe Strummer got up off the PNE's bench and walked over to us to shake hands and say hello. Joe Strummer! *Joe Fucking Strummer!* The guy who, in those days, was the biggest influence in my life. The guy whose songs our band played. The guy whose leftist politics we embraced (even if we didn't fully understand them). The guy who determined the clothes we wore, onstage and off. Joe Strummer!

In photographs, Strummer had always looked a lot like my father as a young man; in person, the resemblance was even greater (perhaps, I speculated, I was Joe Strummer's son). Strummer had a chiselled jaw and was then favouring a decidedly Elvis-style coif; when he stood up, it was apparent (as Joey Shithead had observed) that he wasn't very tall. He had an easy, affable manner. I tried not to stare at him, but it wasn't easy. Though he would probably be irritated by the suggestion, he was one of those people who became the centre of every room he entered. He certainly was at the moment.

When we shook it, Joe Strummer's hand was moist and warm, which made sense—he'd just been playing his heart out onstage, and he was accordingly drenched with sweat. He grinned at us, revealing a mouthful of broken, greenish teeth. Strummer's eyes were a bit glassy, doubtless a consequence of the massive spliffs that were making their way around the locker room. (Mick Jones was off in a corner, meanwhile, satisfying a drug preference that was plainly a lot more expensive.) The other members of the Clash didn't seem all that interested in us at that moment, but Joe Strummer was greeting the motley collection of pale Canadian punks like long-lost pals. "Welcome," he said. "Where y'all from?" We told him, but he didn't seem to know where Calgary, Alberta, was. It didn't matter.

Joe Strummer looked down, in the vicinity of my chest. Beneath my prized black leather biker jacket, I was wearing a homemade Clash T-shirt. Using an indelible blue marker, I had painstakingly recreated every detail of the famous logo found on the cover of the first Clash LP. In those days, there were no stores to purchase punk rock gear—at least not in Canada. So we made our own stuff: buttons, T-shirts, stickers, you name it. We even narrowed the flared jeans our mothers bought for us, by hand, so they would be as skinny and as tight as the trousers the Clash wore.

"Where'd you get that?" Joe Strummer said, jabbing a finger at my T-shirt.

"I made it," I said. "It's not very good, but I did it myself, because . . ."

"It's fuckin' great, man," he said, cutting me off. "You did that yourself. That's great. It's great to do it yourself. Keep control of the means of production, you know?" He laughed—a raw, deep-throated laugh—so I did, too.

By then, the rest of my friends—knowing the unfathomable depths of my Joe Strummer obsession, and how long I could stand there, agog at the brilliance of the Clash front man—had moved off to talk with other members of the band. Pharmaceutical obligations now complete, Mick Jones started to exhibit a great deal of interest in my girlfriend. Fine by me: if it meant I could spend a bit more time with Joe Strummer, the two of them could run away together and get married, for all I cared.

Then and now, punk frowns on the sort of hero worship and personality cults that are too-readily seen in traditional rock 'n' roll. Punk was supposed to be against hierarchies, and it was supposed to break down the walls between the performer and his or her audience, and all that stuff. But the facts were the facts: at that stage in my earthly existence, and in fact for many years thereafter, Joe Strummer was a giant in my life. He towered above most other mortals because he was so passionate, and so political, and so fucking *cool*. On those days when I didn't want to be me, I reckoned I should be Joe Strummer.

Before I said something stupid, I figured I would take advantage of the opportunity the punk rock gods had given me and ask Strummer for a brief interview. Strummer said sure, so I quickly extracted a pen and a tiny notepad from the folds of my biker jacket. Unable to immediately figure out something intelligent to say, I asked the stupidest rock-interview question of all: "Um, er, how is the tour going, Joe?"

He laughed and looked back at Mick Jones and Paul Simonon. "How is the tour going, fellas?" he roared, and they all started to laugh. I wanted to laugh, too, but I wasn't sure what was so funny. Seeing my expression, Strummer explained that the band had no money. None. Zero, zippo, zilch.

"Uh, why not?" I asked. The PNE had been packed to the rafters with punks who had paid a not-insignificant amount to see their heroes. The Vancouver show was the last one of the tour, and in the preceding weeks, the Clash had played to big, enthusiastic crowds all over North America. Where did all that money go? The Clash must be millionaires, no?

"The sound crew we used here were Americans, and they wanted to get paid," said Joe, as I scribbled away. "Before the show, they pulled the fuses on our PA rig and said they wouldn't let us play unless they got their money. We sorted that out, but not for long." (Much later, I would learn that the "sorting out" had involved long-time Clash roadie Johnny Green pulling the sound crew boss into a boiler room deep within the PNE and threatening him with part of a drum kit fashioned into a club. After the sound crew boss was duct-taped to a chair and locked in the boiler room, Green retrieved the fuses and the show went on.)

"Everyone wanted to get paid," said Strummer, "and they got paid. Which meant there wasn't anything left for the Clash." Strummer then loudly launched into a song I did not immediately recognize, and which principally involved tunelessly hollering Frankie Laine's "Sixteen Tons," to wit: "You load sixteen tons, and what do you get/ Another day older and deeper in debt!" over and over. The other members of the Clash—laughing and, by now, drunk and stoned—joined in. For a bunch of impoverished rock stars, they certainly were upbeat.

Eventually, Joe returned his attention to me. "We're not even sure where we're going to sleep tonight, but that's alright," he said. He eyed me and my friends, mischievously, and grinned. "Where are you guys sleeping tonight? Maybe we should stay with you!"

"Well, actually, we're not sure where we're staying," I said. "We don't have enough money for a hotel . . ."

"Then you will stay with us!" Strummer announced. "That's the rule. The Clash looks after its record-buying public!" Strummer wasn't joking. Every diehard Clash fan knew that the band regularly brought fans backstage, and even offered them a floor to crash on, when the circumstances warranted it.

Unaware that my friends had by then made arrangements for us to stay with a friend of a friend of a friend that night, and thrilled by the notion of crashing on Vancouver-area park benches with the Clash, I returned to the interview. "What did you think of the Vancouver crowd? They seemed a little, um, aggressive to me."

Aggressive was an understatement. While the PA system's fuses were being held hostage by the payment-seeking American roadies, the Clash's performance had been delayed interminably. The Vancouver crowd—who didn't particularly enjoy Ray Campi's Rockabilly Rebels, the band that had followed DOA—started tearing the PNE apart. Literally. When the Clash finally dashed onstage, and played "City of the Dead" as the opening number, quite a few Vancouverites took offence. They started to fling bottles and huge bits of wood and metal onstage—at the Clash. The Clash, meanwhile, looked a bit bewildered by it all. The riot squad was called in.

Strummer laughed. "Maybe they didn't like it when we played 'City of the Dead' off the top," he said. "Maybe they thought it was a commentary on Vancouver punk rockers."

There was something to that. The Clash we were hanging out with that night were not the same Clash that had recorded the ferocious anthems found on the first album, songs such as "White Riot" and "I'm So Bored with the USA." The band had clearly become much more proficient musically, and they were experimenting with different genres, such as rockabilly. The Clash looked different, too: the hard punk look that had defined their first two years of existence had given way to a more colourful sartorial style, one that suggested the band was moving on.

Their fans in places like Vancouver, however, were decidedly not moving on. They didn't want punk to change. They wanted the Clash of old. They didn't want dandies prancing about onstage, playing fifties revival tunes. They wanted dark, gritty, fast punk rock. Like too many punks in too many places, the Vancouver punks didn't want change.

While I, too, liked my punk rock loud, fast and snotty, I had always felt there was plenty of room for style, and a sense of humour, in the punk scene. The Ramones had shown that it was possible to be a punk and have fun, and the Undertones and a lot of other bands clearly felt the same. I was therefore always suspicious that the bleak nihilism of the Sex Pistols had too many echoes of Black Sabbath–style heavy metal, and decided to try this pet theory out on Joe Strummer. But the words came out all wrong.

"A lot of these punks aren't really punks, they're metalheads," I said to him, in a rush of words. "Don't you *hate* these guys who *hate* everything?"

Before I could take that last ridiculous statement back, Strummer started to laugh uproariously. He clapped me on the back. "It's okay," he said, seeing me blush. "I know what you mean." He laughed a bit more. "Listen, you're right, you're right. It ain't punk to believe there is no future at all. That's what poor old Sid thought, and it didn't do him any fuckin' good, did it? There *is* a future, and I don't give a toss what the Pistols think.

"That's what Thatcher and the right wing want us to believe, anyway, that there's no future. That way, they don't have to contend with our anger. But they're not gonna shut me up." He pointed at me. "Or you, neither, right?"

Right, I nodded. My God, my God, I worshipped this man.

There was another reason for the PNE crowd's Clash backlash, perhaps. While Joey Shithead's earlier backstage confrontation with the members of the Clash had gone unseen by the 2,200 Vancouver punks in attendance that night, the DOA camp had not hesitated to make clear their disdain for what they considered the Clash's "rock star" attitudes. Right around the time that Strummer and I were chatting, in fact, a few DOA fans—and, possibly, members of DOA itself—were spray-painting the Clash tour bus with assorted imaginative epithets, among them: THE CLASH SUCK! DOA RULE! The Clash's show had fallen victim to punk rock factionalism and nationalism. Vancouver was DOA's turf, and the Clash had angered DOA.

If he was aware of this, Strummer was unfazed. "Yeah, well, DOA was . . ."

Mick Jones, who had been listening in, cut him off before he could complete his sentence. "DOA is a fucking heavy metal band!"

Warily eyeing my note-taking, and as was his wont, Strummer opted for the positive. He reached over to Ray Campi, then strolling by with a beer. "This is rock 'n' roll, right here!" he exclaimed, indicating Campi. "This is real rock 'n' roll! The real fucking article!"

After a bit of conversation, Campi wandered off. I returned my attention to Strummer, who was growing increasingly preoccupied with another cucumber-sized spliff someone had rolled. "Joe, does punk stay the way it was? And if it changes its sound, is it still punk?"

Strummer whirled on me and jabbed an index finger at his temple. "Punk rock is right *here,* my friend," he said. "It's an attitude. It's a way of thinking. It's not just a musical style. Trying out new things, and new sounds, is what punk rock is . . . if you play the same way for the rest of your life, if you dress and think the same way, you're just as bad as someone's parents. You're no punk anymore."

I wasn't sure I entirely agreed with him—I was then mired in my punk purist phase, and was accordingly completely distrustful of anything that smacked of competence or professionalism—but I wasn't about to say so. Much later, I would accept that Strummer was right: punk was a way of *thinking,* not just a way of *playing.*

We talked about a few other things after that, but the details have been overtaken by the passage of time. It doesn't matter so much, now, what Joe Strummer thought about bands that no longer exist. And it doesn't seem as important to recount, twenty-five years later, the minutiae of a rock 'n' roll life on the road. Suffice to say that Joe Strummer was everything I had hoped he would be, and more: he was smart, he was full of life, and he had a heart so big it is hard to believe, even now, that it could stop beating, as it did on December 22, 2002. I only met him that once, just once, but I can tell you that he spoke to me every night through his records. And I loved him like he was a member of my family. I really did. I wasn't alone in that.

As we were making our way out of the locker room, collecting Polaroids and autographs from the Clash, I asked Joe Strummer for his signature. On a page from my little notebook, this is what he wrote—a bit of a lyric from Carl Perkins's "Boppin' the Blues":

WELL I LOVE YOU BABY, BUT I MUST BE RHYTHM BOUND
JOE STRUMMER

Joe Strummer, now rhythm bound with Johnny, Joey, Dee Dee and not a few others, was the perfect punk rocker. Nobody before, and nobody since, has even come close.

Not even close.

Warren "Nuclear Age" Kinsella, Social Blemishes, Hot Nasties: "So, is the culture dead? Is punk dead? Is there any future that punk can reasonably hope to change?"

Is the Culture Dead?

Not the culture that is *learned,* and comprises beliefs, and values, and customs, and behaviour, and so on. Not that. Not some higher state of discernment or taste; not that, either. Not the culture of the soil. Not something growing in a petri dish, or forgotten at the back of the fridge.

Popular culture. You know: the culture that prevails in a given society at a given time. Its content—the "stuff" of culture—is determined, with very few exceptions, by the faceless industries that disseminate, and profit from, cultural material: the movie industry, the television industry, the music industry, the publishing industry and (although they deny that they are a cultural commodity) the news media industry. If you are a cynic, popular culture is simply the aggregate product of these industries: base, venal and without anything resembling a soul. If you are hopeful, as real punks tend to be, popular culture is instead the interaction that occasionally takes place between the culture industries and the people who they want to buy their products; it is something that should, and sometimes does, exist in the narrow space between art and capitalism.

Naturally, popular culture is changing all the time. If it is not unique to a particular place, it is almost always unique to a particular time, like Beatle boots or spiked hair. And, with few exceptions, the things that constitute popular culture typically get their start in darkened corners and under dusty floorboards—in dodgy clubs and at out-of-the-way studios, and with odd-looking people no one ever invites over for cocktail parties. Popular culture, almost always, emanates in a subculture. Like punk did.

The problem, of course, is that popular culture is, well, *popular*. It is carefully designed by capitalists to appeal to the largest possible number of cultural consumers. Paradoxically, the culture industries are not interested in culture per se—they are principally interested in hawking items of popular culture that maximize profit. The "stuff" of popular culture that tends to survive—the stuff that can be seen persisting from time to time, generation to generation—is the cultural merchandise that has propagated itself in the widest conceivable manner. That is, the shit that *sells*.

So what, one might say. So popular culture is popular. So people watch the same reality shows (hell, Johnny Rotten even appeared in one!), and they listen to the same music, and they wear the same clothes because someone they have never met has decreed that they should. So what? Well—and this is the punk's lament—because popular culture is *superficial*. It is *boring*. It *sucks*. And it is made worse by this fact: those cultural "items" that are derived from lots of experience, or training, or reflection, or bona fide creativity—the ones that have actual value, in effect—never, ever seem to end up being "popular." They end up on the junk heap of history, mostly.

In *The Boy Looked at Johnny,* Julie Burchill and Tony Parsons describe the dilemma thusly:

> Capitalism—the godfather of fascism—lives to increase multi-million-dollar profits. In rock 'n' roll, the particular interests of the establishment and capitalism fit together as compactly as a joint, finding an affinity that they are unable to achieve in any other business venture. As soon as any ostensibly dangerous new musical phenomena appear in the sweaty clubs giving a righteous finger to the status quo, they are enticed in from the cold by the same old dangled

carrots of sex/drugs/cash/fame and run through the mill of commercial assimilation. What were once sharp, angry fangs are rendered soft, ineffective gums.

By maintaining the music's illusion of youth rebellion it accomplishes its purpose—a green-back producer channeling not only the money but the time, energy and psyche of young people into what has been their most jealously guarded palliative for over twenty years. Punk started as a movement borne out of No Fun, and ended as a product whose existence was No Threat.

Okay, fine. Burchill and Parsons wrote their book at virtually a single sitting, and allegedly on speed. They have since completely repudiated *The Boy Looked at Johnny,* and have even refused permission for subsequent printings to take place. But the fact is— even now, a quarter-century after their wonderful, over-the-top polemic was first published—they may be right. The punk subculture probably *has* been absorbed by the popular culture. Rendering it, accordingly, dead.

Or maybe not. Maybe—just maybe!—there are things unique to the punk subculture that make it impossible for the popular culture to assimilate it. That make it impossible for the mainstream to swallow, Blink-182 and Good Charlotte notwithstanding. Like the fact that punk is by definition *young.* And *unkillable.* And that it encourages young people to *Do It Themselves.* And that it is leftist in its political orientation—that is to say, *anti-capitalist.* And that it is just more *honest.*

Tony James, formerly of London SS with Mick Jones, is now touring with Mick Jones once more, in something called Carbon/Silicon. On the road, pecking away at his laptop, James acknowledges that there were plenty of people who wanted to profit from punk: "What you soon realize (or more so by our experienced managers, like Malcolm McLaren and Bernie Rhodes) is that, if you create a generation gap war, that is the way to get attention, and to exploit 'youth.' They applied the ideas of the Situationists and the Dadaists and contemporary art [to punk], and then they dressed it up so that it became very attractive and sexy."

But did McLaren and Rhodes—and all those who sought to make the punk subculture "attractive and sexy," and therefore marketable—succeed? No, says Tony James. No, no, no. He writes, "Well, to continue with a different analogy, once you've won the war and seized all the other side's assets and become rich, then it is easy to become complacent and become what you set out to destroy. But hey—the evolution of rock 'n' roll [is that] another icon will come along to be sneered at by the young punks!" Punk is inherently youthful, and young punks are not so easily seduced into capitalist schemes.

Jim Lindberg, the philosopher behind SoCal punk giants Pennywise, is also unafraid of what the popular culture can do to the punk subculture, because, he says, punk is essentially unkillable. "There's a lot of purists out there who say punk was something that happened in 1977 and then died out," Lindberg says. "But I think, like any other form of music—such as jazz, or blues, or even country—it's musical form that will go through many different changes. It will fade in and out of popularity. It will be very commercialized—you will see a very homogenized version of it, designed to be more appealing to the masses. It will be relegated back down to the underground.

"And then," he says, "it will take a revolutionary band to come along and bring it back to its roots. Just because the Sex Pistols don't play together, just because Johnny Rotten is a raging asshole, doesn't matter . . . their music still stands, and young people can still get into it, and get something out of it."

The Do It Yourself ethic provides some measure of comfort to DOA's Joey Shithead. To him, DIY is—ironically—a capitalist notion: it is, in its essence, entrepreneurial. But punk's DIY spirit rebels against another capitalist notion: namely, that you should pay someone else to do something you can do just as well, or better, on your own. "Sure, punk is a little bit on the prefab side at times," says Shithead. "There are bands who are signed with big labels and are, you know, selling millions of records. Punk rock, when you think about it, is a perfectly prefabricated form for record companies to sell kids rebellion. It's angry, it's yelling, all that kind of stuff.

"But it's still political. It's still got the DIY ethic going on. It still kicks the establishment in the groin. All of that—punk will be around for another fifty years because of those things. Unless the world blows up or something like that."

Sham 69's Jimmy Pursey points to another reason why punk is not so easily absorbed by the capitalist popular culture: punk is leftist. It is anti-capitalist. And, at the end of the day, it is more honest than the prevailing culture. Pursey says, "Punk was always definitely on the left, because it was basically always a socialist frame of mind, wasn't it? It was about bringing people together from different kinds of backgrounds, which, again, is a socialist point of view. It was always more about turning to the left than it was about turning to the right. You understand? For the simple reason, again, that the right takes away what you want to say. Whereas the left wants you to speak more."

He pauses. "Punk was a maturing education that still goes on. Because it offers to young people, all the time, the hope that there is a music you can go to that has an honesty to it. That you can use as your guide. That doesn't lie."

Is Punk Rock Dead?

The question gets asked a lot. So often, in fact, that there is an album by Scottish punks the Exploited, a few websites and blogs, and quite a few stickers, buttons and T-shirts you can buy that answer the question for you: punk's not dead.

Then again, maybe it *is*. After all, if punk—as a genre of music, as a subculture, as a way of thinking—is so very vital, and vibrant, and vigorous, it wouldn't be necessary to continually assert that it's alive, now would it? Nobody runs around printing up buttons and spray-painting graffiti to take the position that BROADWAY AIN'T D.O.A. And no one is establishing lines of clothing to advance the thesis that POLKA LIVES 4-EVER. You don't see that much.

But with punks, and punk, you do. In groups, punks will always angrily reject such heresy. They will get pissed off. But when you get them off on their own—and this has happened *every single time* I asked the question of members of everything from the Sex Pistols to Sham 69 to the Slits to Bad Religion—they will get quiet for a bit, and eventually say no, they don't *think* so. But, more than occasionally, they will even say *yes,* punk probably *is* dead. It's gone. Even when they are still in punk bands, still playing punk rock.

So who killed punk, if it's dead? Whose fingerprints can be found on the murder weapon? The most plausible theory comes from a punk who isn't (yet) a household name, but who is one of the smartest I've ever come across: Russ Rankin, vocalist for both hardcore combo Good Riddance and punk "supergroup" Only Crime. Speaking from his home in Santa Cruz, where he started off as a skateboarder and an Ian MacKaye–style hardcore aficionado, Rankin is blunt: "As soon as the culture got its hooks in hardcore and punk, it basically rendered null and void what punk and hardcore were doing for the world. It stomped the life out of what we used to know as punk rock. When I was in high school, there were three of us who were punks. That's it. You had to dig to find your favourite music. You had to go to the toughest parts of town to see it played. Today, punk is part and parcel of the culture industry. It's packaged and spoon-fed to people, but not before it has been bled dry of anything rebellious. It's just another sterile commodity. It is used up and thrown out."

So it's dead, then. It must be dead, given the fact that mainstream culture has murdered it, right?

No, says Rankin, despite all of that, punk is unkillable. "It's definitely not dead. It's timeless. It doesn't matter when you listen to Johnny Cash: he's always going to be cool. Same with punk. Punk has gone away, but it will be back." Because, Rankin says, the mainstream culture—popular culture—will drop punk when it believes that it has made every buck there is to be made. Thereafter, punk will be liberated, and it will return to what it was always meant to be: a music that is about defiance and resistance and self-reliance; a way of thinking that is, in its essence, anti-authoritarian, youthful, loud, creative, independent, unique. All of those things.

There are those who refuse to countenance the possibility that punk is in any way dead, however. They won't even discuss it. The principal spokesperson for this point of view, unsurprisingly, is Ian MacKaye—ex–Teen Idles, ex–Minor Threat—whose passion for the subject is mistaken, by some, for anger. Says MacKaye, the punk who changed a million punk lives (like Russ Rankin's), "What people don't recognize is that there are still kids today who are picking up instruments and they're making punk music. And it may sound nothing like DOA or the Viletones or nothing like those kinds of bands—or it may sound like that—but the fact is that they are wrestling with equipment, and wrestling with expression, and figuring out how to change things. It's almost like an apprenticeship or something . . . for kids, it's still happening. It's underground, so you don't necessarily hear about it."

I try to interrupt to ask him something, but he won't let me because he's afire with an idea, which is partly what makes the guy (and punk) so interesting in the first place. "Look," he says. "I'm forty-two. I've been involved with punk for a long time. I started playing in '79, and I'm not a former punk. It's all a flight of stairs for me, and one step leads to the next. And I feel that I am engaged, still, with what I consider punk. It exists." He pauses, but not for long.

"Everyone assumes that punk is dead, because you sometimes don't hear about it. But in every town, there are kids doing something. *It will never die.*"

—

Is There a Future That Punk Can Change?

Damn right, there is. There *always* is.

In my case—in the case of my friends, and in the case of punks (and aging, former punks) everywhere—punk is not merely a music. It is a way of thinking, one that urges us to take action (as Joe Strummer did) and not just give up on the future (as Sid Vicious did). By demonstrating that anger is energy, and that we have the power to do just about anything ourselves, punk is like a cosmic collision that creates a noisy, colourful, alternative universe crammed with new bands, new politics, new looks, new ways of expressing oneself—new ways of *being* oneself. It's stupid to regard punk as just a genre of rock 'n' roll, or some peculiar new approach to fashion. It has always been more than that. How so?

Okay, *listen:* imagine that you're sixteen again (just like the Buzzcocks song), and you're getting beaten up by jocks at school because you look a little different, or you talk differently, or you're gay, or you wear funny clothes, or you aren't very athletic. Or you're being hassled by your teachers because you're not like the other kids and you've got a bit of a rebellious streak. Or you're being pushed around by some kids because you don't want to try drugs or because you like to read books.

Or imagine that your dad left all of you a long time ago, or that someone at home is pushing you around when they get drunk, or—in the night, when they think no one is looking—someone who is supposed to love you is running their hands all over you. And that you are only sixteen years old.

Or imagine that, like a lot of sixteen-year-olds, you have yet to develop the capacity to be unaffected, or uncaring, about television footage of thousands of children literally starving to death. Or that you still pay attention, and you still cry, when you hear about someone who is weak and alone being hurt by someone who is rich and powerful. Or that you have a rage—a wordless, black rage—

building up inside of you about all of this and none of this, and that you cannot imagine that life could ever have any meaning anywhere, anytime. Or imagine that you cannot conceive that God can exist in a world that is so fucking cruel and bleak and evil.

Just *listen,* and imagine living through any of that. Because a lot of sixteen-year-olds don't have to bother imagining a life like that. It's their life already. That's why punk was invented, and why it will never die. Punk takes a young person's anger and makes them *do* something, and *feel* something, and *be someone.* It makes a kid feel that he or she actually can shape the future—and, sometimes, it helps kids to actually *do it.* It makes those unlivable parts livable again. It gives hope. It sings.

Close your eyes, and slip into that dark, crowded, sweaty, noisy little nightclub and listen to the punk sound, the three-chord sound of fury's hour. And, as you stand against the wall at the back—or as you dance the bad stuff away, right down in the front—know that this is the sound that punk makes, now and tomorrow and forever:

YES!

APPUNKDIX ONE
the top ten punk albums of all time

As any of my friends will tell you—and going back a long, long way, to my adolescent punk days—I am forever preparing lists of musical Top Tens. On scraps of paper, on bus transfers, on the backs of phone bills. The lists vary: Top Ten bands. Top Ten albums with which to be marooned on an island. Top Ten groups we should never be forced to listen to again. Top Ten great band names. Top Ten songs to listen to before Armageddon commences.

Notwithstanding all of that, figuring out the Top Ten Punk Albums of All Time is tough to do. Since 1976, a lot of great punk rock has been released, and a lot more has yet to be heard, too. So any Top Ten list, by definition, is obsolete the moment you put it together.

Also problematic, of course, is that a Top Ten list is entirely subjective. And, really, who cares what I think, right? Accordingly, to make this particular list a bit more relevant, I consulted with the oracles I interviewed over the years—Bad Religion's Brett Gurewitz, Joey Ramone, the Sex Pistols' Glen Matlock, Rough Trade's Geoff Travis, you name it—to ascertain what they thought was Top Ten material. All of them had an opinion.

The list is not in any way scientific. It isn't comprehensive. It is just a take—my take—on the Top Ten Punk Albums of All Time. If you don't like it, piss off. Go DIY and write up your own fucking list, okay?

Herewith, the victors:

1. **RAMONES—The Ramones.** I bought this at a place in my hometown not long after it came out. I had read a little bit about the Ramones in *Creem* magazine, so I knew that Robert Christgau and Lester Bangs were in love with the Ramones, which was good enough for me. On the bus back home, however, I kept the LP hidden away: the black-and-white cover shot depicted a quartet of circus freaks, not the sort of Zeppelinesque cock rockers favoured by my peers (some of whom did not hesitate to express their preferences with their fists). Safely back in my room, I fired up my tinny little record player. A wave of sonic bliss washed over me: Dee Dee and Tommy's stripped-down bass and drums, Johnny's three perfect chords, Joey's yelping. I knew I had purchased greatness when my dad hollered down the stairs, "Can you turn that *down?*" No greater rock 'n' roll ever has ever been committed to vinyl, before or since. And in less than thirty minutes, too. Christly God, I love these guys.

2. **NEVER MIND THE BOLLOCKS—The Sex Pistols.** Mainly a collection of singles, I know. Steve Jones does all the bass parts because Glen Matlock was gone and Sid couldn't play, I know.

More like standard pub rock than the punk sounds then sprouting up in the U.K. and New York, I know. A product of Malcolm MacLaren's marketing savvy, not punk politics, I know. But try listening to "Anarchy in the U.K."—or "God Save the Queen," or "Pretty Vacant," or anything else on *Bollocks*— and believing anything the cynics have to say (John Lydon among them). This is, truly, one of the greatest albums ever, and it came along at just the right time. Circa 1977, rock had become a business—a super-sized, coked-up, irrelevant corporate enterprise run by a bunch of assholes utterly lacking in souls—and the Pistols, and this album, changed all of that. Loud, loutish, pissed off. Of the streets, and for the streets. I'm glad they didn't make a second album, because it's hard to be this great twice.

3. **FIRST TWO SEVEN INCHES ON A TWELVE INCH**—Minor **Threat.** A teenager: that's what Ian MacKaye was when he formed Minor Threat with Jeff Nelson, Brian Baker and Lyle Preslar in their hometown of Washington, D.C., in the fall of 1980. A *kid*, really. But despite his youthfulness (or maybe because of it), MacKaye and his band became the very epicentre of the world hardcore punk scene for most of the eighties. Fast, furious, fresh, forward-thinking, Minor Threat not only invented the entire Straight Edge movement—they literally saved punk from being killed off by poppy new wave shite. The twelve songs on this record (which are all found, with another fourteen terrific Minor Threat screamers, on Dischord's 2003 *Complete Discography*) are an essential part of any punk collection. "Filler," "I Don't Wanna Hear It," "Small Man, Big Mouth," "Screaming at a Wall," "Minor Threat"—and, of course, "Straight Edge"— are testament to the integrity of a young man who was (by any standard of measurement) extraordinary. Can you say you changed the world at the age of seventeen? Didn't think so. Fucking amazing record.

4. **THE CLASH—The Clash.** If you were an aspiring North American punk, and living in suburbia, like me, the stuff Joe Strummer hollers about on this universe-modifying record—the dole, police brutality, race riots, abject poverty—was something to be *read* about, and not ever *experienced*. That notwithstanding, the Clash were able to make all of it seem so bloody real, so vivid, that—after a couple of listens—it wasn't difficult to imagine you were with Strummer and Paul Simonon down at the Notting Hill riots, running like hell to escape the lines of charging, baton-swinging police. Romantic, idealistic and realistic all at the same time (which ain't easy to do, by the way), this album represents the very apex of political punk. Essential, crucial, without equal.

5. **PINK FLAG—Wire.** Twenty-one tracks in thirty-five minutes. Art fused to three-chord punk. Twelve songs running less than ninety seconds. Best cuts: "Reuters," "12XU," "It's So Obvious," "106 Beats That." REM covered "Strange." More punk bands influenced than records sold. Simplicity is a virtue, still. A short, sharp, shock.

6. **IT TAKES A NATION OF MILLIONS TO HOLD US BACK— Public Enemy.** *Yes,* truly, it is a punk album. It is! What else could you call a record this powerful, this political, this pissed off about society's failings (and rightly so)? While most of rap and hip-hop would eventually lose their way—championing sexism, guns, money and little else—Public Enemy's Chuck D always maintained a laser-like focus on the *real* subject matter, but without ever neglecting his obligations to rock out. The phenomenal *It Takes a Nation of Millions to Hold Us Back* was like the very best punk albums: it sought to *enrage* listeners, and then prod them into taking *action*. I, and plenty of others, condemned their dalliance with the intolerance of the Nation of Islam's Louis Farrakhan and Professor Griff's anti-Semitism;

in time (too much time) they expressed their disdain for black supremacy, and fired Griff. Along the way, they revealed themselves to be human, and therefore imperfect. This album remains anything but. One of the great punk records of all time.

7. **INFLAMMABLE MATERIAL—Stiff Little Fingers.** Belfast was clearly no place to grow up, but as punk rock source material goes, it was without equal. Released on the influential independent label Rough Trade in 1979, *Inflammable Material* was the first independent LP ever to make the British Top Twenty. Produced by the brilliant Geoff Travis, championed by the world's greatest deejay, John Peel (R.I.P.), SLF wrote extraordinary, angry songs about the bleak, grinding misery that was life in Northern Ireland's capital: the anthemic "Alternative Ulster" and the most powerful statement of political rage ever to be captured on vinyl, "Suspect Device." SLF were never this good again, but for them the trade-off—leaving Belfast for good—was probably worth it.

8. **CUT—The Slits.** More than once, but not often enough, quite a few of us stood at punk shows and remarked, to no one in particular, "Hey! Everyone onstage is a guy. They're all hollering about guy stuff, 24/7. And they would look naked if their fuzz pedals weren't working." That's why the Slits, and this album, were so important: they were unconditional females, they sang songs about refreshingly different subject matter, and they weren't afraid to play in a way that traditional punk outfits were afraid to. Punk was never about revisiting the same old ways of doing things; it was about trying out new ideas, new approaches, new sounds. The Slits kept punk from getting stuck in a rut of its own making.

9. **THE EMPIRE STRIKES FIRST—Bad Religion.** For a few million people, it is no exaggeration to state that the George W. Bush era will one day be regarded as one of the dark times in human history: when capitalism, militarism and intolerance were in the ascendancy—and when balance, restraint and peace were dismissed as symptoms of weakness. This ferocious, relentless Bad Religion album—the group's sixteenth in a remarkable career stretching over more than two decades— represents the best punk record to emerge from the grim Bush years: for its courage, for its passion, for its intelligence and for its willingness to confront the venality and perfidy of the U.S. administration head-on. The guys in Bad Religion are all Americans, but they didn't let any "patriots" intimidate them into silence. The most powerful punk album of the new millennium.

10. **ROCKET TO RUSSIA—The Ramones.** The Ramones are on this list twice because, in the view of almost everyone, they deserve to be. Released on Sire in 1977, *Rocket to Russia* caught the Ramones at the peak of their powers: inspired tunes, funny lyrics, energy in abundance. "Sheena Is a Punk Rocker" is here (my wife and I were so in love with this song that we named our dog after it). An inspired cover of the Trashmen's "Surfin' Bird." The perfect Beach Boys song the Beach Boys never recorded, "Rockaway Beach." The unparalleled genius of "Cretin Hop." When all of us heard this record, we were certain that if it didn't propel the Ramones to the top of the charts, nothing could. Turns out we were right about that, which still fucking sucks. *Rocket to Russia:* buy it now—and if you already own it, get another copy to play in the car. And a third one for work.

APPUNKDIX TWO
the top ten punk singles of all time

The best ways to receive punk rock wisdom—the best ways to learn the snarling, spitting, screeching, speechifying punk catechism—are to, one, attend a show with your pals and leap about like a spring-loaded nutter and get so sweaty that your leather belt is sopping and needs to be wrung out at the end of the night; or, failing that, two, get your hands on a punk rock single. Not, I emphasize, an album. A punk rock *single,* maaan.

The single: those tiny, scratchy, perfect black disks, 45 rpms, seven inches across, with the one-inch hole smack in the middle. Those things. In the mid-seventies, rock 'n' rollers had completely lost whatever ability they once had to say something in less than twenty-five minutes. They couldn't *say* it if it wasn't on an album.

They couldn't *play* it if it wasn't on a stage the size of your average city block. They couldn't do *anything* if it wasn't too big, too long and too expensive.

Not the punks. They knew the shortest distance between two points was the best. They knew small was good. They knew, ipso facto, that one of the greatest things in all of rock 'n' roll was the single. They knew the Ultimate Punk Rock Truth: if you can't say it in two minutes or less, it can't be said.

So the punks made the single fun again. They insisted on first releasing songs as seven-inchers, not twelve-inchers. They lovingly doted on the artwork for their singles: Jamie Reid's incredible designs for the Sex Pistols, the stunning "Orgasm Addict" art Linder Sterling did for the Buzzcocks, Malcolm Garrett's colourful geometric innovations for the band's 45s thereafter. Honestly: if you were a punk, and you weren't in a band or producing a fanzine or organizing something, it was sometimes enough just to seek out—and acquire—a rare punk rock single. It was that cool.

The Brits understood the beauty and wonder of the seven-inch single better than anyone else. North Americans (bands included) never really caught on, and that is reflected in their poor showing in the list below. Shame on you, North Americans.

This Top Ten list is utterly subjective, unscientific, blah blah blah. But if you are just getting started in punk, try to get started here (and don't download it, either—that's stealing from artists who, unlike some loathsome, lip-synching boy band act, can ill-afford to lose what little income they get).

And, um, *yes:* you will need a record player. And, *no,* I don't know where to find one. Myself, I've still got a fabulous little portable phonograph beside my computer, and I listened to it while writing the book you now grasp in your sweaty maulers.

Alright then, as Johnny Rotten would say: here we go now! A sociology lecture! With a bit of psychology! And a bit of neurology! A bit of fuckology . . . no fun! *Yeee-haaaw!*

1. **ANARCHY IN THE U.K.—The Sex Pistols.** From the December 7, 1976, news release issued by EMI Records, around the time the company signed the Pistols to record and release the very first "Anarchy in the U.K." single: "Sex Pistols is a pop group devoted to a new form of music known as 'punk rock.' It was contracted for recording purposes by EMI Records Limited in October 1976—an unknown group offering some promise, in the view of our recording executives, like many other pop groups of different kinds that we have signed. In this context, it must be remembered that the recording industry has signed many pop groups, initially controversial, who have in the fullness of time become wholly acceptable and contributed greatly to the development of modern music. Sex Pistols have acquired a reputation for aggressive behaviour which they have certainly demonstrated in public. There is no excuse for this." Can you fucking *believe* that? Now, if *that* excerpt doesn't convince you that "Anarchy in the U.K." is the greatest punk rock single ever, nothing will. The song that started it all.

2. **WHITE MAN IN HAMMERSMITH PALAIS—The Clash.** This single, released by CBS in June 1978, is my favourite 45 of all time. Why isn't it the Top Punk Single, then? Good question. Mostly, I think, because "WMIHP" is just as much a *reggae* record as it is a *punk* record; it expertly commingles the two genres, in fact. Therein lie the reasons for the unparalleled genius of this little bit of wax: it fully exposed a whole generation of punks, and Clash fans as well, to reggae music; it was the catchiest tune any of us had ever heard; and, most of all, it was unflinchingly honest. On it, Joe Strummer describes starting an evening at the Hammersmith Palais, where he hoped to listen to Jamaican reggae giants Dillinger, Leroy Smart, Delroy Wilson and Ken Boothe—and finishing the night variously realizing that he was not going to bridge the racial divide, nor stop punk's slide towards commercialism, nor

impede Britain's rightward descent. So Strummer decides, as he ambles home, that he's "the white man in the Palais," who is "just lookin' for fun." He's more than that, and he always will be. R.I.P., Strummer.

3. **SUSPECT DEVICE—Stiff Little Fingers.** When I was sixteen or so, I briefly wanted to join the Irish Republican Army. In high school, I'd wear a black armband on St. Patrick's Day and darkly mutter, "St. Patrick didn't drive *all* the snakes out of Ireland." Stuff like that. And then, on a road trip to Vancouver, I picked up this record, whose cover featured a black-and-white photo of dozens of real, honest-to-God bombs. Released by Rigid Digits in March 1978, the graphic realism of "Suspect Device" made short work of my fondness for the Provo militancy. Howling like a man facing a firing squad, Jake Burns—who lived in Belfast, and for whom Republican and Loyalist violence was much more than a theory—condemned both sides with unbridled fury: "They take away our freedom/ In the name of liberty/ Why don't they all just clear off/ Why won't they let us be/ They make us feel indebted/ For saving us from hell/ and then they put us through it/ It's time the bastards fell." BBC disc-spinner John Peel got one of the 350 copies of the first pressing, and made sure naive romantics like me got to hear it. The most powerful political protest song ever—partly because Burns and his band could have been *murdered* simply for recording it. Astonishing.

4. **TEENAGE KICKS—The Undertones.** Another John Peel favourite—his family played this song at his funeral in November 2004, as his casket was exiting St. Edmonsbury Cathedral— "Teenage Kicks" released on an independent label in September 1978, made the legendary BBC deejay cry the first time he heard it. It is, truly, that wondrous. Like Stiff Little Fingers, the Undertones were from Belfast, but their early subject matter

could not have been more different: girls, dancing, girls, the arrival of summer (we'd sing along joyously to their "Here Comes the Summer," but substitute the chorus lyrics with "Here Comes Joe Strummer"—turns out he loved them too). These five Ramones fans were the first and greatest punk-pop band, whose records anticipated the likes of Blink-182 and Green Day and scores of others. There can be no greater expression of what it means to be a teenager than this song, and in slightly more than two minutes, too. Sayeth Feargal Sharkey, in that extraordinary tremulous voice he had, "Teenage dreams are so hard to beat." True enough.

5. **SPIRAL SCRATCH—The Buzzcocks.** There's not much more I can say about the Mancunians' February 1977 extended play single, having earlier devoted half a chapter to extolling its brilliance and DIY wondrousness. It contains the truest punk anthem, "Boredom," which itself contained the best two-note guitar solo in the history of the human race. Here's Devoto, sounding like he means it: "Yeah, well, I say what I mean/ I say what comes to my mind/ I never get around to things/ I live a straight, straight line." Genius.

6. **SHEENA IS A PUNK ROCKER—The Ramones.** The best singles should make you want to leap up and jump around your basement like a maniac, playing air guitar or singing into a broom handle—they should be catchier than a drawer full of fish hooks. "Sheena Is a Punk Rocker," released by Sire in May 1977, is all of that. The first real punk hit record—it charted at number twenty-two in Britain—"Sheena" should also have made Da Brudders Ramone into zillionaires. If there was any justice in the world, that is. And, because there *isn't* any justice in the world, the gods created punk rock and the Ramones. Kinda circular punk logic, eh?

7. **COMPLETE CONTROL—The Clash.** At first, I was going to grant this coveted spot on the Top Ten Punk Singles list to Alternative TV's "Action Time Vision." After creating the punk zine scene with *Sniffin' Glue,* Mark Perry turned his talents to his band, Alternative TV—and, in May 1978, ATV offered up the amazing "Action Time Vision," on which Perry snarls, "Chords and notes don't mean a thing/ Listen to the rhythm, listen to us sing . . ." But you know what? I sat down and listened to "Complete Control," yet again, and I concluded that, well, chords and notes do in fact mean a thing. And, on "Complete Control," the chords, notes and words are *perfect,* pretty fucking much. Perfect. In the abstract, no one should have been impressed by the song at all—released by CBS in September 1977, produced by Lee "Scratch" Perry, "Complete Control" tells how the Clash were miffed that CBS had released "Remote Control" as a single without their approval. Another song by a band upset with their record company? Is that what the Clash's revolution had been reduced to? And then we *heard* it. My God! Such fury! Such power! Such brilliance! Probably the best punk song the Clash ever wrote—and, when you consider that they were the world's best punk band, that's saying something.

8. **I'M STRANDED—The Saints.** Nobody paid much heed to Australia in the early days of punk, which was a shame, because bands like Radio Birdman were churning out terrific garage rock in those days—and the Saints were already fully formed punk rock geniuses. Unbeknownst to too many, "I'm Stranded" was one of the first four punk rock 45s, released in December 1976, right around the time the Ramones, the Damned and the Sex Pistols were making their recording debuts (with "Blitzkrieg Bop" in July 1976, "New Rose" in November 1976, and "Anarchy" in December 1976). Laid down at a Brisbane jingle studio, issued on the band's own Fatal Records label, "Stranded" was noisy, shambling and chaotic—in short, quintessential punk. Aw-right!

9. **OH BONDAGE UP YOURS—X-Ray Spex.** The feminist, anti-consumerist punk anthem the Slits never recorded, but should've, "OBUY" was issued in October 1977, after X-Ray Spex had played a grand total of three shows in public. Led by a braces-wearing nineteen-year-old former hippie named Marion Elliot (who changed her name to Poly Styrene after catching the punk bug, then later left it all for Krishna consciousness), and featuring the vestigial saxophone sounds of sixteen-year-old Lora Logic (who couldn't play, but would go on to sax distinction with the likes of Essential Logic, the Raincoats, Swell Maps, the Hare Krishna movement and a mid-1990s reformed X-Ray Spex), X-Ray Spex's "OBUY" was a screeching, rollicking rant against chauvinism and consumerism, which have more in common than you might think. "Bind me, tie me/ Chain me to the wall: I wanna be a slave/ To you all/ Oh bondage up yours!" Le Tigre's Kathleen Hanna can try her entire life, but she'll never be as wonderful as Poly Styrene, or write a song as good as this one.

10. **CALIFORNIA UBER ALLES—The Dead Kennedys.** The most effective lampooning of the coma-inducing popular culture of seventies-era North America *ever*. Fucking brilliant. Moving to San Francisco from what he would later call the "new age yuppie cesspool" of Boulder, Colorado, the DK's enigmatic front man, Jello Biafra, was understandably horrified by what he found: hot tubs, FM radio and mellowness in abundance. So Biafra (born Eric Boucher) wrote about it, and in October 1979, his Alternative Tentacles label released the scalding, roaring results. Some of Jello's lyrics in "California Uber Alles" are worth reprinting here, because they represent some of the best satire ever seen in punk: "I am Governor Jerry Brown/ My aura smiles/ And never frowns/ Soon I will be president!/ Carter power will soon go away/ I will be Fuhrer one day/ I will command all of you/ Your kids will meditate in school . . . Zen

fascists will control you/ 100% natural/ You will jog for the master race/ And always wear the happy face/ Close your eyes, can't happen here/ Big Bro' on white horse is near/ The hippies won't come back you say/ Mellow out or you will pay! . . ." Funny, smart and a great tune, too: one of the all-time great American punk rock singles.

Okay, now I'm at the end of the list, and already I want to change it. Best advice: go make up your own list: *Do It Yourself,* right? Right!

APPUNKDIX THREE
the top ten categories of punk writings
(sort of)

Researching this book was a lot of hard work. Honest. It wasn't just cool stuff like hanging out backstage with the Sex Pistols and Blink-182, you know (although I did a little of that with seventy-five percent of the members of both groups, I confess). And it wasn't simply a case of soaking up the ambience at CBGB's or outside the former Sex on the King's Road and chatting about the etymology of punk (although Suzanne and I did that, too, and—yes—I am trying to irritate you now).

Researching the book meant actually *reading* stuff, however. Punk books, for starters: books by punks, books for punks, books about punk. There actually aren't a lot of punk books around to be read, so half the work was finding the fucking things. But find some punk books I did, and rely upon them I did.

Notwithstanding the paucity of such books, in the past twenty-five years or so, there have been published a thousand metric tonnes of in-depth articles—in magazines, in newspapers, on websites, whatever—about punk. A lot of those articles were invaluable to me, and they took up less room than the books did. They were also less heavy to carry around, which helps.

Below I have assembled yet another Top Ten list–this one about the writings I used while researching *Fury's Hour*. Some of the named books and articles are really good, and a few aren't, but I want to give credit where credit is due. Even if the book or article in question ain't so good.

In no particular order, here is the Top Ten Categories of Punk Writings That Helped Me in the Writing of This Punk Book.

1. **As Essential as the First Ramones and Pistols Albums:** Too many punks think punk is something to be heard, or seen, but not necessarily read. Untrue! Along with a favourite, well-thumbed, copy of *Sniffin' Glue* or Holmstrom's *Punk Magazine*—and along with all of the punk albums and singles mentioned previously—no punk should be found without the following books. Presented here in order of brilliance, they are, without any doubt, indispensable:

    *   O'Hara, Craig. *The Philosophy of Punk: More Than Noise!* San Francisco: AK Press, 1999. (One of the best examples of DIY, ever. Passionate and essential.)
    *   Burchill, Julie, and Tony Parsons. *The Boy Looked at Johnny: The Obituary of Rock and Roll.* London: Pluto Press, 1978. (*High Times* said, "What the Sex Pistols did for rock 'n' roll, this book does for rock 'n' roll journalism." I'll buy that. This book influenced my writing and that of plenty of others. Infuriating and brilliant.)
    *   Azerrad, Michael. *Our Band Could Be Your Life: Scenes from the*

American Indie Underground, 1981–1991. New York: Little, Brown, 2001. (*The* most authoritative take on the U.S. hardcore punk movement. Minor Threat, Hüsker Dü, Minutemen, Fugazi, Black Flag: they're all here. Great writing, great insights.)

- Perry, Mark. *Sniffin' Glue: The Essential Punk Accessory.* London: Sanctuary Publishing, 2000. (Essential is fucking right. Every issue of *Sniffin' Glue* is reprinted, plus plenty of Perry's post-punk assessments.)
- Holmstrom, John. *Punk: The Original.* New York: Trans-High Publishing, 1996. (Contains gems from some of the classic *Punk Magazine* issues, including unforgettable interviews with the Ramones and Johnny Rotten and a photographic record of a wrestling match between Lester Bangs and the Dictators' Handsome Dick Manitoba that has to be seen to be believed. From the guy who invented the word "punk.")
- Bangs, Lester. *Psychotic Reactions and Carburetor Dung.* New York: Vintage Books, 1987. (As you may have gleaned—and my editor certainly has, because she slashed away at my adjectival excesses whenever Bangs's name came up in the manuscript— I love this man. Greatest fucking rock critic ever. His gargantuan essay on the Clash is here, and is worth the price of admission for that alone. Lester Bangs Was God. Ha—she didn't take that out!)
- Raha, Maria. *Cinderella's Big Score: Women of the Punk and Indie Underground.* Emeryville, CA: Seal Press, 2005 (The title of this just-published text best describes what it's about—and it's terrific. Exene Cervenka, the Slits, Poly Styrene, Hole, Bikini Kill: they're all here. Indispensible.)

2. **Best Books About the Best Punk Groups:** The Ramones, the Clash, the Sex Pistols and a goodly number of the D.C. punk/hardcore outfits are regularly cited as the best punk rock combos because, well, they were. As such, they attracted the attentions of various authors. Surprisingly few of the resulting

books were any good: some of them were too slavishly fannish, some of them didn't really understand the punk concept all that well, some were trying to cash in, or whatever. But a few of these band-focused books are worth picking up if you are seeking a fuller understanding of your fave group, or (as I did) if you want to look at amusing photos of Joe Strummer and John Lydon with shoulder-length hair.

- Keithley, Joey. *I, Shithead: A Life in Punk.* Vancouver: Arsenal Pulp Press, 2003. (Funny, smart, comprehensive and an essential record of DOA, but also of the entire West Coast punk scene— Canadian and American.)
- Gilbert, Pat. *Passion Is a Fashion: The Real Story of the Clash.* London: Aurum Press, 2004. (I picked this one up while finishing *Fury's Hour,* and found myself wishing it had come out a lot sooner. It's wonderfully written, and the most comprehensive look at the Clash I've read yet.)
- Porter, Dick. *Ramones: The Complete Twisted History.* London: Plexus, 2004. (The best book I've come across about the Ramones—even better than books written by band members. It's revealing, I think, that it took a Brit to write about Da Brudders the right way. Americans never understood the best American band since the Stooges.)
- Andersen, Mark, and Mark Jenkins. *Dance of Days: Two Decades of Punk in the Nation's Capital.* New York: Akashic Press, 2003. (An amazing account of the seminal D.C. hardcore scene. *The* hardcore handbook.)
- Temple, Julien. *The Filth and the Fury.* New York: St. Martin's Griffin, 2000. (It's really just the script for Temple's documentary about the Sex Pistols and, since he lets them say whatever they want, they end up hanging themselves. What did you expect? Redemption?)
- Heylin, Clinton. *Never Mind the Bollocks: Here's the Sex Pistols.* New York: Schirmer Books, 1998. (A slender but incredibly

detailed and impressive account of the making of one of the most important albums ever.)

- Green, Johnny. *A Riot of Our Own: Night and Day with the Clash.* New York: Faber and Faber, 1999. (I loved this book. I loved it. Written by the numero uno roadie to the Clash, this is one of the best books about the band I've read yet. Green plainly loves them, but—like a brother—he's also not unaware of their deficiencies. A classic, with a Strummer foreword.)

3. **Best Books About Punk Penned by Other Punks:** Before we got all unfriendly with each other and whatnot, Johnny Rotten heaped scorn on a couple authors who had written about punk, or Johnny Rotten, without (a) having experienced punk first-hand or (b) having experienced being Johnny Rotten. He was right to do so, I think. Like a lot of subcultures, punk is kind of hard to figure out from afar. It needs to be experienced in all of its sweaty, gritty, noisy glory if you are planning to write something about it: you need to immerse yourself in it. So, naturally, some of better punk books are written by products of the punk movement, such as Craig O'Hara (although O'Hara's book is in another stratosphere for its DIY purity). Here are some of better ones:

- Lydon, John. *Rotten: No Irish, No Blacks, No Dogs.* New York: St. Martin's Press, 1994. (He may be a jerk now, but the facts are the facts: the guy practically invented punk. And he did a rap with Afrika Bambaataa. For those two reasons alone, he's a god-like genius. Good book, too.)
- Armstrong, John. *Guilty of Everything.* Vancouver: New Star Books, 2001. (Stupid title, but not so Armstrong's book. I knew him, a little, back when he was Buck Cherry, the immensely talented lead singer of Vancouver's Modernettes; this slim book reveals him to be immensely talented at writing, too. Along with Shithead's book, all you will ever need to know about the

West Coast punk scene. Also contains the best slicing-and-dicing of Gerry Hannah ever.)

- Ramone, Dee Dee. *Lobotomy: Surviving the Ramones.* New York: Thunder's Mouth Press, 2000. (Dee Dee admitted that some of the stuff in this book, published a couple years before he OD'd, is made up or exaggerated. Who cares. He was a Ramone, not Walter Fucking Cronkite.)

- Diggle, Steve. *Harmony in My Head.* London: Helter Skelter Publishing, 2003. (The Buzzcocks' Diggle is a wonderfully funny and easygoing guy, and his autobiography is the same. Not just for the Buzzcocks fanatic, either.)

- Matlock, Glen. *I Was a Teenage Sex Pistol.* London: Omnibus, 1990. (Worth it for the title alone, because it's not strictly accurate: most of Matlock's Pistol years came when he was in his forties!)

4. **Best Overview-Type Books About Punk:** Quite a few of the books I came across are collections of essays about punk, or books that provide a snapshot-style overview of the punk rock scene. Some of them are pretty good, and they are particularly worthwhile if you are seeking short, snappy stuff for trips to the crapper, or if you have the attention span of a housefly, like I do.

- Manley, Frank. *Smash the State: A Discography of Canadian Punk, 1977–1992.* Montreal: No Exit Press, 1994. (Pure DIY, lovingly illustrated and laid out. The kind of book that should be written about every country's punk scene. Clone Frank Manley now!)

- Bessman, Jim. *Ramones: An American Band.* London: St. Martin's Press, 1993. (Good overview. Fun pix. Worthwhile.)

- McNeil, Legs, and Gillian McCain. *Please Kill Me: The Uncensored Oral History of Punk.* New York: Grove Press, 1996. (There's a wee bit too much New York stuff in here—and way too much stuff about Andy Warhol and his boring hippie crew—but some of the verbatim narratives are priceless.)

- Lahickey, Beth, ed. *All Ages: Reflections on Straight Edge.* Huntington Beach, CA: Revelation Books, 1997. (Women were pretty thin on the ground in the Straight Edge scene, but Lahickey stuck with it, and we should all be glad she did. This book provides the best look inside the Straight Edge scene ever committed to paper.)
- True, Everett. *Hey Ho Let's Go: The Story of the Ramones.* London: Omnibus Press, 2002. (Solid, detailed, beginning-to-end look at Da Brudders.)
- Marcus, Greil. *In the Fascist Bathroom: Punk in Pop Music.* Cambridge, MA: Harvard University Press, 1993. (Greil also published this book under the title *Ranters and Crowd Pleasers.* Not sure why. It's not just about punk—I mean, there's too much fucking Elvis Costello in here, for starters—but he's such a gifted writer and thinker, you forgive him for it.)
- Sinker, Daniel. *We Owe You Nothing: Punk Planet; The Collected Interviews.* New York: Akhasic Books, 2001. (Everyone is in this book, from Ian MacKaye to Jello Biafra to, er, Noam Chomsky. *Punk Planet* is the most authentic punk magazine around.)

5. **Top Academic Books About Punk:** Hey, look, I agree: academic punk is an oxy-fucking-moron, man. No argument here. But if something stays still long enough, or stirs up the slimmest amount of media coverage, the chances are excellent it will end up the subject of someone's Harvard Ph.D. thesis. It's just the way things work, you know? If you walk around with a safety pin through your epiglottis, a sociologist somewhere is going to endlessly analyze the significance of your decision for the rest of us. Some of the resulting books aren't as bad as you might expect—and some of them are quite good, in fact.

- Sabin, Roger, ed. *Punk Rock: So What? The Cultural Legacy of Punk.* London: Routledge, 1999. (Sabin has put together an impressive collections of essays here, on every aspect of the punk experience. Top-notch.)
- Thompson, Stacy. *Punk Productions: Unfinished Business.* New York: State University of New York Press, 2004. (Damned if I can figure out, still, what the title means. It's dumb. Professor Thompson's book ain't, however: it's a comprehensive socio-economic look at punk, from Riot Grrl to the CBGB hardcore Straight Edge scene. Impressive.)
- D'Ambrosio, Antonino, ed. *Let Fury Have the Hour: The Punk Rock Politics of Joe Strummer.* New York: Nation Books, 2004. (I had a coronary when I heard the title of this book prior to its publication. My editor told me to calm down. She was right: while the titles are a bit similar, the content really isn't. D'Ambrosio's book is a pretty sober collection of essays about Strummer's politics, and it's pretty good, too. Chuck D and Billy Bragg on Strummer: can't beat that.)
- Brake, Mike. *The Sociology of Youth Culture and Youth Subcultures.* London: Routledge and Kegan Paul, 1980. (This guy was a social work professor at Carleton University when I was studying journalism there, and his book isn't all about punk, but a lot of Brake's observations have guided a lot of my subsequent thinking about subcultures.)
- Hebdige, Dick. *Subculture: The Meaning of Style.* London: Routledge, 1979. (The most influential sociological take on punk and other youth subcultures, Hebdige's little book is cited as a source in virtually every punk book I've read. Smart cat.)

6. **So-So- Books About Punk:** I don't want to be mean to anyone who went to all the trouble of writing a book. It's a lot of work, writing a book. And, naturally, I fully expect to be on the receiving end of plenty of good-natured ribbing myself (e.g., "Kinsella is a fascistic manipulator who props up the capitalist

establishment and should be summarily executed for trying to write about a wonderful anti-capitalist, anti-establishment subculture," or "Kinsella is a cynical, aging punk wannabe going through a pathetic mid-life crisis, and is crassly attempting to capitalize on the art of others," or "Kinsella is a loudmouth and a dickhead, and his book sucks the big one," blah blah blah). Fair enough. That said, I feel it is a geriatric punk's duty to steer his readership away from books that are a bit of a waste of time. Life is too short as it is, and if I've wasted a few precious hours on a stinker, there's no reason you should be obliged to do the same.

- Savage, Jon. *England's Dreaming: Sex Pistols and Punk Rock.* London: Faber and Faber, 1992. (On the day I met him, Johnny Rotten had just finished a rant about this book, which is one of the bestselling books about punk . . . and I have to say, a lot of Rotten's criticisms weren't so far off the mark. Lots of detail herein, which is always useful if you are writing a book, but I, too, found some of Savage's theories—like the Situationists and the Pistols—unconvincing. A bit pretentious.)
- Gray, Marcus. *The Clash: Return of the Last Gang in Town.* London: Helter Skelter, 2001. (I have to say it: I really disliked this book. There's nothing wrong with writing a critical biography—just like there's nothing wrong with guys like me being less critical of Joe Strummer and his band. But Gray is just so unrelentingly negative about the Clash, and so nasty, you just end up wondering why he ever bothered to write this fucking thing in the first place. I also stopped counting after finding quite a few factual errors. Pass.)
- Parker, Alan. *Vicious: Too Fast to Live.* London: Creation Books, 2003. (I didn't want to be too critical of Parker, but when he tried to absolve Sid Vicious for the murder of Nancy Spungen—a murder Vicious confessed to, among other things—it irritated me. Also irritating is the book's very existence. Repeat after me:

Sid Vicious wasn't punk. Sid Vicious was the moron who almost *killed* punk.)

- Thompson, Dave. *Punk*. Burlington, ON: Collector's Guide Publishing, 2003. (I've seen it for sale all over, but I'm not sure why. Want my copy? It's yours, no charge.)

7. **Books with Cool Pictures:** Punk was, and is, visual. With the exception of the North American hardcore scenesters—who were not, in and of themselves, all that interesting to look at, but were pretty eye-catching when they assumed mob formation— punks have always been pretty colourful folks. They stand out from the rest of the mainstream crowd, quite deliberately, because they don't want to be considered *part* of the mainstream crowd. Thus, there are lots of cool books with cool pictures of punks. I wouldn't necessarily recommend them as coffee table mementoes for your grandmother at Christmas, but a few are still worth picking up.

- Smith, Pennie. *The Clash: Before and After.* London: Hollen Street Press, 1980. (Amazing, incredible, immortal photos of The Only Band That Matters, taken over the course of several Clash tours. Some of the best rock 'n' roll photography you will ever see, whether you're a Clash fan or not.)
- Stevenson, Nils, and Ray Stevenson. *Vacant: A Diary of the Punk Years, 1976–1979.* London: Thames and Hudson, 1999. (Nils, who supplied the words, was road manager to the Pistols and Siouxsie and the Banshees; his brother Ray was there to take the best punk photos—mainly of the Brit bands—in the early days. Nils died, too soon, in 2002.)
- Colegrave, Stephen, and Chris Sullivan. *Punk: The Definitive Record of a Revolution.* New York: Thunder's Mouth Press, 2001. (Don't be put off by the big picture of Sid Vicious on the cover, or the fact that the book weighs as much as a small automobile. Leave it around the house and frighten the elderly.)

- Coon, Caroline. *1988: The New Wave Punk Rock Explosion.* London: Orbach and Chambers, 1977. (It's long out of print, but I got my copy the year it came out and found myself—and still find myself—staring at Coon's amazing photos. Which is a good thing, because her prose is a bit, er, underwhelming.)

8. **Pretty Good Books About Punk:** I found all of these books helpful. Most of them were pretty good.

- Vale, V. *Search and Destroy: The Authoritative Guide to Punk Culture.* New York: RE/Search Publications, 1996. (Reprints of the terrific San Francisco punk fanzine from the seventies, compiled by long-time counterculture authority V. Vale—yes, that is his name.)
- Monk, Noel E. *Twelve Days on the Road: The Sex Pistols and America.* New York: William Morrow, 1990. (Written by the Pistols' American tour manager, this book details the Pistols' death throes, and is therefore a bit depressing. But it's still worth a quick read.)
- Wells, Steven. *Punk: Young, Loud and Snotty.* New York: Thunder's Mouth Press, 2004. (Not-bad alphabetical mini-essays about individual songs by the bigger punk groups. Good pictures.)
- Melnick, Monte. *On the Road with the Ramones.* London: Sanctuary Publishing, 2003. (Beautifully illustrated—and with a Holmstrom cover cartoon, too. Melnick was the Ramones' tour manager for twenty-two years, and clearly loves them as much as I do. For fans.)

9. **Great Magazines and Magazine Articles:**

- *Uncut Presents Punk 1975–1979.* Steve Sutherland, ed. Uncut Special Edition, Vol. 1, Issue 2, 2002. (This is a near-book-length collection of punk articles, reviews and pix taken from *New Musical Express,* and it's simply outstanding.)

- *Never Mind the Jubilee: Here's the True Story of Punk!* Chris Hunt, ed. Special Q. Edition, Summer 2002. (Another great book-length collection, but this one contains new profiles of punk bands, trends and people. It also features a handy timeline of notable punk events, mainly in Britain.)
- *The Clash: White Riot.* Steve Sutherland, ed., Uncut Special Edition, Vol. 1, Issue 14, 2003. (Prompted by the death of Joe Strummer, this mag contains virtually every article *NME* ever published about the Clash. Lots of fabbo photos, too. A must-have.)
- *Mojo Magazine.* Pat Gilbert, ed. March 2003. (This one is noteworthy because it contains a raft of articles about the Clash and the Damned, and it lists the Top 50 Punk Albums, too. Great stuff here.)
- "100 Punk Scorchers." *Mojo Magazine.* Paul Trynka, ed. October 2001. (The top 100 punk singles, according to *Mojo.* I didn't agree with a few of their selections—*Blondie* making the punk list? C'mon!—but I'm a sucker for lists. Even a flawed one.)
- "New York Punk." *Mojo Magazine.* Paul Trynka, ed. February 2001. (This article, which profiles every NYC punk combo in the 1976 era, is worth it for the cover photo alone: a shot of the Ramones seen through the worn-out knee of someone's jeans. Cool.)

10. Not-So-Great Magazine Articles:

Aw, fuck it. If you buy any, you'll figure it out soon enough.

ACKNOWLEDGEMENTS

Some of the stuff I write about in *Fury's Hour* goes back—way, way back. To, like, when I was sixteen years old. The beginning of time, in other words.

As a consequence, when I sit down and try and figure out whom to thank, I find myself thinking about folks I haven't clapped eyes on in close to three decades. And, in more than one case, I find myself vainly trying to remember the *name* of someone with whom I was in a particular punk band, or of the guy who connected me with Joey Ramone one afternoon in March 1980, or of the many people who gave me an insight about punk that stayed with me, or whatever. Time marches on, relentless and cruel, etc., etc.

So, to those whose names I have forgotten, I offer sincere apologies. My excuses: I am a boring old fart, and I have a boring old fart's piss-poor memory. Moreover, when I was slam-dancing with you at the Rotter's Club in Edmonton back in the winter of 1979, I wasn't also simultaneously and secretly taking detailed notes as part of the research I was conducting for the book I planned to write a quarter-century later. I was, in fact, drinking lots of beer and slamming into other guys, and whatnot. That's it.

I'll go at this chronologically, to make this exercise easier on both of us, okay? Here goes.

In the seventies, when punk was starting up with a vengeance, there were a lot of people who were (whether they realized it at the time or not) helping to shape what punk would become. From the NCNA and Social Blemish era, circa 1975–1977, I offer thanks to the following: Marty and Elizabeth and Gisela and Christina and Evelyn Schenk, Ron and Doris and Nona and Carol Macdonald, John Heaney, Neil Sanderson, Dan Nearing, Pat O'Heran, Sonic Don Finstad, Lionel Sawatzky, Jim Keelaghan, Dale Franklin, Marcel Savoie, Steve Gajda, Bill Corcoran, the Baldridges, the Lufts, the Class of 1979, Conan Daly, Sarah Humphreys, the 531 gang, Brian McGoogan, Joan Bedard, Dave Beatty, Brian Brennan, Glenn Bontje, Lee G. Hill, Allen Pseud Baekeland, Lynn Gray, John Vickers, Mike Stotts, Colin Tomlins, Terry Tompkins, Bill Reynolds, the folks at CJSW, and—most of all—Dr. and Mrs. Macdonald, as well as Mr. and Mrs. Schenk, for putting up with the godawful racket originating in their basements. (R.I.P., Dr. Macdonald.)

A bit later on in that same decade, in the rockin' 1978–1980 Hot Nasties period, things were getting really interesting. "Interesting" is measured by the scores of people who showed up at gigs, the explosion in the number of bands that formed (see below to get a sense of what I mean) and the dwindling numbers of guys who wanted to beat us up. By 1979, punk was becoming more popular—although nothing like it is these days. I offer tons of thanks, therefore, to Just Plain Tom Edwards and Wayne the Sane Ahern of the Hot Nasties, our manager and friend Nasty Bob Haslam, Kevin and Troy (Screeching Weasel Rules!) Kinsella, Mark and Alvin and Pete of the Sturgeons, Lori Hahnel, the Virgins, Moe Berg, the Silicone Injection, Leeanne "LeeAnimal" Betzler, Julie the Hot Nasties Fan, the Mild Chaps, Paula and Tim Christison, George Wall, the Rock 'n' Roll Bitches, Bruno and the Golden Calgarians, Mark and Eric Johnson, Adele and the Ripchords, Tom and Adele Wolfe, the Modern Minds, the Sandwiches, Murray Edwards and Brad Clark, Virginia and her Breeders, Jerry Jerry, Junior Gone Wild, Animal Kingdom, Barrie and Gail Wright, the Malibu Kens, Mike Bezzeg, Mick Memorex, Linda and the thousands of card-carrying members of the Hot Nasties Fan Club, Barry Morice and Pete Slupski at Fog Eye, Joey Shithead and DOA, the Dishrags, 999, and all of the bikers at the Calgarian and elsewhere who did not kill us. Thank you for not killing us.

In the eighties and nineties, when not attending classes, I kept writin' about music, and I kept playin' it, too. But, on balance, it was once again a terrible, awful, shitty time for rock 'n' roll. The groups that kept me sane—the ones that kept *a lot of us* sane—were the Replacements, Public Enemy, the Ramones and quite a few of the SoCal bands. Musically, the musicians I knew weren't themselves necessarily sane, but we all helped each other get to the other side of the cultural wasteland. Thanks, therefore, to my bandmates Chris Benner, Gayle Nakamoto, Yazmin Laroche, Terry Flanagan, Alvin Charlton, Mel Kennedy, Brian Carson, Tom Griffiths, Chris Tuck, the Sheridan brothers, and quite a few other guys whose names I honestly, truly cannot remember. (You can guess why.)

In the brand-spanking-new millennium, with more shite choking the airwaves than ever before, I found myself playing punk less and writing about it more. Thus, this here book. Lots of folks helped out—musicians, managers, publicists, fans, record company reps, you name it. Let's go at it geographically, shall we?

In England, I was generously assisted by Charlie with Sham's organization, Matt Bristow at Cherry Red Records, Doug Hart with the Siouxsie/Budgie/Banshees group, Jeanette Lee at Rough Trade (and formerly of PIL), Jack McKillion at Precious P.R., James Dutton at Motion Records, Shirley Sexton with the SLF gang, Patsy Winkelman at Rough Trade, Lois Wilson at *Mojo,* TV Smith and Gaye Advert of the Adverts, and the remarkable Geoff Travis at Rough Trade.

In the U.S. of A., meanwhile, I received invaluable assistance from many folks who do not necessarily wield guitars or drumsticks. Thanks go out to Martin Hall at Merge Records, Jonathan Rice at Virgin Records, Mitch Schneider, Libby Henry, Jonathan Elder, Melanie at Fat Wreck Chords, Andy Grabia, Tasha Shermer, Legs McNeil, and various folks at CBGB's.

Here at home in the Great White North, help came from a variety of places. Thank you, then, to the gang at Punk History Canada, Craig Pyette at Random House, Steve Blair, Shinan Govani, Peter Scowen, Karim Bardeesy, the Evaporators, Catherine Davey, Mark Brady, Kerry Goulding at Sanctuary Records, George Stroumboulopoulos, Jaime Watt, metalhead author Martin Popoff, Jari Kurri at Sudden Death Records, Kerry Doole, Don Guy, the guys in Gob—particularly Tom, Theo and Craig—Sum 41, Emily Hill, assorted St. Denis folks I will not embarrass by naming, Jimmy Warren, Mike Miner, Doug ("Nasties CD") Mercer, James Villeneuve, Avril Lavigne's guy, Peter Simpson at the *Ottawa Citizen,* Sean Litteljohn, Paul Ferguson, Jean C., Bob Richardson (even if your taste in music still is horrible, Bob), Maria and Karl and Ted and Marce and Mark and Joanne and Deb and Al from the supportive W.C. network, Dave Pryce, Adam Radwanski, Josh at Swerve, Rob Benzie, Cathy Allman, John S. Kendle, Gordon Prieur, Frank Manley and his vast *Smash the State* empire, and all of the many folks who bought Hot Nasties CDs or sent punk-related tips through www.warrenkinsella.com. (And to all of you www.warrenkinsella.com regulars, thanks too, although I still don't get why you keep coming back!)

Special, unqualified, super-sized punk thanks go out to *accessmag* publisher Keith Sharp, my column editor Sean Plummer and, most particularly, Cam Carpenter and Karen Pace, without whom this book simply would not have happened. Thank you, Karen and Cam—you both *rawk!*

Now, when researching the book, I wasn't particularly interested in interviewing people because they were famous, or because they sold a lot of records, or whatever. I didn't give a fuck about that. I wanted people who were *smart,* and who I figured had thought about punk's relative position in the musical/ political/cultural universe. With the exception of nasty old Johnny Rotten, all were very generous with their time, and the book wouldn't have happened without their help. Thank you, then, to Eddie Vedder of Pearl Jam, the incomparable Joey Shithead, Tobi Vail of Bikini Kill, the brilliant Ian MacKaye, Ari Up of the Slits, Nardwuar (for his lengthy radio interviews with Gerry Hannah, upon which I relied heavily), the much-missed Joey Ramone, Steve Diggle and Pete Shelley of the Buzzcocks, Hüsker Dü, Joan Jett (even if she is less of a feminist than I hoped), Bruce Foxton of the Jam, Mark Perry of *Sniffin' Glue* and Alternative TV, Tony James of London SS and Generation X, Craig O'Hara (author of the essential *Philosophy of Punk*), the guys in 999, Billy Idol, Andy Partridge of XTC, Gene Simmons of KISS and original Straight Edger Ted Nugent (I'm not kidding, either), the amazing Hilly Kristal of CBGB's, Jane Wieldin of the GoGos, James Spooner and *Afropunk,* Jake Burns of Stiff Little Fingers, Jim Lindberg of Pennywise, Mensi of Angelic Upstarts, Jim Walker of Public Image Ltd., Brett Gurewitz of Epitaph and Bad Religion and his staff, Bernie Farber at the Canadian Jewish Congress, Lee Hardy, John Lydon and Glen Matlock and Paul Cook of the Sex Pistols, the eternal Jimmy Pursey of Sham 69, the guys in the pre-Rollins Black Flag, Bob Geldof of the Boomtown Rats, Lux Interior of the Cramps, Jerry Casale and Mark Mothersbaugh of Devo, Terry Chikowski (for his courage), John Holmstrom of *Punk Magazine,* Seymour Stein of Sire Records, Mark Hoppus and Tom Delonge of Blink-182, Joel Madden and the guys in Good Charlotte, Colin Newman of Wire, the wonderful Vic

Godard of the Subway Sect, Russ Rankin of Good Riddance, Topper Headon and Mick Jones and Paul Simonon of the Clash . . . and, of course, Joe Strummer, who (in these dark days) we all miss more than ever. God bless you, Strummer.

Most of all, I thank my brilliant editor, Anne Collins; my friend and advisor and publicist, Scott Sellers; über-agent Helen Heller; my tireless assistant, Jo Reath; colleagues Cameron Summers, Beth Clarkson and Sandra Leffler; Charlie Angelakos, Derek Raymaker and Chris Bingham of our destined-for-greatness nameless punk combo; my brother Lorne (for unflagging support and valuable insights and watching my back); my mom and dad (for putting up with all of our noise and cursing and troublemaking, and whom I will love forever, for those and a million other reasons); my punk brothers and musical Svengalis Ras Pierre Schenk and Alan "Flesh" Macdonald; and, most of all, my beloved Suzanne, Emma, Ben, Sam and Jake, who are life itself.

And to all of you punks who bought this book (or swiped it), thanks to you, too. Now put it down, *immediately,* and grab a guitar, or a pen, or a microphone, and get up on stage . . . THE WORLD NEEDS CHANGING, AND YOU CAN CHANGE IT!

Warren "Nuclear Age" Kinsella
Toronto, Canada, 2005 AD

INDEX